the best years of their lives?

pupils' experiences of school

Cedric Cullingford

KOGAN
PAGE

For Mary Morrison

First published in 2002

Kogan Page Limited
120 Pentonville Road
London N1 9JN
UK

Stylus Publishing Inc.
22883 Quicksilver Drive
Sterling, VA 20166-2012
USA

British Library Cataloguing in Publication Data

A CIP record for this book is available from the British Library.

ISBN 0 7494 3795 2

Typeset by JS Typesetting Ltd, Wellingborough, Northants
Printed and bound in Great Britain by Clays Ltd, St Ives plc

Contents

Contents

Preface

The origins of this research lie in a project designed to explore all the most positive links between the experience of schools and young people's subsequent careers in employment, whether they go straight to work or gain more qualifications through university. The approach taken with the many interviews with pupils in Years 10 and 11 was to find out what they had learnt in school and what had been most helpful to them in their subsequent careers. It was also to discover their attitudes towards different possibilities of future careers. The positive approach taken here deserves emphasizing as it highlights the contrasts between the tone of the interviews and the subsequent findings. What this research reveals might not be a surprise to many, and will probably stir up corroborative evidence in those who reflect upon it, but nevertheless the results are, as in the best empirical research, unexpected as well as consistent.

The analysis of the data has taken a considerable amount of time, during which the experience of conducting other research and writing other books has naturally had an influence. The time taken on analysing the transcripts is due to trying to make certain that what was emerging was valid and reliable. The unexpected nature of the consistencies comes through a process of constant interrogation of the evidence. This scrutiny arose out of questioning the possibilities of either a tendency to deny what the interviewees revealed, or a temptation to seek for corroborative evidence for a personal bias. Every care was taken to make sure that, despite all the individual differences and many small idiosyncrasies, the results are a true statement of a deep-seated problem. One of the ironic difficulties of the analysis is the splendid resilience of the pupils – putting up with what is happening to them and trying hard not to complain.

In the analysis of the manuscript there was not so much a tension between the surface answers and the underlying revelations as a slow realization of the implications of what the pupils were saying. Their revelations might be unexpected but they are not shocking or meant to shock. What is surprising is the consistencies of young people's experiences and the challenges they present.

The sample comes from a wide spectrum of socio-economic backgrounds, from schools different from each other in many ways. Whilst the interviews are with pupils from Years 10 and 11, as well as with some school leavers as yet jobless, the experiences they present are a reflection on the whole of their experience of school. This is the chance for them, in the context of their leaving or going on to the next stage, to analyse the overall meaning of school.

The pupils are summarizing the accumulation of years of schooling, or many thousands of hours – Rutter *et al* (1979) reminds us it is 15,000 hours in secondary schools – a large amount in this context of their lives as a whole, with other influences, other learning experiences, and relationships with a wide range of people, some intense and many ephemeral. These reflections are not just about their immediate circumstances but are the outcome of years of observation.

People are rarely asked to express their thoughts on their experience. What they say might be not only surprising but challenging. There will be some people who find the truth too shocking or undermining. One reason that young people are not heard, or if they find their voice are not listened to, is because people are somewhat afraid of what they say (Pugh, 1997). They challenge the unexamined assumptions of the educational system, a system to which many people are directing their careers. It can feel undermining to have the routine bases of action challenged.

The problem is that there seem to be almost separate worlds of schooling or, at least, the perceptions of schooling. We know the rhetoric of school effectiveness, league tables, standards and accountability constantly employed by all of those involved in politics whether supported by a political party or a newspaper. This language, with its acronyms and terminology and underlying assumptions, is understood by pupils, but is almost completely alien to their experience (Jeffrey, 2001). Pupils are aware of what is going on but their own world is quite different, quite separate. One of the most telling challenges in understanding what the interviewed pupils were saying was to distinguish between different uses of similar terms, to deconstruct some of the seemingly familiar rhetoric into quite distinct meanings. Pupils hear the rhetoric of effectiveness and targets every day. They are imbued at the one level with the official notion of what schooling means and have to adjust to the demands of the core curriculum and to exams. This is at one level of the 'truth'. There is another. The world of school, as experienced by pupils, is different from the assumptions about it made by politicians and those operating the system. Pupils challenge these assumptions and, when they do, this is often interpreted as an unwelcome intrusion into the hardened and sacrosanct purposes of the operators, as the voice of the disaffected or the failures.

This leaves teachers in a somewhat ambiguous position. They are there to 'deliver' the educational policies, and yet are too close to the realities of pupils' experience not to feel at least discomforted. One of the reasons for such a high incidence of teacher stress is the tensions between the appealing rhetoric and the uncomfortable facts. Teachers also have to submit to the conditions. They are the ones who actually keep the whole system going whether they like it or not. If pupils in this research seem to criticize teachers I must stress that they do so only concerning the role teachers play, rather than suggesting that blame rests on teachers as individuals. All pupils recognize the dedication, self-sacrifice, resilience and subtle awareness displayed by teachers. I am the more astonished at how well teachers do in circumstances that this research reveals as far more difficult than we have imagined. That is why the book is dedicated to a representative of the best of teachers, Mary Morrison.

Introduction

The idea of a school

We tend to take schools for granted as a natural and unquestioned part of the human experience. They are, however, a relatively new phenomenon especially in terms of a common universal application. As institutions, schools have certain unique features in common, however much they vary from each other in terms of buildings and ethos. They are compulsory. They hold together two distinct bodies of people for a fixed amount of time before releasing one of those bodies of people into the outside world. One group of people is there to enforce certain experiences on the other, however reluctant that other group might be. There are rules that must be obeyed by groups of people organized into spaces created especially for this purpose.

To remind ourselves of the peculiar condition of schools – and it could never be mistaken for anything else – is to enter a world that we no longer recognize in its stark clarity, since it has become so much an intimate and complex part of our circumstances. If we were to enter schools fresh from an alien planet and observe them with the close intensity of Swift's Gulliver we would be taken aback at the simplicities of what they have in common. Such a scrutiny should make us consider many matters that we otherwise take for granted. Underlying the central place schools have in our lives are a number of ambiguities, mostly to do with the relationship between schooling and other aspects of people's lives. The most significant ambiguity of schooling is that between school and the experiences of home, neighbourhood, community and society as a whole.

Analysts of the educational experience point out that the influence of school, as opposed to socio-economic circumstances, is relatively small. Schools that measure up to the government's highest standards of results are invariably from somewhere like Surrey rather than Birmingham. The early experiences of home, the immediate surroundings and the attitudes of peer groups have a deep impact on the attitudes and motivation of children whatever the school they attend. The outside world continues to have a profound influence on the outlook and understanding of life. And yet there is a tendency, exemplified in the regimes of inspection, to see schools as hermetically sealed units unaffected by what takes place elsewhere.

This leads to a second ambiguity: whether school is a purely academic centre, concentrating on passing on testable knowledge, or whether it is a social centre where pupils learn standards of behaviour and the means of working with others. The ways in which schools operate highlight the tensions. Schools are clearly hierarchical and yet do not refer this type of organization to any wider norms in society. They rely clearly on the enforcing of rules and on standards of discipline as if this did not derive from the home. They concentrate on the formal, nationally imposed curriculum, as if nothing else was being learnt through other children or the media. Schools that seem to be successful are those that concentrate best on the more academic matters and the clearest outcomes – but these are the schools that are more easily in tune with the aspirations of their communities.

The relationship between schools and the 'outside' world is a matter of time as well as place. Schools take up a distinct passage of time from the moment the children are deemed ready to take on the discipline of formal learning and behaviour – this varies from country to country – until that time when the result is unleashed on the unexpectant world. There was a time when schools were seen as a protection against the abuse of children, a means of postponing the moment when young people would be placed in the harsh conditions of factories. Schools were temporary havens. Since then schools are justified by the very way in which they prepare young people for employment. The wonders of the world of work are often invoked. The examination successes are implicitly justified as a way of measuring this introduction of industrial skills. Just as powerful as the rhetorics of child protection are the languages of 'relevance' and 'fitness of purpose'.

From the point of view of those running schools, the crucial elements are the outcomes, the examination results, especially in relation to other schools, all competing against each other. From the perspective of pupils, however, there is far greater emphasis on the people, especially the peer group (Gill and Howard, 2001). The experience of schools is more like that of an extended family rather than a microcosm of society. If schools are a 'rite of passage', are they deliberately sealed off from the world that will embrace the leavers afterwards or are they a preparation that makes the inmates undergo a miniature version of society as a whole? Are they just concerned with academic skills, those matters useful for jobs, or are they preparation for citizenship? In most schools these questions remain rhetorical since schools are so busy with the processes of teaching and testing that there is no time to examine the questions.

Concepts of childhood

It is widely accepted that the concept of childhood, as a distinct phase like adolescence, is a comparatively recent invention (Aries, 1962; Elias, 1978, 1982). The distinction between the public and the private, and the commensurate protection against being confronted by too much adult reality, only gradually came about as a result of the bureaucratization of society. Schools, with their distinct ethos, are also a result of the same social tendencies. There are certain aspects of school in particular that symbolize types of social organization. The preponderance of terminal examinations with the ranking of individuals in a list of classes might be ancient, as in choosing the Civil Service in Confucian China, but is recent in its widespread application to everyone in every walk of life. The notion of sport as organized competition, with groups of people formed into houses or schools challenging each other, is another example of the peculiar discipline of schooling. It could be said that we live in the age of schooling, where institutions are the expression of the norms, if not the values, of society.

Schools are so deeply embedded in modern culture and in the experience of individuals that they are rarely questioned. All the debates are about the margins, about the balance of the curriculum or about whether it is better to teach in larger of smaller classes. The outcome of the schools effectiveness research industry is to try to isolate those instrumental variables that might make a difference. Seen from the perspective of pupils these matters are hardly fundamental. On one level there are all kinds of distinctions between schools, in the teaching and learning styles, in group work, in the rules and in the expectations, but these distinctions are very small compared to the similarities of all schools and the effect of schooling on the individual.

For all the differences there are some fundamental experiences that are true of all schools. Teachers are in command and pupils need to learn, or guess what is demanded of them. Teachers are the arbiters of tests; they reveal the expectations of the assessment system. The tasks for pupils are to answer closed questions and to make sure that they at least keep up with their peer group. Schools are also seen to mould or fit pupils for the society in which they operate. One does not need to put forward a thesis tinged by socialism to recognize this (Gramsci, 1977; Bowles and Gintis, 1976; Cole, 1988). Indeed most governments would see the preparation of a compliant workforce and content citizenry as an accolade rather than a criticism. This social initiation is what happens, even if this aspect of schooling is rarely examined in itself, when so much attention is paid to the delivery of knowledge rather than attitudes.

The implicit purposes of school lie in introducing young people into the order and discipline of groups and in fitting them for future employment. This is quickly understood by all those entering school (Cullingford, 1991). It is rarely discussed, either because it is taken for granted or because there is no time or need to do so. Whether the pupils are properly prepared for employment is often debated. This debate is concerned with whether the system works in the way intended, measured against the accepted norms, rather than whether this it what schools should be for. The pupils themselves are caught up in the language of 'outcomes', of planned instruction, of meeting targets, of achieving levels, of orders and standards, of efficiency and effectiveness (Nutbrown, 1998). They are aware that they are being made ready for a smooth transition into the world of work rather than taking any critical stance towards it (Petherbridge, 1997). When aspects of industry are introduced into school they are presented as something important and central but, like schools, quite separate from the wider context of the society in which they are embedded.

At one level schools are taken for granted. They are a central part of a competitive society. They support those who are able to take advantage of their facilities in gaining access to further study and better employment. These offerings are general and clear. Whilst pupils might express fears and doubts about the values and experience of school and about the future, the schools are cajoled into presenting a positive image (White, Bruce and Ritchie, 2000). Indeed, that is the only way in which they can survive.

Policies or practice

We have talked of different worlds of perception and there are some conflicting uses of languages. Listening to the rhetoric of politicians is an experience distinctly different from hearing teachers, let alone pupils, and it is the language of politicians that dominates the discourse for all kinds of reasons we do not need to explore here. All we can do, apart from presenting the evidence, is to plead that it is evidence rather than rhetoric that is listened to.

There is always a reluctance to take in new information especially when it challenges set assumptions. The literature on 'habit' and 'change' in individuals and institutions is large. This is why the rhetoric of support for the systems of school, and their improvement, for the language of standards and targets, is so widespread and so unexamined. Any doubt is ascribed to being negative or expressing a wish to return to the past. The evidence that is acceptable and listened to is supposed to add to the positive, to support the achieving of targets, to accumulate, in stages, such accretions of knowledge as will help the journey of improvement towards its culmination. It reminds one of the kinds of evaluation that inform some debates about educational reform, interpreted as strengthening governmental policies in bringing about improvements. As a light example, suppose a vast questionnaire with many items, all subject to a Likert scale of 'Strongly agree' to 'Strongly disagree', is distributed widely. The statements begin with 'Teachers ought to be good.' Of course the results are consistent and unsurprising. Suppose the statement is 'Teachers are good.' This might set up some quite different reactions, and might produce complex, even difficult, results. This example might be a parody but it illustrates the level of enquiry that sometimes supports policy.

For those who are involved in a system or a political party, it is very difficult to stop and question what is happening and what the point of it really is. It can be undermining to do so and is always uncomfortable. Even when evidence is admitted, it is difficult to make uniform policy or change practice. To take one example, there was an experiment tried with primary teachers who were asked to insist that the pupils worked by themselves, helping each other, seeking information from other sources and never relying on the teacher for anything except in the very last resort. All the onus of learning was put on the children themselves. There were two results. The standards of work went up markedly; but the teachers felt guilty. They thought they ought to be there delivering the curriculum, testing the results and justifying themselves in their very busyness. The 'competencies' and 'accountability' are all to do with teacher performance, rather than what children are learning. The chances of teachers being able to implement the findings of such research are small. The psychological pressures to conform to personal standards of performance are too strong to be changed by a dose of verifiable fact.

There are many studies about learning that all come to the conclusion, whether we like it or not, that people learn best under the least pressure. The more vigorous and strenuous the emphasis on teaching the less that is learnt. In one typical example three groups of European students were given a day to produce a pamphlet that described cultural familiarities and differences beyond distinctions of language. One group was given clear instructions about what was expected. Another was told to enjoy the discussion and if they could get round to putting a pamphlet together that would be much appreciated. The third group was given a clear target and reminded of the high standards required. An added incentive was that if they did well they were to be rewarded and if they did badly they would be named and shamed. Those who have read research reports on learning and on motivation will not be surprised that the group with the least pressure produced a brilliant result and that the one that was set a clear target failed abysmally, despite the threats.

Most of the research on 'ownership', on giving people responsibility for their own learning, is on teachers rather than pupils (Dalin *et al*, 1994). The outcomes, however, are consistent. Encouragement, the generation of personal excitement and the freedom to learn all promote the best outcomes. At the same time educational policy in the Western world would appear to depend upon 'targets' or 'standards' or 'racking up' standards and, most powerfully, on punishment through inspection (Alexander, 2000). The rise of accountability and the testing of results, as well as the monumental central control of the curriculum, are all fairly recent trends, and there are some indications of their effects in this research. The way that teachers are viewed by pupils, for instance, is influenced by the realization that they are in thrall to inspection. Even if teachers do cajole their pupils to work harder, this is interpreted as being motivated not so much because they care about their students but because they in their turn depend on the successful outcomes of the standard assessment tasks (SATs) and examination results. Teachers are seen by pupils and parents alike as being 'driven' by the expectations of accountability (Cullingford, 1999a). Nothing is done disinterestedly for the sake of the pupils; at least, that is what it looks like, and that, indeed, is how it is supposed to be from the point of view of those who create and impose policy.

The ethos of policy

This current emphasis of policy, however, is not the subject of this research. There are deeper concerns than the phenomena of blame. Certain aspects of schooling, including the differences between some schools and others, between greater success and more widespread failure, might be exacerbated but there are some fundamental structural problems in schools that go deeper that that. The sense that the *raison d'être* of a school lies in the actions and being of teachers rather than pupils is fundamental. Some might argue that it is also inevitable. The sense that there are given subjects that must be learnt, that what is learnt must be in a form that can be tested and that some pupils and some institutions must do better than others, measured in the same way, pervades the idea of school. The organization of the school from the individual's entry to the playground, from tentative waiting, to the assemblies, to the incarceration in school, to the release, is dependent on a structure and ethos of homogeneity. Within this circumstance most teachers remain creative and driven by missionary instincts but they are having to prevail in difficult conditions, whether consciously or not.

The world of schooling can present itself to the pupils as monumentally forbidding and alienating. Amongst those pupils who have difficulties this is not surprising (Cullingford, 1999b). This impression is not however confined to the minority of those who play truant or who find themselves excluded. There are all kinds of private reasons for pupils to wish to 'drop out', since they feel they cannot keep up with the particular demands made on them in such institutions. More significant are those who are psychologically excluded, who go on ostensibly working and attending school and who are in fact doing the minimum in concentration and the maximum in devising means to avoid being noticed. When we explore the inner thoughts of young children and what interests them we are reminded of a real gap between the formal demands of the curriculum and the parallel, sometimes quite separate, lives of the pupils. This juxtaposition between personal ideas and sensibilities and the formal curriculum continues and sometimes becomes wider during the years of school.

The most powerful learning is often inadvertent. It depends on conversations with peers, on items of interest picked up in passing. Any close inspection of our own learning processes, with so many disconnected thoughts and so many wanderings of the mind, will reveal how significant are the moments when we are not concentrating. It is in these moments that attitudes and opinions are formed in the subtleties of the inadvertent rather than by what is supposed to be imbibed in a prescribed way. It is this level of interpretation with which this research is concerned. Perhaps experience ought to be different; but this is how it is.

What children bring to school

When they enter school, and throughout schooling, pupils bring with them several important characteristics, although these are often deliberately or conveniently forgotten. The first is a critical intelligence that observes the environment with an intense personal scrutiny. From the shape and meaning of objects to the analysis of personal relationships, including different points of view and distinctions between truth and falsehood, young children show a sophistication and objectivity that we tend to forget under the guise of sentimentality and ignore when we wish to assert our intellectual superiority as adults (Cullingford, 1999c). The intense search for interpreting meaning continues throughout school. Pupils are clearly not mere passive receivers of knowledge, and yet they are treated as if they were. What they are actually doing is observing the actions of other people, understanding tone and mood, and seeing how people treat each other. Whilst teachers are intent on the subject matter they are conveying, pupils are analysing teachers as people.

The most important part of the environment that pupils observe is the behaviour of people in their inconsistency and vulnerability. Relationships, intellectual as well as emotional, are crucial. That sense of shared understanding, respect for the individual, and the potential of dialogue underlies confidence in learning and the requisition of the cognitive tools of learning. Relationships are vital but can also be traumatic. They are turbulent and changeable and dominate all other aspects of the experience of school. If it is easy to forget the native intelligence, or acutely learnt instinct in young children, it is even easier to ignore the importance of social relationships. From the myths before going to school to reflections of the experience, it is the behaviour of other people that counts and the effect on each other's psyche. Intentions are not as important as effects, and the inadvertent remark can do as much psychological damage as the deliberate attempt to do harm. All pupils, like all readers, will recollect how easy it is in school to be humiliated. The competition both inside and outside the classroom is fierce and exposed. In that volatile mixture of the individual and different groups it is very easy to feel ignored or 'picked on', insecure or arrogant. Relationships are never again so constantly fierce and changeable. This is the real inner core of the school rather than the formalities of control and obedience.

This is not to say that schools are always sources of trauma. Schools are extremely mixed as an experience. There are many good moments as well as terrible half-hours. They are full of joys as well as difficulties, of humour as well as blights. We should never forget the resilience of the human spirit and the intention of so many teachers to make school as pleasurable as possible. Schools are complex and full of contrasts. They are also full of contradictions, and this is another aspect of what young people bring with them in their understanding of their environments. Policies and mission statements are clear, consistent and unambiguous in their writing, even if not carried out in practice. What a school ought to do, and tries to do, is often conveyed to those in it in terms of behaviour policies and the demands of the curriculum. The reality, in terms of individual experience, for teachers as well as pupils, is not like this, whether we approve of or admit the fact or not.

Complexities of real experience

When young children observe the behaviour of others they see at once the distinction between the statement of intent and the actual point of view. They understand, as they experience, the contradictions of human behaviour, the inadvertent hypocrisy. They know that people are capable of holding two conflicting opinions at the same time. They are aware that what is said can never be so exact as to be incontrovertible. They are natural epistemologists. All this, again, should be accepted as philosophically obvious, but the problem is that we lead our lives, and run our schools, as if it were not so. The curriculum and the tests are supposed to be without any complexities or ambiguities. The clearer the outcomes and the more simply they can be measured the better we are supposed to feel about the organization. Clarity, transparency and consistency are worthy goals, but assertion of their very worthiness does not make them automatically a reality.

The underlying culture of school consists of many layers of meaning and interpretation. All the time, individual pupils in school are scrutinizing what people do as well as what they say. They interpret the social structures and hierarchies of school, the way that people struggle between juxtapositions of power and of autonomy. The distinctions between the published, proper intentions like policies, and the actual everyday interpretation are well understood. It is at this level, not the public presentation, that schools are experienced and understood, as displays of contradiction and ambivalence.

The ontological contradictions of the human experience are given social and cultural force by the school. The contrast between the lectures and statements made by teachers and others, and their idiosyncratic interpretation by each individual in the mass audience is obvious, in the same way as different people read the same book and draw out their own quite distinct meanings. Under the surface there are many events influencing individual pupils, which they are doing their isolated best to make some sense of. This is all very well, but it needs admitting or accepting rather than the denial that is expressed as the assertion of all that is more systematic and managerial. Organization and good intentions as well as accountable systems are admirable, but they are only one interpretation of reality. As the term 'managerial' suggests, there is an attempt to control and close all that happens, and this means denying all the cultural complexities of the emotional, as well as organizational, hierarchies of school, denying the effects of what actually takes place and not just the intention.

One of the contradictions of the experience of early childhood and schooling is the fact that, whilst more people, in their individual memory, will know that there is as much unhappiness as happiness in their early lives, there is at the same time a denial of this knowledge. Childhood is too easily depicted as unproblematic, as a period of innocent and optimistic bliss. One result of this subsequent interpretation is the psychiatric problems that so many experience as they become older, the deep insecurities never having been resolved. Childhood is depicted with the same warm glow as the anthropomorphic heroes of illustrated children's books. There is a strong and unacknowledged tendency to reinterpret one's own childhood and the experience of school as untroubled and free from worries. This is the powerful work of nostalgia, but it is made systematic in the way in which the school system is envisaged. But then even young children understand nostalgia, and look back on themselves as only blissful and safe when they were themselves babies. Even if we at one moment accept the realities of other people's lives we will almost at once or at the same moment reinterpret them in a way that suits our, as much as possible, untroubled and untouched existences.

Pupils learn a great deal from school about the implicit theories of life. The formal curriculum is only a part of school. More long-lasting than the facts are the attitudes, the motivations, the understanding of other people, the interpretation of behaviour and the analysis of society, the way in which humans beings behave in groups and as individuals. As we will see from what the interviewed pupils report, the fundamental learning lies in the interpretation of events, in the picture of cultural assumptions observed in the organic whole of the school rather that the expressed intentions.

School as societies?

This puts schools into an odd position. What they ostensibly do is all published in league tables, in the success or failure of their results. Those schools that do best are also deemed to have formed the most positive and long-lasting attitudes in their pupils. The more easily the pupils seem to fit in with the ethos of the school, the more the experience of school becomes a valuable attribute. This immediately raises the distinction between schools in terms of their social and economic circumstances. The best-endowed schools have the most resources and the smallest class sizes. At this level the 'ethos' of the schools is relished and promoted. The many schools that do not achieve excellence are easily forgotten unless they are punished with 'special measures'. The distinctions are obvious, and they highlight the crucial social aspect of schools, the shared assumptions and the distinct personal relationships.

The contrasts between schools are clear and this in itself raises some questions of what is supposed to be an inclusive system. Are schools so different? Is there anything about the experience of schooling as delivered in most countries that is homogeneous as well as varied (Alexander, 2000)? In all schools relationships, for good or bad, count both with teachers and with peers. The forming of groups, formal and informal, creates an attitude towards society that is long-lasting, if varied. The sense of self-worth or its lack derives largely from school. Prejudices are formed there. Attitudes towards other people and their motivations are set. The crucial distinctions between the personality and the role people play are revealed.

Schools, like larger societies, tend to take for granted their purpose and their ethos. There is a job to do. What the job is can be problematic. As Egan (1997) points out, schools try to carry out contradictory tasks. Following a deeply academic tradition they try to create scholars in the mode of Plato, questioning, thinking, applying logic as far as it will go. They are cajoled into the maintenance of high intellectual standards. The power of thought as well as knowledge is invoked, and the sense of the importance of a discipline. This intellectual scrutiny can imply a criticism of the society in which schools are set.

At the same time schools are deemed to fit their pupils for the society of which they are part. The skills learnt and the culture imbibed are to make them into useful citizens, not making too many or too obvious academic demands. Schools are the rites of passage that prepare their leavers for employability, with the basic means of economic survival and of making a useful contribution to their particular community. This is not about questioning what happens but accumulating whatever is most useful in its furtherance, whether as children working or as citizens.

At the same time schools, following the tradition ascribed to Rousseau, promote the idea of children discovering their own unique personalities, expressing their natural individual tendencies and learning about themselves through actions and experiences. This places pupils in a different position again in relation to the school, becoming ostensibly the unique centre of attention, and continuing the discovery of play and emotional intelligence in the patterns of school life.

These aims are all recognizable, and most schools would protest that they do all three, even if they are incompatible. The difficulty is that schools do not have to examine what their implicit intentions are, and are even discouraged from doing so. They muddle on. They are driven by public accountability and published expectations. They produce the results.

The discomfort of this for some teachers is readily apparent but rarely treated sympathetically. It is easier to ignore the contradictions and not to explore the realities of what schools are conveying. If the difficulties of schools are sometimes instinctively clear to teachers, they are even more so to pupils. At the heart of their rich experience of school is the constant juxtaposition of the set of formal requirements made upon them, and the more complex inner meanings that they derive from the everyday events of school. The need to make some kind of sense of the experience of the social system is not helped because its essential purpose is rarely if ever examined. Indeed it is hardly mentioned, perhaps in itself a sign of disquiet or deliberate ignorance.

The result of these cultural contradictions is an ever more elaborate experience of school for the pupils. They do their best to make sense of it. They articulate the meanings of their experience as best they can, usually keeping quiet about their bewilderment, and doing their best to accept and to submit to their hidden desperation. When they do talk about the real meaning of their experience it is more surprising.

1
Research methods: hearing what pupils say

The sample and method

One of the authors of a study of early childhood headed a chapter, 'Early childhood education finds its voice: but is anyone listening?' (Pugh, 1997). It has recently become more fashionable to assert the rights of children to be heard, but the implications of this right, in terms of responsibility, are rarely taken up. All the demonstrations of the will to include the voices of pupils in school show how limited is the effect when this happens. Listening is all very well, up to a point, but to act on what is heard remains quite another matter. The fact that we can gather crucial evidence about the reality of schools from paying careful attention to the experiences of those within them appears only to be acceptable if the views concur with those who have control. If the views challenge the very nature of schools then they are somehow put aside.

This research depends on listening to pupils and analysing what they say so carefully that what is said can be believed in. School is just a part of the lives of young people, however significant, and they bring with them a number of other experiences than the reception of a given curriculum. This other life might seem to be separate from the objectives and measurements of school, but it is a reality that is significant to the individual if not to the system. The gap between the voice of the pupils and the imposition of policy is huge. If we really listened, would we go on doing what we do? This is the challenge that we will face when we have heard what the pupils say.

The pupils are old enough to be both informed and articulate. That is a deliberately laconic assertion. Far younger pupils are just as objective, and just as capable of giving their views. This outline of the methodology will therefore concentrate on the ethical dimensions of listening to young people, or, indeed, to any individual. Do views count in the face of policy? Can we learn from them? Whether we define pupils as 'children', or children as older or younger, and whatever the demarcation lines surrounding infants and adolescents, the personal experiences of the individual should count, given sensitive and thoughtful treatment.

The research basis for this book can be presented simply, but there are implications that need further explanation. The essential facts are these. The main core of the book is taken from 195 lengthy, semi-structured interviews, carried out in conditions of anonymity and confidentiality. The sample was derived from a mixture of schools from deprived to advantaged areas, representing a range of socio-economic backgrounds and minority ethnic groups, and carefully balanced in terms of gender. Every care was taken to make sure that, in an area that is often used by market researchers as the most 'typical' and representative of the rest of Great Britain, every possible permutation of social background was taken into account.

The interviews, recorded and transcribed, were structured to the extent of making sure that all those involved covered the same topics; but many of the most significant questions were those concerned with following up answers with subsequent probing – 'why?' Respect for the opinions of each individual was paramount. What was said was received seriously, without bias or expectation.

The significance of the results derives partly from the fact that there was no chance for the interviewees to guess what it was that the researcher wanted to hear. The theme was both ostensibly and in this case actually what pupils felt about their future employability, and about the attitudes of the world of work – from industry to the professions. Their relationship with schools was introduced as a background to this; the framework was the future, and the experience of school as the context of their lives as a whole. The probing was of their personal experiences and attitudes, not about their views of schooling as such. We did not wish to encourage criticism or give any indication of a line of argument.

Much has been written about ethnographic research and there are many books about methodology, possibly as many books as those that present the results of research. The facts of the sample, the qualitative approach, and the analysis are essentially simple, even if they could be elaborated. The ethical implications of the methodology – and their alternatives – are another matter. Pupils are to all intents and purposes treated as 'children' without an adult voice until they leave school. If this remains the case, will they ever be taken seriously?

Rather than elaborate on all the nuances of the sampling, or the particular approach taken in the interviews, or the complexities of the analysis, some of the wide implications of the methodology and its application will be explored, especially the question of 'informed consent'. In reality the problematic questions that surround research are not so much to do with intricate questions of methodology as such but with motivations and the uses to which the research results will be put.

Ethical issues with pupils

In registering for a research degree students are often asked whether their research raises any ethical issues. What is meant is whether they are dealing with particularly sensitive subjects, like fertility or cancer, where revelations of findings could have great consequences to the participants, and where participants themselves are vulnerable to emotional stress through the research. Clearly there are some subjects that do not raise such fundamental ethical issues, but this does not imply that there is any research that does not raise any ethical issues whatsoever.

When we discuss the issue of ethics in relation to research with children, however, we bring together two areas of moral difficulty: on the one hand, that comprising the host of questions concerned with the limits of behaviour in the activity of gathering data for research purposes and, on the other, that concerned with the status of 'the pupil or child'. The response to the difficulty and ambiguity of these two issues is that there is a wish to institutionalize and codify, a response that can be described as 'authoritative absolutism'. This is flawed on two principal grounds. The first is that the claims to provide moral solutions to ethical problems are undermined by the cultural and political character of many of the judgements involved so that what is revealed is ignored. The second is that it is the very existence of procedures and principles that obscures these cultural–political judgements under a cloud of apparently neutral objectivism, so that there is unawareness of the implications of the empirical data. There

15

is a need to apply skilled professional judgement with integrity, rather than to seek indemnity through the application of flawed procedures. The real question revolves not around the sample but around a variety of dimensions to the practice and philosophy of 'ethical procedure' in research. One essential question that both emerges from research and affects it is the 'status' of the pupil or the 'child'. It is no longer ethical, let alone true, to regard the child or pupil with a patronizing superiority, as if greater experience led to greater wisdom, or as if the child were somehow not fully human. Ethical questions apply to all research, and apply equally to all subjects. And yet there is an influential mind-set, bolstered by sentimentality, that sees children as separate subjects for research, somehow intellectually disenfranchised.

The most fundamental ethical question that shadows all research is the uses and misuses to which it is put. Questions of motivation, of deliberate or inadvertent manipulation of fact or hypothesis, of attempting to prove what the sponsor wishes to have confirmed, the use of methods of research as a sign of cleverness by the researcher rather than the seeking of what is valid, the mistaking of correlations for causes: all these are the most important ethical concerns, but are more often than not dismissed or disregarded.

Amongst the many reasons why the more fundamental issues remain unexplored is the diverting of attention away from them to other, safer areas of concern. In the place of the status, motivation and approach of the researcher, the focus of attention is placed on the participant in the research. (It needs a spectacular case like that of Sir Cyril Burt to draw attention to these aspects of the researcher. Burt was obsessed with the significance of measurable intelligence – IQ – as a worthy social instrument. His research happened to fit the prevailing belief that society would be better off if pupils were divided into ability streams at the age of 10 – the Eleven Plus. After his death it was revealed that he had systematically falsified the statistical evidence.) Instead of looking at the overall context of the methodology and findings, the question raised is that of how much those who are being researched, especially children, know or should know of what is going on.

Informed consent?

The British Psychological Society (1993) lays great stress on obtaining informed consent from those involved in research, and tellingly and unselfconsciously suggests that for children under 16 years of age consent should be sought from those 'in loco parentis'. One can understand the principles. The famous case of Milgram's (1974) research on obedience drew attention to two issues. The first was the heavy reliance on deception. As in the case of Latané and Darley (1970), the 'volunteers' thought they were participating in one piece of research when they were in fact being observed for quite different reasons. The experiments would never have succeeded without deception (Rosenhahn, 1973). The second issue was the effect of the experiment on the participants. Those who took part, with one exception, were horrified at their own actions. They had been proved willing to administer lethal electric shocks to innocent victims on the grounds that there were those in authority who sanctioned their actions.

The debate about Milgram and others symbolizes the debate at one level on informed consent: can deception ever be justified on the grounds that the research outcomes are so important that the means are subsumed in the ends? The question is, however, more complex than this. What exactly is 'consent'? This could entail merely the agreement to be interviewed, without having to see, or change, the transcripts, or it could be an implied support for the overall results as if each contribution were a kind of public document. What does the 'information' itself consist of? This could be the whole context of the research, the key questions that underlie the hypotheses, indeed all the indications of what a 'correct' answer would be. If Milgram had 'informed' his subjects he would perhaps have been able to prove that the Holocaust was impossible and that no single act of cruelty to Jews could ever have taken place. The very sensitivity of the approach can imply a particular point of view, or an attitude to the subject's age, or to the notions of what is meant by educational (David, Edwards and Alldred, 2001). 'Information' can mean declared bias.

The more that notions of informed consent are analysed, the more complex they appear. In an overview of the literature, Morrow and Richards (1996) note the fundamental contradictions that impinge on research with children. On the one hand children are regarded as vulnerable, incompetent and powerless in society. This is the basis of parental, or adult, consent, as in the British Psychological Society guidelines. On the other they possess rights and voices that need to be heard. There is an ambivalence about both children's capacity to be informed and their understanding of what they are consenting to. Plummer (1983) defined two positions: that of the ethical absolutist, which at its extreme allows almost nothing, and that of the situational relativist, which is open to any suggestions. Both are, however, somewhat undermined by the continuing ambivalence about children, their vulnerability and incompetence, their powerlessness and irresponsibility in law, and the lack of a culture of listening to children, despite an incipient recognition of their rights.

Listening to children

Children's rights, including the right not to be abused in any way, are only taken really seriously in extreme cases. The prevailing culture of regarding children as uninformed and unready to take part in social debate runs deep. It is enclosed in the whole edifice of the system of education where a set curriculum is placed before pupils for them to imbibe. Children's voices or opinions are the last to be heard in a school, even if the pupils form the vast majority. Even child-centredness, as a concept, can become a cliché of patronage. As Alderson and Goodey (1996: 114) put it: 'Child-centred ethics would simply be a form of the psychopathological egotism often attributed to young children by Piagetian schools of thought.'

The question of listening to children should rest on respect for what they say, with the assumption that as individual human beings they have information of their own, and that, in classrooms and other places, they are consistently giving their consent to answer questions. In the classroom, however, their willingness to answer is often abused by the dominance of closed questions, where there is only one right answer and the question is being posed as a test. The result is the opposite of listening to what pupils have to say. This does not stop pupils being willing to try.

These views on the subject of ethical considerations attached to research work with children illustrate how complex are the issues associated with research ethics, and how difficult it can be to provide clear and unambiguous guidelines for practitioners. Many ethical dilemmas can only be fully understood in the process of the practice of research, since it is in this arena that the problems of definition of terms such as 'fully informed consent' or 'competence' emerge as critical. To take one actual example with children, what do we mean by fully informed consent, when the *more* that is explained to them, the more feedback, the less valid the result? If for example we are seeking to discover the effects of television programmes on them and show a particular relish for any mention of sex or aggression, then children will be tempted to provide us with what is perceived as useful or gratifying. Consent can mean being merely allowed to talk, to be listened to, to be able to communicate things on their mind. If children *knew* what the research results might mean they might well treat the questions, like the questions that are used in schools, as 'closed', as to be guessed at rather than freely given. When one 'fully informs', is one actually treating the subject with respect, when respect comes from the personal dialogue and the taking of whatever the subject says seriously? Morrow and Richards (1996) highlight the complexity of the issues of protection and informed consent; Alderson and Goodey (1996) challenge conventional assumptions about the relative lack of competence of children, whilst Kelley, Mayall and Hood (1997) argue through transcripts of their research the fact that informed consent is (or should be) a feature of the whole research process, not simply a precursor of it. But how can one give complete information to the very subjects whose anonymity is being respected, and when the confidentiality of the whole exercise is paramount? The transcripts that arise from interviews are merely the beginning of interpretation and the quality of the result rests on the analysis. It could be more disturbing to feed back the analysis of what is said in a particular transcript – signs of deviancy or child abuse – than not.

Institutionalizing ethics

The preoccupation of individual researchers with the ethical character of their research is mirrored by increasing institutional concern, illustrated by the enshrinement of 'ethical principles' in social institutions and practices, such as ethics committees, and the codes of practice that govern their activities and decisions. Part of this stems from the defensiveness of institutions and the fear of litigation. Many codes of practice would actually make qualitative (not quantitative) research impossible. What is most interesting about these rules and procedures, such as those of the British Psychological Society, is that they assume that only *some* types of research have ethical implications. Not to take the view that every piece of research raises questions of ethics is a curiously 'unethical' position to take. We should constantly be reminding ourselves about the misuses as well as uses of research, and of the need for the validity and integrity of the findings and the interpretation, rather than defensiveness about the way of reaching them. Many institutions are following the lead of medical research in meeting situations of moral uncertainty and ambiguity by codifying ethics. Typically, institutions have introduced ethics committees 'charged with the task of ensuring that all research carried out by, or under the direction of, staff of the University has received adequate consideration with regard to its ethical implications' (Lovat, 1994). The growth of institutionalized ethics has its origins in the medical profession, and it has been argued that the approach adopted in bioethics should and could serve as a model for the general process of 'discerning the parameters for good, and encouraging the practice of good, within the professions' (Lovat, 1994: 197). In particular, this is an argument that recognition of the key principles of 'autonomy', 'non-maleficence' and 'beneficence' can support teachers acting as researchers in an era when these principles are beginning to be enshrined as quasi-legal 'rights' of research subjects. There are however cases where 'deception', which sounds so bad, can be the only way of gaining the truth. Is an under-cover police officer, trying to discover who is responsible for the selling of contaminated heroin, acting in an unethical manner because the subject has not given 'informed consent'? Is the action researcher trying to find out behaviour patterns by joining in as a member of a group not acting in a 'beneficial' manner?

Many of these research procedures proceed from an inadequate theoretical base, and they contain the seeds of a kind of negative inertia inhibiting research in general, and certain research procedures in particular. This tendency to inertia is accentuated in the case of research with children by the complicating factors of children's social status as ascriptively vulnerable individuals, by the debate over the character of any rights that they may have, and by natural and socially con-structed cultural differences between children and adult researchers. There is a range of ethical issues and their interpretations, within a framework provided by a set of oppositions that present themselves as key dimensions of the process to any researcher trying to establish an ethical position.

The first of these concerns the status of ethics: whether we wish to derive absolute principles and criteria for measuring them that will facilitate processes of judgement, or whether we wish to understand how varying institutions and individuals construe the process of conducting research ethically.

Prescriptive versus descriptive approaches

Whilst many institutions approach the business of developing proce-dures in a prescriptive fashion, by developing codes of principles and practice that may act as a quasi-statutory framework for making quasi-judicial decisions about individual cases, the distinctions between the codes produced by the different professional bodies serve to underline the fact that ethical stances frequently derive from the social construc-tion of the professional context of the body that produced them. It may be more useful to adopt a descriptive approach that analyses the ethical guidelines in order to understand what they tell us about how a given institution construes the research process and those involved in it. Examples of this analysis may help to caution against the wholesale importation of ethical codes from very specific professional environments.

Lovat (1994) advocates an approach to research ethics that is based partly on its lengthy and successful history as the foundation of ethical practice in medicine and medical research. There are aspects to this 'bioethical' approach that require careful consideration. The professional context from which they arise construes ethics as concerned not only with the relationship between individual professional and individual client, but also with the benefits provided 'in the interests of society' by medical research (quoted from the Constitution of the Huddersfield Health Authority Local Medical Ethical Research Committee, developed from Department of Health guidelines). However, the sense of balance between competing interests (the collective and the individual) provided by this formulation is frequently lost in the development of ethical procedures, where concern for the individual may be seen as overriding collective benefit. Just as an interest in research methodology can become an end in itself, so can pseudo-ethical considerations, such as the principle of information, inhibit all the benefits that come from seeking those 'truths', those enlightenments that could transform our understanding of the human condition. The Socratic search for knowledge can be taken not only openly to criticize the easier belief in sophism, but implicitly to question the fascination with methodology in which 'ethics' is just the final weapon of prevention. The Socratic concern with ethics has much more to do with the outcomes: how they are reached and what use is made of them. It is the uses and misuses of evidence that raise the greatest questions of ethics.

Screening procedures in medical ethics developed as a result of the practical problem of what Lovat describes as 'maleficence', the possibility of harm resulting from a research intervention. Again, consent, of the passing back of information, can have adverse effects on the children who have freely given information, unaffected by any designs that the researcher might have, not on them, but on the research question. Full information suggests a very clear research design and purpose, without any possibility of surprise. When dealing with the complexity and dignity of individuals, what kind of research is that? The consequentialist approach to ethics that this implies is often transferred to contexts where the prediction of consequences is not really possible, and a false analogy between physical intervention by researchers, and the act of human enquiry is therefore sustained.

Real consent

'Informed consent' is anything but neutral. The deep participation of children in research implies the need to explain exactly what is being done and why. It suggests an iterative process of a kind that removes all neutrality. It leads to a relationship more like that of a teacher and pupil, with one important difference, that is that pupils are rarely listened to, let alone have their opinions informing action. Consent in this form can be interpreted as contamination, bringing the desire to please, or annoy, to bend the listener to a partisan point of view.

There are those who, whilst recognizing the need for a neutral objectivity rather than turning research into a personal counselling session, maintain that the epistemological ideal of neutrality is imposs-ible to attain (Hammersley and Atkinson, 1983). This arises partly because of the still somewhat defensive position of ethnography and partly in reaction to the set 'hard' scientific principles of positivism. Instead of attempting to attain the ostensible veracity of scientific fact, the richer, more complex, more inward data are positively welcomed. The entry of the cultural identity of the researcher is seen as part of the research process, as if the explanation of ethnicity, gender and clan could explain the individual point of view or, at least, mitigate or neutralize accusations of bias. In the feminist tradition such an embrace of the individual researcher becomes a positive factor, as if the research were in fact a personal journey, carried out as much for the sake of the participant as for the outcome. The concept of 'truth' is even more distant: no longer even difficult to attain but unattainable, no longer even unattainable but not worthy of attainment. The journey is all.

This puts children in difficulties, whether their position is defined as vulnerable or simply as the weaker partners in power relationships. If the researcher, unlike the teacher, is exposed as participating in a personal journey, some of the rights of children, to have their voices heard, are lost. Instead of seeking to guess what the teacher wishes to hear, the individual is cajoled into the world of the researcher, playing a different kind of intellectual game. The idea of informed consent has a quite different meaning when imposed on children. Whilst this is not the place to raise the question of teacher/pupil relationships, the fact of their importance makes a great deal of difference for the research process.

The role of the researcher

The researcher will always be a factor in any research, even if inadvertently so, just as the teacher is a personality even when fulfilling a role. But this is not the same as being partisan. Being a participant can have all kinds of outcomes. There is a long tradition of participant observation, of exploring research findings by entering as subjectively as possible the inner experiences of those observed. The argument is that by sharing the same experiences as the researcher, the same insights, shared, commented on and analysed, are clearly understood by the researcher. With children this is much more difficult, if not impossible to do. The adult will remain an outsider – overhearing but not party to the conversation. One could argue that this is true of all participant observation; there will always be a sense of intrusion, however much the researcher cajoles him- or herself into the confidence of the group. With children, with their experience of peers and adults, such an entry into complete insight, if not confidence, is barred.

There is also a tradition of action research, of teachers in particular pursuing lines of enquiry that arise from their daily experiences. Far from tending towards neutrality such research is supposed to make an immediate impact on actions. It is a constantly evolving experiment. The subjects in this case do not know even that they are part of research. The daily occurrences take up so much of their attention, and the researcher/teacher so much of their time, that there is an unawareness that there are attempts being made not just to teach but to learn something that can be communicated to others. In action research the subjects are given a status and importance that has significance not for them but for the researcher. They are the unwilling participants.

There is a fine distinction between partnership and partisanship. It rests on the uses that will be made of the research. Action research is, after all, popular because it is designed to inform what the teacher would anyway routinely carry out. It is supposed to be personally useful, personally, that is, to the teacher rather than the pupil. But partisanship implies designs on the results. It is not just a matter of entering into the processes of thought and action that are empowered or revealed by the subjects, but an awareness of what ought to come out of it. The most significant ethical question of all is the bias, intended or not, given to research. The partisan, after all, wishes to gain significant findings, significant for him- or herself if not for others. The worst research results can be deemed to be the ones that are sought. And yet, this is just the motivation behind action research.

The relationship between teacher and pupil, between child and adult, is never one based on complete neutrality if this is interpreted as equality. Just to emphasize the point it is worth reminding ourselves that children resent those attempts to make the relationship neutral (Cullingford, 1999c). For 'neutrality' is not only a lack of order or discipline, but a sign of *laissez-faire*, ultimately of indifference. Children are clearly aware of adult personalities; they see the individual quirks and idiosyncrasies. But the 'neutrality' they look for is that of role and status. As a framework for individual endeavour children seek that common ground of shared rules and expectations. This implies that in any research they wish the researcher to fulfil his or her *function*, and carry out what needs to be done rather than explain it. The individual needs, the personal endeavour, merely intrude.

'Neutrality' is therefore a difficult concept. For some it is impossible, for others an impossible ideal. From children's points of view it is something they expect on a personal basis. The teacher, after all, is supposed to be fair and unbiased, to put personal feelings aside. The teacher fulfils a duty. So does the researcher, without having to add all the extra information of causes and personal outcomes. Individual children, in those circumstances of anonymity and confidentiality, can raise all kinds of topics. Listened to, at length, there is the opportunity to say whatever they wish to say, rather than seek out the answer to a series of 'closed' questions, either right or wrong. The good teacher is, in the eyes of children, someone who is fulfilling a role. The private concerns and personal problems do not intrude. The same is true of the researcher.

The boundaries of confidentiality

This raises another complex ethical issue. In interviewing children we occasionally come across startling revelations. We have assured all of confidentiality, like a priest. When the child then reveals sexual abuse is it the breaking of confidence to pass that information on? If the child makes a criminal tendency and experience clear, should anonymity be broken? How is one to interpret what children say: as personal as a knowing confession, or as free as anything that they would say to anyone, if only the person would ask? Our inclination is to treat what children say as the latter, but this begs all kinds of questions about our views of childhood. An adult would say all manner of things to all kinds of people, as long as he or she could be assured that it would not be passed on.

Given the relationship between children and adults, the question is whether there is an implicit understanding that there will always be something about the status of *in loco parentis* that implies individual responsibility. When we argue at the end for the child's right to be heard, this is because children have a hope, if not an expectation, that they will be given a voice, a hope often blighted. It is because they are not listened to at an early age that they end up with those major characteristics of adults, of dissimulation and the projection of the ideal self. This is not to suggest that children do not lie. It is one of the first social arts they master. But knowing how to do so is not the same as wanting to.

Responsibility, accountability and democratic control

It is emblematic that the debate about social research has little to do with the difference that it might make to the future of children's lives. It is, indeed, far from questions about empirical data. Instead it is concerned with power and control. Who defines the policies? Who adjudicates in matters of practice? The central ethical question is whether research is respected because it offers up empirical evidence, whatever the consequences, or whether research is at the service of policy. Does research test out those matters that any system needs to explore, or does it dare question those selfsame policies it is supposed to test and even protect?

This conundrum is encapsulated in one simple fact. Any study of the academic journals that report research will reveal that, for every piece of research that is designed to explore the experience of children, there are nine that measure the effectiveness, or otherwise, of teachers. As is the case of standard assessment tasks, even if the children's performance is measured, it is often for the purpose of ascertaining whether teachers are performing adequately. The overriding concern is to test the efficiency of policy, to find out what is most effective in what is imposed (Tooley with Darley, 1998). It is far less to do with the evidence that emerges from the witness of children, from the accumulated hearings of what we, as adults, are constantly told but have learnt to ignore.

What children say seems like 'soft' data. Sometimes we would prefer to see it that way, especially when it undermines many of the cherished assumptions about educational delivery. Children do not *seek* to question (Davies, 1982). They have an inbuilt conservatism and yearning for the status quo. They will not readily criticize the circumstances to which they are trying so hard to adapt. What they say is revealing, almost despite themselves. True responsibility might suggest giving them such a voice that their inner experience, and its effects on their future lives, might make a difference, even by influencing policy. But this is to give a status to and insight into the experience of children that only those researchers who have actually worked with young children understand.

Young children are not deemed accountable. This is because of the preservation of the myth of childhood innocence, or more particularly of adults' superiority. No one can argue against changes in maturity and understanding. The question is whether the ideal of wisdom can ever be achieved without at least understanding the base from which it comes. Children's rights are both mentioned and ignored in the Children Act 1989. The rhetoric that suggests a change in practice has not been borne out by events.

In contract research there is always the drive to be committed to certain answers, either to arrive at given conclusions or to test an a priori hypothesis (or better still a null hypothesis). The problem with the evidence that accrues from children is that it does not fit into this framework. It remains relatively unexplored. The researcher then finds him- or herself in the position of being both an explorer and a guardian of the results. These should not be mitigated or changed by expectation. But how can they be conveyed convincingly when expectations including the readers' are so firm? On the one hand it is an essential issue for children to be individually and democratically heard. On the other hand they fall into the most obvious category that can be ignored or dismissed. They are the 'other'. Gender issues and ethnic issues can be accounted and allowed for. The issues of age are far more complex.

Suggesting that children have rights, even as the subjects of research, immediately invokes the rights of parents. Legislative attempts to blame parents for their own children's misdemeanours reiterate the deep-seated mistrust of the rights or accountability of children (DfEE, 1998). At what age or stage are they responsible? When the analysis of the Bulger case was carried out, and the distraction of the horror video put aside, the whole question was on the concept of age (Smith, 1994). Is there a fixed point at which a person becomes fully human? Do children remain innocent, passive and unknowing until a legal age? To what extent are they, therefore, the proper subjects of empirical research? At the heart of the ethical dilemma lies the real issue, which is that of adults rather than children: the way they see themselves and the way they acknowledge all participants in society. As this chapter has argued, there is an element not only of defensiveness but of arrogance in the injunction of ethics over research. If every part of the advice were to be fulfilled the result would not be that research would cease, but that research involving children would be at an end. And that would be the most unethical conclusion of all.

Conclusions

The ethical principles for conducting research with human participants laid down by the British Psychological Society, which threatens disciplinary action against anyone who disobeys them, gives the impression of treating children as less than human. This is surprising. Educational psychologists, after all, did in the past obtain Qualified Teacher Status (QTS). This involved two very important elements. The first was the ability to be trusted with children, the demonstration that behind the closed doors of the classroom there were no acts or innuendoes that could possibly be dangerous or offensive. When we consider how rare are the instances of overt abuse of children by teachers, as opposed to psychologists or social workers involved with children in their care, one must assume not only that there are fewer opportunities but that there is a success in the sanctions of and more particularly the principles of QTS. To be a danger to children is defined as far more complex than any physical or emotional attack. It means not abusing the possibility of damaging the motivation and the intellectual potential of individuals.

The second, and most significant, element of QTS is the respect accorded to the individual pupil. Each pupil is deemed to be of interest not because of some psychological aberration or peculiar individuality. The 'inner life' of the individual is not some almost hidden manifestation of impulses to be uncovered by psychoanalysis but the recognition of an individual voice: a point of view, a habit, an attitude that is at once unique and strongly, in the Vygotskian sense, social. Whilst there might be so many constraints in the education system and in the National Curriculum in particular that listening to the voice is difficult in practical terms, it is nonetheless both axiomatic and proven by research that a central tenet of the qualified teacher is the ability to accept that each learner is more significant than the making available of what is learnt. All the research on attitudes and motivation confirms this (Pollard with Filer, 1995).

It is then only half a surprise to find that the ethical principles of the British Psychological Society contrast with those laid down by the

British Education Research Association, which talks of the 'care. . . that should be taken'. It is more of a surprise to find that on inspection the paragraphs of the British Psychological Society document (1993) treat children as if they were not real people, but rather misfits, displaced, ignorant and unable to find their own real voice.

This is in itself a fruitful area of debate. Does one, as Spradley (1979) implies, show each transcript of the interview to the interviewee for his or her consent? This is not the place to describe the consequences of such an action, although it will be implied in what follows. Does one, as Farrington and West (1990) conspicuously do not do, tell interviewees that one wants to see how they will become criminals and end up in prison? Does one really have the confidence of the subject if one confesses to a curiosity about particular sexual deviations? The paragraphs in the British Psychological Society document talk of the 'welfare and dignity' of the participants but they don't seem to mean it. On the contrary they imply labelling. There is not dignity there. '*You* are a criminal. I am interested in criminals.' '*You* are a pervert. That is the subject of my research.'

The British Psychological Society pamphlet spells out what is really thought of the welfare and dignity of the participants. Children 'have impairments that will limit understanding and/or communication' (Para 3.2). There is no sense of the real dignity of the individual or the importance of the human voice.

Of course one sees what they are getting at, and well meaning it is. But it is worth reminding ourselves of the inner world of children. They long to speak, to be listened to. The greatest problem in any education system is the distinction between the information given and the information received. To many children all questions given by anyone in authority are 'closed'. There is only one right answer. They spend their time trying to guess what it is the teacher wants. For example, 'What is a watershed?' Even an ostensibly open question like 'How are you today?' put before an adult in a university elicits the psychological response, 'What does the questioner want? What is the questioner after? What am I supposed to answer?'

The kinds of questions children themselves posit are the most open and profound. 'Why is there a world? Why are we here? Is there a God?' (These are the hands-on questions that some hurourists say justify sending children to school where they are taught not to ask any such difficult questions.) Does the adult respond by asking what are the objectives that underlie such a form of questioning? When children guess that there is yet another test in the form of an interview, all their powers of intellect will be directed towards giving the answers they deem to be right. They will conform to their everyday notions of school – 'right; wrong; do it again'. Thus if I had told children in my research on television (Cullingford, 1984) that I wanted to know the effect of violence they would never have revealed what they really thought. It all depends on what you ask. The BBC objected to my findings that children of under 11 watched television late at night (long before the advent of videos). They said they had figures to prove that children would never watch anything after 9 o'clock, the watershed in the metaphoric meaning of the word. The difference was this. They asked children (in a minor survey) what time they went to bed. 'Seven o'clock, sir' was the official answer. I asked children what they had watched the night before – and checked their accuracy against the programmes. Quite a different picture emerged, and far more accurate for not having any ostensible designs behind it. After all, children are perceptive enough to know what the BBC researchers wanted to have confirmed.

But then, the real problem of integrity within the ethical dimension is that of knowing what answer is wanted. The 'objectives of the investigation' are so well known by the researcher that he or she is determined to obtain them. As an example, another clash I had with the BBC was over *Blue Peter*. I discovered, to my surprise, that, with certain significant exceptions, children did not rate the programme highly. 'Nonsense,' said the Head of Broadcasting, 'and we have figures to prove it; so there: it's a very, very popular programme as well as our flagship.' In the end, they allowed me to inspect their viewing figures. Children were hardly part of the audience. More than 70 per cent of the viewers were over 40.

Telling people what you want to research is like telling them what you want to hear (David, Edwards and Alldred, 2001). In that context children would be the most inappropriate subjects. They are not like managers defending their record or hopeful candidates for a job. Their very openness seems like 'impairment' in the eyes of the British Psychological Society.

In research with pupils that involves not just observation or experi-mentation (Bandura, 1973; Berkowitz, 1962) but access to their own thoughts, there are certain principles that are very important. The first, and it cannot be stressed enough, is the respect to them as people who have their individual voices. Why do we not accord them the dignity they deserve? One reason is that it is threatening. Their gaze is absolute. A thousand references from the journal *Child Development* (published in the United States six times a year by the Society for Research in

Child Development) could suffice to demonstrate children's advanced social skills developed by the age of five. Adults do not wish to admit that. It has such profound implications. How on earth can we handle it? But there they are, complete, individual, thoughtful, whether we like it or not, by no means 'impaired'.

Children have things to say. That means that they can talk about whatever they want, and not just about those particular facts that the researcher wishes to hear and confirm. The subjects are more important as a locus of interest than the objectives of the research. They need to be allowed time and expression. And they appreciate it.

The interviews with children therefore need to be anonymous. This implies that the researcher not only respects the confidentiality of what the children are saying but enables them to accept that the researcher is not a teacher/official/manager/inspector trying to discover their secrets. The inner life of children after all is not the same as the 'secret' life. They talk about what they wish to, not according to some pre-planned objectives. The interviewer is not 'present' as a manager. The confidentiality of the proceedings is marked by the informality.

The question of integrity therefore depends on the fact that children do *not* know what the researcher is after. There is always a placebo. The interview is no more than a talk about a subject of general interest. Thus we would not dream of researching children's views of politics and society by saying exactly what we were after or we would have received party political attitudes second-hand (Cullingford, 1992). We allowed young, convicted offenders to talk about their experiences without them knowing what in particular interested us. It was *they* who brought up subjects and definitions such as truancy and bullying (Cullingford, 1999c).

Respect for the individual needs to be matched by the validity of the findings. The essential conundrum is the tension between the legality of ethics and the integrity and validity of research. It seems to me to be important to find out the 'truth', rather like a historian or possibly like a psychiatrist. That is more important than proving the cleverness of the methodology. To find the truth entails being pragmatic, changing our mind, being open to the evidence, being surprised. This is the opposite to some educational research, showing off, self-reverential, full of the symbols of the instrumentalism.

Of course there are issues of difficulty with pupils about which we should be sensitive:

- They can change their mind (just like all human beings) but this does not invalidate what they say.
- They can range widely over events, and tell anecdotes that are off the point, but this does not prevent unexpected insights.
- They can be lazy, as in the 'don't know' syndrome, which means 'Don't ask; I can't be bothered', or defensive: 'This is too painful to think about.' (This, however, can also be a finding, if one can know the differences between 'don't know' and 'don't care'.)

Nevertheless, children make good subjects. They are at the opposite extreme from politicians (and ethics committees):

- They are not defensive and have no lies to tell.
- They do not want to deceive themselves, or you.
- They like to talk.

This last point is true of all human beings. Provided the points of dignity are met (confidentiality, objectivity, anonymity, interest and concern), as well as the essential elements of validity (the ability to be surprised, analysis *follows* empirical evidence, and no preset hypothesis), then research with children touches on real ethics when we realize that we should have a responsibility to *act* on what we learn, a responsibility that is often wholeheartedly and unethically eschewed.

The subject matter of this book is how pupils experience and understand their schooling. It is not about what schools ought to be doing. It is not, in fact, about the success or failure of particular schools let alone individual teachers. It is not about the official curriculum or about tests and standards. Pupils here are being given the chance to talk openly and freely in summarizing their understanding of the meaning of schools in their lives. The fact that the results are unexpected, or challenging, or disturbing, should not undermine their reception.

The crucial methodology questions are all ethical. The approach taken is to try to find out what the pupils really think in a consistent way, rather than prove how clever the researcher is. The attempt is to explore the inner reality of pupils' lives in their overall social context rather than praise, blame or shame the schools. This search for the meaning of pupils' lives is not normally part of the research on effective schools. It does not try to isolate those particular variables that could make an instrumental difference in a particular circumstance. The open questions and the readiness to hear the answers mean that the results were a surprise rather than the confirmation of a well-theorized hypothesis.

Despite the centrality of ethics it is worth reiterating some of the methods used here. The essential techniques of the research can be briefly described and it is important to acknowledge the context in which the interviews took place. The original theme of the research was to explore the transition between school and employability, between the experience of school and subsequent careers. The tone was positive to the extent of finding out who had influenced pupils, what pupils had most usefully learnt and what were those skills that they most valued. It is useful in semi-structured interviews to have some kind of 'placebo' – or at least no clear indications in the opening questions of what would be of particular interest to the researcher. The ostensible subject was the pupils' own futures in the world of work. It was important during the interviews not to give leading questions, and not to provide clues or definitions of what was expected or wanted.

The literature on semi-structured interviews is extensive, and the ground rules simple to describe if far more sophisticated to put into practice. The importance of the interviewees not being aware of what information is being sought, and why, cannot be overemphasized, but has invoked the question of informed consent. All we need reiterate here is the importance of confidentiality, anonymity and the respect for the views of the informants. Pupils want to talk, and are even relieved at last to have a chance to do so. They need to have an appreciative if neutral interviewer who respects what they say. It is the duty of the researcher to make sure that all pupils have a chance to cover the same topics – for the sake of validity and reliability – and to make sure that all answers are appropriately probed for reasons or extensions, and to ascertain that there are no contradictions.

Given the right conditions there are no reasons to doubt the honesty of what the pupils were saying. It would be a far-fetched conspiracy to suppose that they could create such consistency. The 195 lengthy interviews from the core of the research were from pupils equally divided in terms of being in Years 10 and 11 (15- and 16-year-olds for the most part) and in terms of gender. The pupils represented five different socio-economic areas according to the standard Department for Education and Skills definitions, from the privileged to the deprived, and included a higher-than-representative number of minority ethnic groups. There were no significant differences according to any of these variables.

The fact that the same negative views were presented by those whose expectations were of a university career (one who even aspired to be a professor) and those who felt they had no particular prospects is significant and surprising. The analysis of the transcripts is a very important and lengthy process, and as delicate as the conduct of the interviews themselves. It is important, as in good anthropological research, not to impose a preset theory, but let the insights emerge from the empirical evidence. The transcripts were analysed several times as the true nature of the findings emerged. Looking at first for attitudes to industry or employment, the actual experience of school, in its profound effect on the thinking of pupils, was slowly and painfully made apparent. Neutral analysts should allow themselves to be surprised, and keep challenging their own assumptions. Every transcript was meticulously recorded for consistencies, or for variations, so that any conclusion that was general could be trustworthy.

The respect for listening to and hearing what pupils have to say depends on finding the best means to ensure validity and reliability. Up to a point this can be measured simply enough by the consistency of their statements and description, and by the fact that this consistency covers a wide range of social, academic and economic circumstances. Some of the pupils are going on to universities and assume their own success in the future as professionally qualified. Others feel their personal disenfranchisement and have few expectations. Whether self-confident or academically successful or not, the experiences presented here have a fundamental consistency that goes deeper than superficial or circumstantial differences.

In order to gather this fundamental evidence it was important to ensure that the conditions of the interviews were right. Consent was not only given but the interviews were welcomed as far as the information of the research was concerned. This was, as far as the pupils reflected on it, a matter of speculating on their future. The starting point (and many of the lead questions) was to do with their future employability, and what they had learnt in school that had equipped them. This had two implications. The first was that pupils were invited to take as positive a view of their experience as possible. There was no set agenda for them to be negative. The second implication is even more important. The interviews were not carried out with a view to seeking out criticisms or even doubt of the experience of schooling. There was no researcher bias in the approach, nor in the analysis of the transcripts.

The book rests on the ethical challenges of trying to discover the truth, and even more on making sense of it by listening to whatever emerges. If ethical questions arise the moment research is contemplated – 'What is its purpose?' – then they also reverberate long after it is ostensibly over – 'Will people be willing to listen or will they reject what is uncomfortable out of hand?'

2
Submission? Pupils' attitudes to school

Formative stages?

Schooling is a rite of passage that we take for granted. Beyond the idea of a stage in the development of young people, school is distinctive. Whatever happens at home or in the wider community, schools have an ethos of their own both collectively and individually. The building and the discipline, the expectations of what is learnt and of behaviour are all unlike any other experience, even if there are some unexpected similarities to other institutions.

All this might seem obvious but it is also taken for granted. There is an assumption that schools are an inevitable part of life and that the modern state cannot do without them. They are there to instil the necessary skills for economic survival and the social understandings of obedient behaviour, and are assumed to be the place where personal development takes place. Some might argue that these are three mutually incompatible goals (Egan, 1997). Nevertheless a great deal of reliance is placed on schools. They are seen to be responsible for all kinds of patterns of behaviour and success. Parents have a tendency to expect schools to develop not only academic prowess but social skills (Cullingford, 1990). Pupils are placed in schools as though the schools are hermetically sealed, and the pupils seem to emerge with particular qualities. The fierce regime of inspection is certainly centred on this premise (Cullingford, 1999a).

Schools are taken for granted, but they are also assumed to be generally pleasurable experiences. Would parents relish them so much, apart from the moments of freedom to work without disturbance, if schools were not seen to be enjoyable, safe and useful? Would parents be so encouraging, apart from being free from the constant 'Why?' questions that schools are capable of repressing, if schools were not assumed to be teaching all kinds of useful knowledge? Schools are taken for granted, certainly in the memory of those who have undergone them, and those who control them, as being positive and useful.

It is rare for people to examine, neutrally, whether schools are quite so positive and unmitigated in their efforts. It is rare to question what the experience is like for the pupils. The acceptance of schooling is such that those who even start to question how they operate can be accused of being 'de-schoolers' or overtly radical (Meighan, 1995). To underline the point, the fact that 'de-schoolers' are seen as mildly radical rather than subversive is a sign of the blandness of acceptance that makes schools so well padded with complacency.

And here, with implicit theory, we take a fresh look at the meaning of schools from the point of view of pupils. There is no imposed construct that measures what schools do for their pupils against what they ought to do, nor a measurement of internally driven performance standards against set targets and based on competition. The context of this research is simply to examine the inner lives of the pupils, taking into account the overall context, the social dimension and the 'hidden' as well as the formal curriculum.

Finding the positives

As the methodology section made clear, the pupils were asked to say positive things about their schools. Whilst they were allowed to be comparative – 'Would you recommend your particular school, and why?' suggests there might be alternatives – the questions that followed were open in the context of the general positive pleasure of school. Some of the answers might seem obvious, but sometimes, just as in great music, it is the seemingly obvious that is the most profound. One of the many reactions to empirical research on the inner lives of young people is to say 'They would say that, wouldn't they?', which is a kind of unwilling concession to the truth.

What the pupils said might seem obvious but it was, to those who listened, startling. They were asked to praise their schools, to pick out the best points, those things that they would recommend to their friends. There are so many possible ways such a question could be addressed, from the particular to the general. There could be a wide range from the utterly contented to the disaffected.

The overall judgements made about school were consistent and the variations in tone were small. What could have been expected was a general sense of well-being or contentment or general appreciation of all that was learnt. There might have been signs of small dissatisfactions or minor impediments to the generally smooth and satisfactory experience of school. In fact, whatever the expectations or the hopes, the opposite was the case. The attitudes towards school were uniformly negative.

At best the response would be a grudging 'It's all right.' Pupils cited a range of dissatisfactions, which will be analysed later, but these were all deemed to be part and parcel of school life. Critical incidents were symbolic of a shared, consistent, negative view of the experience of school.

The question policy makers would then posit, in an automatic denial, would be whether the pupils were merely saying this for the sake of it, to surprise, or whether they were saying it because the question was being asked as they were contemplating leaving school, or whether this is just the kind of attitude pupils would express, even if it was not the case. The first charge, that pupils were trying to shock, is not borne out by the consistency of the results, both across and within interviews. Those interviewed were in Years 10 and 11 and many were looking forward to university careers and well-paid jobs, so that the second point about an end-of-experience malaise can also be dismissed. They were openly reflecting on years of schooling. It is unlikely that pupils would consistently turn positive questions into negative answers: the chance to communicate to a receptive audience is not so common that it would be eschewed.

Rites of passage of a kind

It could be argued that schools should always be a difficult rite of passage that challenges and confronts the pupils with difficulties that they have to learn to overcome. This is not, of course, the official approach, which emphasizes the accumulation of knowledge and the readiness of pupils for a future in employment for which they need specific skills. From the point of view of the pupils, schools are uncomfortable places whether designed to be so or not. For some commentators, like Holt (1964), schools are joyless, repressive places in which children learn to be afraid of failure. The constant testing certainly has an effect. The curriculum in the guise of a means of comparing students' achievements with each other certainly lends itself to passive or active rejection (McFadden, 1995). The whole nature of inspection that makes visible the uncertainty of teachers in their own performance and puts the onus of failure on pupils undermines any notions of creature comforts in schools. The kinds of judgements that Ofsted makes, and the criteria that are employed, are open to question but they are rarely discussed (Gray, 1997).

It is as if the whole edifice of school were so implacable that pupils have to learn to submit to it. Teachers were always to be seen to be in control, the people with the power who had to be pleased. The duty of the pupil was to guess how to fit into this expectation. Now the teachers are seen to be representing other people's wills in turn, seeking out the best means to adapt to the requirements of results and inspection. Children conceive of schools as places where power is distributed downwards, and where they themselves have little or no voice (Gilroy and Wilcox, 1997). Nowadays every effort that a teacher makes to cajole the pupils into more work is interpreted as a sign of the teacher's selfish insecurity. All appears to be done for the sake of the external powers (Wharton, 1997).

This general theoretical perspective comes about because pupils have a sense of helplessness. Control is in the hands of others: pragmatically with teachers on a daily basis, but really with some unseen social forces vested beyond individual real personalities in the form of inspection.

There are certain kinds of control that depend on who is supposed to be 'boss'. This is a pervasive feeling:

> She says that if you get under this certain mark you get detention even if you're not really brainy. She like punishes even if you try your best. It makes me not want to do anything. It makes me feel I used to like it at first but now I just don't want to go any more. I have to though.
>
> (Female, Year 10)

The essential condition of school is obedience. The teachers make rules. In addition, the teachers set tasks. Rules of discipline are abetted by rules of standards. Poor work is punished whether pupils can help it or not. The result is the pressure to give up. 'I have to' embodies the essence of submission, doing what you do not 'want to'.

The demands of school

This form of teacher demand is a pervasive and regular routine of school. The assumption is that the pupils must be forced to work. They are not seen as wishing to work, seeking out knowledge, but as reluctant learners who, at the slightest sign of trouble, will rebel. Whilst this is a matter of the peculiar relationships embodied in the roles of teacher and pupil, there are more general symbols of control that convey the atmosphere of school. There are all kinds of rules, some explicit and arcane, that pupils need to follow:

> It's like you've got to be in boundaries. You're not allowed over that side of the school or down there. We're not allowed in the field and we're not allowed in the form rooms a lot at break. We're not allowed in there but we always get chucked out at dinner-time.
>
> (Female, Year 10)

Boundaries are everywhere, physically as well as embodied in rules. Inmates are moved from place to place, excluded from certain places at certain times, and always acquiring the sense of being incarcerated or excluded – 'chucked out'. It is all a matter of being carefully controlled:

> Because you can't do anything without being tagged by any-one; if you go one way you get done. If you go around the front of the school you get done. If you go around the back you get done. If you go to the side you get done.
>
> (Male, Year 10)

There is nowhere to escape. The control lies not just in the rules but also in their implementation. It is as if the rules were there in order to give excuses for people to punish them. The symbolic order of onto-logical insecurity is the construction of rules with equal opportunities to catch people out. You 'get tagged'. It is a question of being restricted. School is associated with being 'too impersonal. . . the whole sort of factory routine of it all' (Female, aged 18).

The lack of independence, the controls and the sense of being 'moved on' are all essential parts of school life. How do other places differ? Is this a subliminal view of life that pupils acquire? Do other places like city streets or terminals treat people in the same way? Some could argue that this could be a necessary part of the learnt submission that is expected of people as dutiful citizens. Others will say it is purely a concomitant part of the necessary procedures of school in which space is restricted, where there are too many people and in which order must prevail, assuming, of course, that the pupils would be out of control otherwise.

There are analogies with the rhythm of control, of moving bodies around, that the pupils are instinctively aware of and that have been brought out in some of the literature:

> Rules that they've made. Like they say this place is out of bounds and all that stuff and like they made it as if it's a prison or something because you've like a little area and then like we can't go down on the field and that's where the sun shines anyway. I don't like it here. . . It's a bit boring.
>
> (Female, Year 10)

The importance of order and control is clear in those who run schools, and the most pragmatic of teachers will address issues of discipline first. This is understandable.

The consequences on the thinking and responses of the pupils are, however, rarely examined. 'They' make the rules. 'They' control which places are 'out of bounds'. It is as if prison were the only analogy. The forbidden place is even symbolically where the sun shines. The space the pupil is allowed is full of gloom and controlled.

There is a sense of arbitrariness as to which spaces are forbidden and which are used. There might be logic to the rules but it is not a logic explained to the pupils. To them it is the rules and not the explanations that loom large. There is a sense of personal helplessness within an anonymous system:

> Timetable doesn't give you much information where the lessons are and which part. It just says maths and you've got to find out because when I first came here they didn't find me anything out, they just bunged me into a lesson: whatever they said they just bunged me into a lesson.
>
> (Male, Year 11)

On a first day the anonymous systems and the sense of ignorance combine into a nightmare, like not knowing where to go and being guilty of ignorance. Such a sense of helplessness captures the tone of the continuing experience of school. Others know what is expected. The individual is supposed to find out. Even when he or she does, the control and the power over information rest elsewhere.

There is an irony in this. On the one hand the individual pupil feels he or she is under control. The rules and the restrictions are clear. This should create a sense of relative safety:

> They're very strict, the teachers here too: they'll keep you in line and order that you won't do anything wrong and they'll teach you everything that you want to know.
>
> (Male, Year 10)

Despite this, many pupils feel unsafe in school. The first experiences make a deep impression: the sense of size and anonymity, with other people knowing what is expected, and with traps for the unwary. The mythology of the first day in school – 'having your head pushed down the toilet' – is quickly dispelled but the reality is just as uncomfortable:

> Because you didn't know your way around school or anything; you didn't know none of the teachers or anything. Everybody else seems a lot bigger and you were looking up to them.
>
> (Male, Year 10)

The pupils are naturally expected to adapt to the requirements of school. This is the first ritual submission. But thereafter the sense of constraint, of having rules forced upon them, or being locked in or locked out, grows rather than diminishes. The restraints are obvious. At the same time there is a strong and pervasive sense of unease.

Control and disorder

Despite the rules and regulations all kinds of events take place beyond the orderly control of teachers. Teasing, bullying, victimization and pain are a central experience in school. All mention bullying. Sometimes they mention it as witnesses rather than as victims (Smith and Sharp, 1994). Sometimes they see it within the classroom as well as outside. Bullying is a central experience:

I don't think when I've done at college I'll have to put up with this abuse and rubbish that you have to take at school. It's unbelievable, to be honest. I'll be glad to leave, definitely.

I think it's just anybody that they don't really like. Anybody that is different, really, just because, don't know, I'm not a swot, not like that at all really. . . just because I'll sit down and I'll get on with my work, 'Oh, you're a swot.' I'm like, 'Get lost; leave me alone.' They call me a freak and I'm just not a freak at all, it's just because I don't wear my trousers really baggy and you see it's just like a fashion statement and I'll wear what I want.

(Female, Year 11)

Bullying is a far subtler and more pervasive phenomenon than many people think (Lee, 2001). It does not depend on intentionality, on deliberate cruelty. It is often inadvertent, a matter of silence rather than of provocation. As this pupil points out, any form of difference can be the excuse for a collective attack. Whether it is the colour of skin or the clothes worn, the individual can be ostracized. More common and more pervasive than these superficial excuses for abuse are differences of culture or outlook. It is typical that pupils are bullied for being 'stupid' or a 'swot'. Conforming to the norm of peers is expected and those out of line by taking their work seriously are marked out for attention.

One of the surprising complaints that students make about teachers is that, despite their insistence on rules and obedience, they are often indifferent about bullying. There is a marked distinction, observed and noted by pupils, between personal insistence on behaviour and on avoiding personal trouble, and indifference to the suffering of others. Children learn that teachers insist on rules only for their own sake, and not because they are good or helpful for others. The conflict of norms is great: control becomes a weapon even of defence, and only invoked at times. In the cracks between symbols of order comes the counter-culture of undermining pupils' work and self-confidence. Sometimes the formal and informal systems of school continue to hurt pupils.

If 'swots' are despised as not being part of the accepted codes of behaviour, then there is something about the very way they try to keep out of trouble that attracts the atavistic instincts of bullies:

> They don't defend themselves, that sort of thing. . . I think it is
> because, well, it's mainly because they are quiet personality.
> They won't answer back or anything.
>
> (Female, Year 11)

These pupils remain unprotected. The very desire to remain 'invisible'
attracts attention, as they are different. Pupils observe the pleasure that
some of their peers have in pursuing victims and in creating an
atmosphere that is counter to the normal academic routines of school.
In some schools these bullies are controlled; in others they are rampant:

> They're quite violent and I don't know, they don't seem to have
> that much respect for anybody and everyone's coming up. . .
> I'd be really polite but the amount of abuse you get from them
> is amazing. It's just horrible. They've just got no respect for
> anybody.
>
> (Male, Year 10)

Beneath the rigid codes of control lie other alternative codes of
behaviour. The experience of school is a mixture of both. It is impossible
to understand the daily tensions in school without taking into account
how bullying, teasing and the undermining culture of peer group
pressure overlap with differently expressed but just as formidable
pressure from teachers to do certain things and to fit in to expected
norms.

The demands of teachers and peers create pressure. They are a certain
kind of excitement even if unwanted. There are certain moments when
such tensions come to the surface. They might always be implied, but
there are also moments of freedom from those points of attraction. The
general dismal tone of school is somewhat different. It is not so much
a sense of untoward demands as a lack of them, not so much fear as
boredom.

If schools are 'all right' as the highest point of praise this is because
expectations have gradually been whittled away. The problem for
schools is that in between the moments of tension or excitement are
vast plateaux of boredom.

Whilst the routine description of the quality of school is at best 'all
right', the common perception of day-to-day life in school is of hours
during which there either are meaningless tasks to be carried out or
there is 'nothing to do'. Words like 'pointless' and 'waste of time'
abound. The sense of pointlessness might lead to boredom or vice versa
but they are strongly linked.

The routine of school

The languor comes about because school seems meaningless: it seems without purpose. All the bullying clearly has no immediate purpose in terms of learning outcomes, but is significant in shaping the attitudes of pupils. The lack of a sense of meaning makes the imposition of rules the more distant. The less there is to do the more artificial the necessary control:

> Not really good, there is nothing to do. There are certain areas where you're allowed and certain areas where you're not and there's nothing to keep you occupied. . . I think most of the things that you hear and see go on in most schools.
>
> (Female, Year 10)

In circumstances where the main task is to follow the dictates of others it is hard to be creative or to invent interesting occupations. There are empty passages of time within and outside lessons. Boredom is part of the fabric of school: hanging around, waiting for something to begin and waiting for it to end. Routines are imposed on pupils so there is no flexibility of personal judgement. This emptiness is deeper in the school than the rumours that pupils hear of being 'told the wrong directions' or 'being beaten up'. Those things happen too but the individual experience of marking time is significant. In the context relationships with friends (and with enemies) become more significant. They fill the gaps, and give a purpose for coming to school:

> Sometimes it's all right and sometimes it's not and I can't be bothered to come because of all the tests that we are doing and that. Waste of time. My friends, I get on with my friends.
>
> (Female, Year 10)

School, in this instance, becomes something marginal. To some extent the experience of school as formally constructed, devised by policy makers and implemented by teachers, is of a marginal activity in the strained and complex personal lives of pupils.

They are learning about each other, about relationships and personal ambitions. They are learning about the world in which they live mostly from each other. They are trying to put meanings on to what they observe about other people's behaviour and their motivations. Teachers, driven by external demands, protecting themselves and imposing rules, become like another part of the peculiarly complex relationships within school – passing, but intense, juggling for authority but impersonal. One of the associations with teachers is boredom, but relationships can be worse than that:

> Getting away from the teachers. It's their attitude towards us pupils. Always shouting at us instead of being reasonable. Not hearing us out.
>
> (Female, Year 10)

The alternative is 'meeting other people and just getting the hang of other stuff, being out in the world, really' (Female, Year 10).

'Just getting away from it all' (Male, Year 10) marks out the final dismissive judgement of the school experience. There is no sense that this was a passage of time valuable in itself, exciting, pleasurable or useful. Instead the pupils look on their experience as a mixture of boredom and purposelessness, underlined by a sense of threat, from peers and teachers.

Pupils' attitudes to schooling, responding to attempts to elicit positive judgements, make consistent reading. What they are learning, for all kinds of reasons, is not what they are supposed to learn. Perhaps, towards the end of their school career, they are ready to pass on. We should, nevertheless, wonder at the consistency of their negative judgements, the lack of excitement or purpose, the sometimes brutal sense of normlessness. There are many characteristics of school that are off-putting (Lewis, 1995). There is also the lure of the outside world. If the two – the present and the future – were connected, schools might make more sense, a meaning that pupils seek. The fact remains that pupils find themselves in an impossible circumstance. Even more to the point, this sense of personal normlessness and grievance is seen in those who have power over them. It is genuinely pervasive, this 'lost cause':

> The teachers. . . I can understand the point of view that they can't be bothered with it any more, because like I say most of the people were just turning up at school because they had to. They didn't have to do any more work when they were there. Teachers basically weren't there to teach them; they were just to look after them, basically. It's rather pointless if you're doing this. Well, some teachers were still trying to discipline

them in the fifth year, but other teachers just gave up. It was a lost cause.

(Male, aged 18)

In such conditions of pupil disillusionment it is no surprise if teachers give up. More significantly, even if they do not, they are perceived to do so from the pupils' point of view. The teachers cannot be bothered. They try in the face of implacable odds. The malaise is too deep. The pupils 'just turn up' 'because they had to'. In school there was nothing meaningful to do. Discipline was the only chance: an outside will and an intransigent group of people. This is an absurd situation. No wonder there is a sense that teachers 'give up'. No wonder this is a 'lost cause'.

What the 'cause' is will be explored later. Schools need a purpose that makes sense to the pupils. What the pupils learn, however, is some very significant observations about the nature of society, about rules and regulations and how to overcome them, about motivation and distraction, about the personal power of individuals and the imposition of their will and, above all, about submission, long-term or temporary, resented or accepted. What schools teach, essentially, is submission.

3

Pupils' perceptions of the purpose of school

What purpose?

The purpose of schooling is a subject rarely mentioned either in individual schools or in the wider community. This is partly because it is taken for granted that schools have both an explicit social and an economic purpose. The place of schools in society is seen as obvious. The 'broad and balanced' statements behind the National Curriculum talk about the need for skills, for employability, for good citizenship and for keeping up with the economic competition of other countries. Whilst there are both philosophical and historical accounts that delve into the underlying purposes of school, education systems being relatively new phenomena, the purpose of schools is still generally taken for granted.

Those who question some of these assumptions have tended to be considered eccentric. The traditions of Gramsci (1978) and Bowles and Gintis (1976) that try to uncover what the pupils are actually learning about their place in society tend to be demonized as politically motivated, and when the underlying messages that teachers give are deconstructed (Sharp and Green, 1975) there is a tendency to conclude that this is how things should be. Society will always impose its structures and cultural assumptions on the young in its care. Economic purposes are paramount, even if the social destruction between the skilled and the unskilled is overdone.

Others who question the underlying purposes of school have had little impact on the ways in which educational systems go about their business (Holt, 1972; Illich, 1971). They are associated with deconstructing the whole structural organization of schools, rather than questioning the philosophical systems. They are accused of negatively pulling a social system apart, rather than constructing an alternative way of thinking. These contrary views merely highlight the fact that schooling systems are taken for granted and rarely examined. The debates are *within* the present circumstances of school, like that between school improvement and school effectiveness (Elliot, 1998). The arguments are at the edges, like what should be in the core curriculum or what should be the age of entry and of leaving the compulsory school system, or whether schooling should include religion and morals, or the extent of parental choice. Rarely is the purpose of schools a subject of educational debate.

Even if some of the marginalized arguments about school are occasionally the subject of educational debate, there is one group to whom the purpose of school is never explained. It is clear from previous research as well as here that schooling is so much taken for granted that there are no further issues to be debated. There are two clear examples of the consequences of taking the purpose of school as read. When White with Brockington (1983) explored the lives of school leavers who were without jobs and therefore likely to be disaffected with school – the school leavers could have blamed all on their experiences – they were surprised to find that the tone of the young people was more of regret than anger. The young people wished that schooling had been different, as if they would like to have had a second chance. The first point they made was that they wished that the curriculum had been made more relevant to them; and they also wished they had seen its relevance. The major point, however, was that they wished that someone had explained to them the purpose of school. No one ever had. Anything that could have been relevant passed them by.

In research that led up to *The Inner World of the School* I explored the experiences of pupils in primary schools (Cullingford, 1991). One of the clear findings was that from an early age they had to guess what they were at school for. It was not a subject ever raised. They drew their obvious conclusions from the time they entered school when they said that the purpose of school was to get jobs. Primary schools were there to prepare for employment. Clearly, in order to get a good job pupils had to learn things and gather skills and, in particular, pass exams. The ultimate aim was clear, whatever pupils had to undergo on the way: to get a good job in a competitive world.

Perhaps society as a whole does agree about the purpose of schooling. If young people, in the wilderness of silence, come to the same conclusions about economic and employable skills as the rest of society, perhaps there is an overwhelming if unexamined consensus. We do, however, need to remember that the absence of debate on the subject means that all kinds of interpretations are placed on the experience. What is observed, about hierarchies and power, about control and inspection, about fear and stress, becomes the more powerful. Comedians make jokes about the actual purpose of schools: 'Can children keep asking these questions – "What is eternity? How could the Universe start with a big bang? What is the meaning of God?" We can't answer these questions, so what do we do? Send them to school where they are taught not to ask questions like this.'

Children also come to their own conclusions. They observe the behaviour of teachers and peers. They meet a given curriculum and undergo batteries of tests. They have to make sense, in their own way, of their experiences. Those big questions about meaning with which they are born and which trouble them have nothing to do officially with their experience of school, which is increasingly pragmatic. What they understand as the purpose of school is the more interesting because so rarely discussed.

By the end of their experience of school pupils should have a clear perspective on what schools are for, what they have learnt and why. Especially as they are nearing employment or preparing for the next stage of education, the whole of the compulsory educational experience begins to make some kind of personal sense. The questions being sought from them here are specifically about whether anyone talked to them about the purpose of school and, whether anyone did or not, what this purpose might have been.

The social context

Pupils are brought up to accept schooling as an inevitable rite of passage. Schooling is received as an initiation into society, although this is never spelt out by the authorities. Schools might give a distorted view of society as a whole, and the fact that schools are not promoted as symbolic of social institutions might suggest that people do not wish to suggest that schools encapsulate the subsequent experiences of adult life. Schools might not be typical of society as a whole but they are interpreted as being so by the pupils. It is always difficult to express a coherent sense of what a large community means. Indeed it is easier to dismiss the notion of society altogether, but schools, whatever their size, do give a vision of society, however imperfect the analogy.

Schools are the first significant environments in which children are taught to socialize with each other and with adults, and they interpret their experiences according to their own definitions, using their own observations as a systematic template. The implicit purpose of school is suggested by the ubiquity of the common experience. Virtually everyone goes to school. It is taken for granted. The only debate is about when, not if, children should go to school, and the only controversy that affects them is when they should leave. For the most part schooling is presented, and to a large extent accepted, as inevitable. Schools are part of the larger political system. They are inevitably linked with the economy and with upholding the existing state of affairs. This is natural, but schools are also expected to instil their pupils with the experience of social values and behaviours, at the same time as developing pupils' independent critical judgement. It is because these purposes are never articulated as well as mutually contradictory that the influence of schooling is so unexpected (Egan, 1997).

The social expectations of schools are profound. Schools are assumed to instil discipline as well as knowledge. Parents in some countries rely on schools rather than themselves for developing good manners and behaviour as well as knowledge (Cullingford, 1985). These expectations might seem extreme, or a derogation of parental responsibility, but they are readily, if inadvertently, taken on by schools. Whilst the regimens of inspection ostensibly concentrate on standards of achievement and the delivery of the curriculum, reports almost inevitably comment on all the other, more social, aspects of schooling that affect learning, like behaviour and discipline, and even 'spirituality' (Cullingford, 1999a).

The beliefs that parents have in schools are often very strong. The assumption is that schools are safe and happy, as well as essential. They not only pass on learning and administer tests but act *in loco parentis* in maintaining order and fostering obedient relationships. Whilst parents are also concerned with some aspects of schooling like bullying or the stress of teaching, they are the more shocked or surprised when these aspects are revealed because of their implicit belief in the necessity of the experience. Whatever their children go through, parents had to do the same themselves. Whilst parents compare their own experiences to those of their children, they rarely question the centrality of the experience in their lives. Schooling is supposed to provide for all the needs of children, the moral, the spiritual and the physical as well as the academic, as so many curriculum documents have articulated. Schools are seen as inevitable and, as such, the more unquestionably necessary.

Schools are such a central part of the modern experience that anyone who stops to examine them and their effect is considered to have a personal agenda or be politically radical (Meighan, 1989). It is the pupils, however, who by their personal and unaffected analysis really question the nature of schooling. In their acceptance of the given purpose of schooling – they would accept what they are told but need to interpret what they can – they realize there is a tension between their own experiences and the implicit theories that surround schools. This tension is usually suppressed in a kind of vehement obedience.

The differences and distinctions between the whole paraphernalia of society and the individual perceptions and experiences in the young deserve fuller exploration. What pupils reveal about the purpose of school demonstrates a yearning for greater comprehension and the rarity of the chance to articulate their concerns. They are so often taught that the answers are already given, that all questions are closed. Naturally these tendencies to prevent a proper scrutiny of experience can be overcome but it is not a process fuelled by many opportunities.

One important social fact that pupils learn in schools is that their opinions can easily be dismissed. There are always only the right or wrong answers, and personal opinions do not fit into that agenda. Seeing pupils able to start to articulate unexamined and unrehearsed feelings suggests a great deal about the authenticity of their statements. They have, after all, been taught not to talk about certain things since these either are seen as not fitting the official ethos of schools or are interpreted as subversive.

Outcomes or judgements?

The way that pupils talk about schools reveals more about their shared and mutual experiences than about the way that schools are officially judged. There is a constant juxtaposition between the two since pupils know what they are supposed to have learnt and what they are expected to say. At one level they do their best to present the formal judgements about the purposes of school. They do their best to conform to expectations. They also suggest that their actual experience is not quite like this. The implicit purposes of policy give them the chance to recognize both the unexamined practice and the actual realities of school. People do their best to be positive. They try to put together what their experience is like, assuming that all the practices of society are entirely benevolent. They try to make the best of things. This is never easy.

It is unlikely that pupils would consistently turn positive questions into negative answers: if they did that when they had a chance to talk, it would overturn all assumptions about human nature (and, incidentally, undermine completely the nature of schooling).

Schools are used by their inhabitants in a variety of ways. We know a great deal about the ways in which they can become alienating places, and how young people feel essentially excluded from them (Cullingford, 1999b). We also know how many young people silently accept and put up with the systems they are in (Pye, 1989). There is also a tradition in which schools are, for some, a kind of safe haven. When the school system was set up, social reformers, seeing children in factories alongside their parents, were interested in postponing the transition from school to work (Reubens, 1977). Education was a postponement of drudgery, and the virtues of school were placed against the evils of work. Whilst social conditions have changed, there is still an element of thinking about, and within, schools that continues in the same emotional framework. 'The best years of your life' might be a cry of nostalgia but within schools there is a clear juxtaposition between those parts that are safe havens and those parts that are threatening. Every pupil realizes those moments of peace within school (Cullingford, 1991). When school is contrasted with the world of work, there can be an element of fear of the unknown:

> The only thing that scares me is that I'll be there and I won't know anybody. . . some of that I'll just have to get used to or something.
>
> (Female, Year 11)

School is a place to meet friends. It is a place where the routines are familiar. The world outside could easily pose a threat; a place of employment or a new institution will demand new and different relationships:

> because a few of my mates who have already left school, they said they wished they were still here. All their friends and things like that, like they're on their own now. You don't get

> bossed about too much if you went to technical college because
> you're told what to do all the time in school.
>
> (Male, Year 10)

If school is a matter of being told what to do, of following rules and
instructions, it might be oppressive, but it is also easier, without
responsibilities for decisions. To this extent school can present itself as
a social haven. It is, after all, a gathering of peer groups. One should
not be surprised if there were a certain reluctance to enter the large
and potentially more threatening world of employment. In fact, as we
will see, despite missing friends, the vast majority of pupils could
hardly wait to leave school. Perhaps this could be partly attributed to
the fact that the purpose of school, from the beginning, lay in its ending.
It is a process through which all people have to go, in order to emerge
at the other end. If the purpose of school is employment, then pupils
will have fulfilled it by leaving.

If the ending of the rite of passage is the implicit purpose of schooling,
then the more common interpretations of that ending are the GCSE
exams, which either mark a new beginning, in a sixth form, or the
termination of all. Fifteen thousand hours will have been spent in school
(Rutter *et al*, 1979). All kinds of experiences, formal and informal, with
intrinsic and extrinsic factors shaping them, will have taken place. The
question remains how much time has been spent during those years
of explaining their purpose. Do pupils have a chance to make sense of
it all, and relate the experiences of school to their personal lives and to
their futures?

Reasons for being in school?

In passing, and given as a subsidiary question to the interpretations of
what had been learnt, the pupils were asked whether anyone at any
time had talked to them about the purpose of school. This question
was met by a mixture of puzzlement and bewilderment. With the few
exceptions to be recorded here, and which themselves are telling, there
had been no discussion about the meaning of school or what it was
for. The very idea of raising the question met with bewilderment, partly
because for years the pupils had brought their own assumptions to
bear, and partly because there must be an implicit social purpose,
understood, if not shared, by all. The real bewilderment came about,
however, because the experience of school was so far from any
exploration of such a theme.

No one had talked to them about the purpose of school; no one in a school would. There might be implied answers – if you don't work hard you won't get to college – but no one would, it seems, dream of exploring the question.

The response to whether teachers ever talked about the purpose of school was blunt and consistent:

> No. Not really. I don't think they tend to spend a lot of time with people who just get on with it and do whatever they want. You know, it's like the people who don't tend to behave. They're the ones who get talking to all the time, so. . . If you do what they want you to do they don't bother talking to you, really, so. . .
>
> (Female, aged 17)

There are themes here, which illuminate part of the essential facts of school. People 'get on with it' without stopping to think about anything as arcane as purpose. The pupils get told what to do, and as long as they do they are essentially ignored. Those who receive all the attention are those who misbehave, who challenge the system. Perhaps it is those who ask such awkward questions. 'Getting on with it' is all:

> I didn't really speak much to the teachers. I normally got on with my work and stuff. I'll be honest. I didn't really communicate well with teachers because, like, I communicate better with my fellow pupils.
>
> (Male, aged 17)

The lack of communication with teachers at a level of such detail is part of the ethos of school for many, possibly most, pupils. Real conversations about matters such as purpose take place with the peer group. There is a deeply held view that schools are essentially for the teachers and that pupils have to learn to accept this fact:

> Most of them at my school just never bothered with it [purpose]. They concentrated more on just getting the lesson over and done with – getting one lesson after another all the way really, instead of trying to get on with you.
>
> (Female, aged 18)

The very fact that there could have been a dialogue about a common sense of purpose or a shared vision struck most of the pupils as a strange thought. It was so far from their experience. This does not mean that they had not thought about it, or that they had no reflections. It demonstrates that there were no formal mechanisms for discussion about issues beyond the curriculum, or issues about society:

> No. They never said that this is what you have to do. It's something that you knew anyway, didn't you?
>
> (Male, aged 18)

> Most of it they don't. But I suppose you do in a way as well, but you don't realize it. It's only when you think.
>
> (Male, aged 17)

All that is learnt about the purpose of school is implicit. One might add that it is at this informal level that all emotional and attitudinal learning takes place. Reality is observed rather than taught. What is clear is that the pupils are supposed to strive to do well in examinations. That is the end in itself and the accepted justification is that good qualifications lead to good jobs. This reveals the social system as a competition in which only some – who work hard and have the ability – succeed. On those rare occasions where there has been a message spelt out by teachers it has centred on that fact:

> I think we once. . . a couple of times they've taken us into the hall and the teacher spoke to all of us and said like. . . you've got to buck your ideas up 'cos you're going to work and. . . they really just told us it were about working. . . get an education to go to work. . . and get through life.
>
> (Female, aged 16)

The message is clear – 'to learn and how to get a job and that lot' (Male, aged 15).

Getting 'through life'; getting on. School is seen to be about 'bucking up' and working hard. There is no mention whatsoever about what is actually taking place in school, no mention of any possible pleasure in it. The message is all about outcomes, whether it is implied or made explicit.

The underlying purpose of school seems to lie in leaving it. The pupil looks toward the end, the qualifications, the skills, as a preparation for the next stage in life, as if the inexorable march of time were a meaning in itself. Whilst some pupils regret not any longer having a meeting place for their friends, and whilst there were occasional glimpses of apprehension, the prevailing tone of the comments is relief and pleasure in leaving, 'getting away' in the general phrase: 'I think it will be good to be able to get out' (Female, Year 10). The sense of relief in going makes it sound like some kind of escape:

> Not tied down to this school any more and you've got, in a way, more freedom. You're not just at high school any more. . . you're not under strict rules any more, like at school.
>
> (Female, Year 10)

> I'm just tired of school now, like I put everything in for the last few years and. . . I'm just feeling like, oh, I can't wait to get out. I'm at a stage where I can't wait to get out of school because I'm tired of working hard with all the homework and everything.
>
> (Female, Year 10)

One of the consistent themes is the experience of school in the sense of being incarcerated, of being forced to do things, however unwillingly. Even if these are 'for their own good'. The rules, the inflexibility, the unshared assumptions become ends in themselves. It is as if that is what school is perceived as being *for*. It is not just for teachers but for its own sake:

> Rules that they've made. Like they say this place is out of bounds, and all that stuff, and like they made it as if it's a prison or something because then you've like a little area and then like mostly we can't go on to the field down there and that's where the sun shines anyway. . . it's a bit boring.
>
> (Female, Year 10)

Rules and obedience to them. Is this the purpose behind the leaving? One of the implied reasons for schools is that they are there to teach future citizens. These need skills but also to fit into existing society.

Perhaps there is some truth in the Gramscian assumption that schools teach their inmates to accept and adapt to the hegemony of the organization.

It could also be, as Egan (1997) so forcibly expresses, that the purposes of school are contradictory and impossible, drawing pupils in all kinds of directions, social, academic and personal, all of which undermine each other. From this research, however, it seems that it is the schools' lack of stated purposes that causes the problems. Students are not just pulled in different directions but left directionless. Apart from the contract with the outside world, schools seem to have a life all of their own, out of context, even meaningless in broader terms. The last illuminative quotation struck a recurring chord: the analogy with prison. School might need rules but these are imposed. The pupils long to escape them.

From work in school to paid work

The main escape from school, as well as its justification, is the acquisition of a job:

> To get a job at the end of it. I used to just sit back and think, 'Oh, I'll get myself a job', but really I shouldn't have done, do you understand what I mean? I should have put my head down and done what I should have done.
>
> (Male, aged 17)

As in earlier research findings, there is a genuine sense of regret at the missed opportunities, at not realizing the possibilities of school. Some look back and wish they had 'put their head down'. Others feel that would have made little difference:

> No, I don't think any of it prepared me for what. . . really for jobs and that.
>
> (Female, aged 17)

Both witnesses reiterate the close connection between the school and employability. If the whole exam system and the schools that mount all the tests have any *raison d'être* it is in one kind of outcome: jobs. It could be important that all schools should rethink this strategy, which in itself would question the nature of the traditional curriculum. It is, however, an assumption that creeps in for the want of any other. Schools are for qualifications, for jobs. That gives them a single dimension of the social context. Schools are sometimes seen, by Ofsted in particular, as being hermetically sealed, complete in themselves, and unaffected by socio-economic circumstances. This is not, however, as pupils experience them. One dimension of the social context is the looming reality of the world of employment. Another is the everyday reality of life at home and in the neighbourhoods.

It is sometimes hard for those who study schools and what takes place within them to recall that, for the pupils in them, this is only a minor part of their lives. The formal curriculum and the examinations seem to dominate, but there are two other aspects of life that are just as important, if not more so, for the pupils. One is the 'hidden' curriculum, the social interaction and the informalities of school. The other is the life outside, the full context, the private passions and interests that are a mark of a fuller life. The emotional meanings given to the individual life are of such depth and of such a different context that, as Hodkinson reminds us, it is only really possible to understand the meaning and purpose of school in this way (Hodkinson, Sparkes and Hodkinson, 1996). Each individual has a different story to tell – and only through such stories do we fully understand the ways in which the purposes of school are understood.

We must acknowledge the influence of others and the insights provided by particular experiences:

> My Dad. . . wants me to do well. 'Cos my sister didn't; so, well she were a bit of a bad 'un at school. She really never used to go much. Got herself pregnant when she was 17 and that, so. . . He thinks that she's failed him and he, like, wants me to, you know, pick up from where she left off. It's just that he wants me to do well but he still sort of looks at me as if I'm a little kid as well, as though I can't do it.

> He doesn't realize, you know. I told him last night that, you know, 'I'm leaving on Wednesday, Dad'. . . and he's. . . he didn't really seem interested half of the time. But I think that's because of his job as well, you see. 'Cos his job's hard on him, so. . .

> She's happy. But I think that she wishes that, um, if she didn't have Ellie, her little. . . my niece, that she could go to college and do a course or something. Or, she keeps saying if I had my time again I'd go back to school and definitely work this time and everything. She used to be at home most of the time, like, so. . . I think she just thought I wasn't capable of. . . and this lot, and she says it'd be pretty difficult to find another job,

especially all people you know just leaving school and they've got so many grades and stuff. And she keeps saying, 'Oh, I'm getting too old', and all this.

(Female, Year 11)

There is a different perspective on the purpose of school where a quite different event dominates. The sense of outside pressure – from the disappointed father to the cajoling school – is strong, but both seem to provide the opposite reactions to those intended. And yet there is also a strong sense of both regret and personal inadequacy. If only things had been different. This is a common cry for many others whose lives have not been so diverted by incident. There is a sense of limitation of personal prowess or in relation to someone else or in relation to expectations. At the same time attempts to communicate with her father are as unsuccessful as many attempts to communicate in school. She wants to be listened to. But most of all she reveals the profound and ambiguous influence of her sister. With such realities, the school's limitations, or her own, have the more poignancy.

There are all kinds of factors that influence attitudes towards school. The parents and peer groups are far more explicit in their attitudes, whether they are negative or positive. There are judgements being made about school all the time. Schools are compared to each other. Experiences are compared. When there are judgements made about school they come about both because of the personal experiences within school and because of the examples of others outside. Individuals have both reputations and personal experiences in school:

You didn't get much work to do and that and with my brother and sister going to that school, my brother was a bad person and I got a lot of teachers blaming me for what my brother was doing and things, calling me John, when I wasn't like my brother at all, so I got fed up with that so I came to somewhere they wouldn't know.

(Male, Year 11)

The teachers have a clear view of particular students that can shape attitudes, but the views of the purposes of school are nearly always forced from outside. The same young man goes on:

My sister. . . she's 22 now. She knows how important it is to do well at school and because she didn't do very well. . . she had a lot of trouble with her eyes and that. . . They messed her around, well, most of her year, they messed around because they were sort of, like, guinea pigs for testing different exams. . . and there was a fire so they got messed around a lot going to different schools and that and then she didn't get the grades she wanted because the teachers told my sister you should be in this set and my sister knew that if she'd stayed in the set that she wanted then she'd probably be able to get the grades that she would have done. Then she went to the tech. And half-way through, she was about 18, she had a baby so she had to leave and then go back to it, but she passed for childcare and then, well, she's really the one who realizes how much you need qualifications for a job and my brother, well, he's a bit like my dad really because he left school in the fifth year, after Christmas. He didn't take any of his GCSEs or anything like that so he's not bothered or anything like that.

(Male, Year 11)

What do these comments tell us about school? One message is that he needs school, for qualifications, but the school does not need him. His sister, who preaches the necessity of doing well, had a time disrupted not just by accidents but by changes to the system. Many pupils feel like guinea pigs in the system, not just when new regulations are introduced but as a matter of routine. They are moved on from school to school. They feel helpless in the face of the impersonal and implacable will of the school. It is not surprising that some, like his brother, find it easier to be 'not bothered'.

In the context of a larger world, with emotional ties and responsibilities, the school has a particular part to play. This reinforces two aspects of school that are familiar. One is the processing of qualifications, the supply of exam fodder and results. The other is the preparation for employment. In that sense the views of young children even before they enter the system are, in a pragmatic way, correct. Schools are to do with jobs. As for personal lives, that is quite another matter.

4
Nostalgia or regret? The summary experience

The past is another country?

Remorse is not a fashionable concept of our time. That sense of sturdy independence encapsulated in the popular song by Edith Piaf – 'Je ne regrette rien' – is as lauded as if it were the motto of politicians. A little reflection on the meaning of a refusal to regret, as if no mistake were ever made or, if made, brazenly ignored – 'Never apologize, never explain' – might make us realize that such assertions are also potential signs of brutal insensitivity. Independence of mind might be better served by at least a hint of thoughtfulness, of weighing up the costs of experience. Perhaps we live in a time that suffers from the strong belief in self-assertion, and that places learning from mistakes in the same despised category as 'U-turns', so dreaded by politicians. The age of self-promotion has little time for reflections or for changes of opinion in the face of new evidence.

One thing is certain: young children know all about regret. They dwell on mistakes that they make and their 'sorry' is much more than lip-service. The sense that matters could be, or could have been, different is strong and encapsulated both by young children's sense of relativism and by their understanding of nostalgia (Cullingford, 1999c). Even in primary school children we detect a strong longing for the lost safety of babyhood, as if their present lives were undermined by a new sense of insecurity. That blithe belief that hard work will auto-matically be rewarded by success is by the age of eight replaced by a greater awareness of the unfairness of personal achievement, and the great disparity of different talents. Hard work and good results become distinctly different concepts. The insecurity of normlessness and the growing sense of being disenfranchised is not a sudden fall or 'simple alienation' (Williamson and Cullingford, 1998), as if that were a condition almost without emotion. The shadow of personal involvement, of a deep and personal sense of sadness, is also a part of the actions that lead to exclusion. There is a tendency to associate disaffected pupils with a lack of sensitivity – as if they had no regrets – and also a tendency to assume that they are a case apart, unusual and to be treated as a separate category. The tribulations of school, like any other manifestation of social relations, are deeply and personally felt, and only expressed more publicly and more insolently by some. All pupils are sensitive to what happens. Some just react to events differently. Many hide their feelings, even from themselves. This is part of their resilience and adaptability. They assume that what they feel, however uncomfortable, is part of the norm, part of what is expected of them.

Pupils have a capacity to reflect with sensitivity and personal responsibility on the experiences they have had and the mistakes they have made, from simple wrong choices to acts of which they should be ashamed. It does seem odd to have to remind ourselves of the sensitivities of being human, but we need to do so partly because of the tendency to deny the importance of reflection and partly because those inner, personal voices of individual pupils are so often so blatantly ignored. The experiences of school and of the many relationships there and at home have an emotional impact far deeper than the outcomes of the curriculum or the competition of tests. The dismissal of remorse might be a particular coping strategy much prized in the ethos of our time, but it is also a habit of mind that is learnt the hard way, by the very sensitivities that indifference and assertion wish to replace.

Young children understand the complexities of personal emotions in others as well as themselves (Dunn, 1988). What they learn at home as well as at school is the capacities to hurt as well as be hurt. Both can be regretted. That constantly heard complaint 'It's not fair!' shows both the vulnerability to pain and injustice and the deep sense of ontological rectitude that is so constantly being challenged. Nothing is so easily bruised as optimism. That early sense that it would, could and should be just, which is the source of all hope (Chukovsky, 1963), is constantly exposed to disappointment. One way of coping is to cease to care: to accept what is with a greater indifference than is natural in the fierce emotional lives of young children.

If young children express a realization of regrets, at what stage is this knocked out of them? One could argue that the acceptance of unfairness as a way of life is deeply embedded by the age of eight (Cullingford, 1994), but this does not necessarily mean that children have learnt so easily to fit in to the particular anonymous demands of school (Sharp and Green, 1975). Many argue that schools are there to teach emotional indifference or to ignore the sensitivities of bullying, or to teach pupils how to fit in to social demands in a particularly pragmatic way. This would suggest that pupils in school should be impervious to what happens to them, or that they adapt so well, so quietly, that most of what happens passes them by. School, in this analysis, would be a particularly unemotional and unintense experience, at best a mildly bleak passage of indifferent time.

If it is argued that schools teach social coping strategies – how to keep out of trouble, how to avoid confrontation, how to understand just how far to go with teachers (Sluckin, 1981), and how to avoid disappointment by reducing expectation – then we might expect pupils to have no regrets. If they have really adapted, and properly submitted, then they will have been just a part of a process, and they would accept all. And yet, despite these hidden assumptions about what school teaches – indifference, adaptability and the avoidance of challenge – the pupils all retain a sense of regret. They do not simply accept schooling. It might be better if they did, but a sense of disappointment prevails. This is always a personal matter, a sense of personal regret and not simply a blaming of the system. One deep regret is the fact that the purpose of school (let alone life) is so rarely discussed. If only, say the pupils, school itself had been a matter of discussion. This is seen as a pity; but the sense of remorse is held more personally than this. One result of the nature of school is that pupils themselves regret the mistakes they have made. When it is too late, they realize that they could have made different choices, and could have worked harder, and could have had more fruitful relationships with teachers.

This is not a matter of simple blame, although we will argue that schools could be quite different, but a matter of personal feeling and the lack of proper involvement in decision making. Looking back on the experience of school, this sense of personal optimism is replaced by a sense of loss, of opportunities not taken, or denied. This may be because of the ethos of schools, but it is taken personally. If pupils blamed anybody, they blamed themselves.

Looking back on experiences

We should make a clear distinction between matters of personal remorse or regret and the sense of imposed failure or lack of success. Schools are institutions that are adept at inducing feelings of failure. Every test within and beyond the classroom is a potential source of anxiety and comparison. Only one person will come out on top; and the sense of distinction between pupils is very strong. They are always aware which are the 'bright' ones. They point out that they themselves are labelled 'stupid'; as if this were not enough in itself, they are also brought up to compare their actual achievements with what they ought to achieve. If ever there were a system geared to brand individuals as failures, schools could hardly be bettered. The sense of failing, against standards, against targets, against each other and against themselves, is pervasive. A number of pupils always find this humiliating; but the majority are inured to it. It is part of the 'system' of school. The tests become routine, and the assumption is that pupils are hardly affected at all. The arguments for testing are that they are necessary and inevitable, and that all people need to be assessed in order to fit them into suitable posts in the future. The personal consequences and the deeper attitudes towards society are ignored.

'Failure' is not, however, the same as regret. Pupils respond to it in different ways. They give up, or they try to improve. Some give up, not because they do not think they are capable but because they do not wish to expose themselves to disappointment (Galloway *et al*, 1996). Whilst there was a tendency to regret not working hard, thereby expressing disappointment at not doing better, the pupils accept the impersonal judgements made by tests. They try to treat such outcomes, especially if they are uncomfortable, as impersonal, as not really personally affecting. Tests are, after all, imposed on them as part of a system. Of course, they all wish to come out on top, but if there is a purpose that is implicit in schooling it is the constant grading of the pupils. They are there to be assessed; the curriculum is what is assessed. At least pupils have the comfort of knowing that they will do better in their most favoured subjects (Pollard *et al*, 1994).

One peculiar condition of school is that some of the favourite subjects – the most practical and individual – are the least tested. There could be a connection between those subjects that lend themselves easily to assessment – memorizing and regurgitating facts – and those subjects that are found most boring and routine. It is almost impossible for children to anticipate what will turn out to be a subject that is demanding because of its centrality in terms of tests. Soon they learn that there is a connection between the importance of the subject and its style of delivery. The more central its place in the scheme of things the more it will be associated with routine and repeated tasks. One of the regrets of school has to do with the choice of subject. Given the nature of testing and the reliance on grades, it is very important to choose not just the subject that is most interesting but the subject they know how to handle. The objective way in which pupils assess the choices in school is revealed in the crucial distinction between those subjects they are 'good at' and those they 'enjoy'. Some of the differences come about because of the relationship with different teachers, but choosing a subject that guarantees success in examinations is also important:

> The subjects I chose. I wish I'd done better from the past and my exams and things. . . If I turned over a new leaf.
>
> (Female, Year 10)

> If I could go back I don't think I'd have chosen design and graphics. I'd have chosen some other kinds of technology.
>
> (Male, Year 10)

Pupils often have to make choices, and these become more important as they progress through school. Some subjects remain to them both disliked and unavoidable, but often remain a source of constant regret or antipathy:

> Well, I wish the language wasn't compulsory because at this school they make as though you've got to take one. I wish I'd only taken one of them because I did my exams. . . and I got them sort of muddled up a bit and lost a few marks on this.
>
> (Male, Year 10)

Examinations also expose the sense of failure, from the sense of disappointment at not performing very well on the day and anticipating the sense of deflation to the shock at the actual outcome after the insidious growth of hope has done its work. Many subjects turn out to be different from how they were anticipated:

> Well, I wish I did different subjects. I wish I didn't take business studies because it's really hard but then I suppose it opens a

lot of doors. It doesn't shut any. You know, if I decide, if I get a good grade, but it's not something I could carry on, I don't think.

(Female, Year 10)

This judicious appraisal of the subject, balancing the demands against the potential utility, also suggests how the judgement of a subject depends on the outcome. The pleasure of a subject is closely linked to success.

Having said that, there are some choices to be made, which can also lead to difficulties. The bulk of the school curriculum is prescribed and affords no individual choice at all. It cannot, therefore, even be regretted, in terms of personal responsibility or choice. It is imposed and has to be accepted. The assumption is that all pupils learn exactly the same things and that some do better than others. Ultimately, testing is all.

Pupils are accustomed to competition and adapt to it in different ways. Some give up. Some try not to care. But all know how much depends on the grades they get. If there is one major regret they all share, it is the fact that they could have done better, by working harder. It is interesting to note that this is a constant afterthought. The regret is that they did not work harder at the time. This suggests that the purpose of learning – even defined as preparing for tests – was never clearly defined. Despite the battery of tests there is little sense of urgency in the curriculum, either in terms of thirst for understanding or in meeting the demands of examinations. Afterwards this is regretted.

There is a gap between the curricular expectation of schools in their demands on pupils and the desire by pupils to be more involved in the learning process (McCullum, Hargreaves and Gipps, 2000). Pupils want to be responsible and to share understanding but so much knowledge is presented to them as a *fait accompli* that they find it difficult to generate the required motivation. Of course, schools vary. Some are far more independent and creative in their activities than others; and this is sometime attributed to the socio-economic backgrounds of pupils when they match those of teachers (Bowles and Gintis, 1976). Those who feel that the curriculum is imposed upon them regret the missed chances that could have been taken had they been more aware of the nature of the demand. There is a pervasive sense of loss:

> Not working as hard as I should in some subjects. Because
> they're a bit boring sometimes I just think I could have done
> better. . . a little bit harder than I did.
>
> (Female, Year 10)

> I wish I'd tried harder in Year 7 and 8 class. That was just like. . .
> I just messed about then and it's just Year 9 and 10 when I've
> just calmed down.
>
> (Male, Year 10)

Many pupils experience a hiatus of interest in certain years in secondary
school, those years where all the incipient tendencies to exclusion
become manifest. There are times when a whole year group has a
collective ethos of negativity and when it becomes a norm not to learn
(Measor and Woods, 1984). Individuals also experience phases of
disenchantment, particularly when away from the immediate pressures
(and consequences) of exams:

> I wish I'd worked harder in the first year and the third more
> and concentrated. Then you just think you can mess about until
> you get to the fourth year and then you realize, it's such a shock,
> and you wish you'd worked.
>
> (Female, Year 10)

Nothing could make clearer the implicit purpose of school – to pass
exams, to have a satisfactory outcome. The teaching itself is not the
point. All that matters is the big test. This concentration on the
importance of examinations has the inevitable consequence of dimin-
ishing the significance of other years – and other practices – that do
not contribute directly to the tests.

The very concern with the consequences of qualifications can have
an effect on the working practices of pupils:

> I was willing to work but I messed around a lot really. I didn't
> put my head down as hard as I should have done. And I had a
> family outside school, which guaranteed me a job, so it was
> like it doesn't matter about my work. I can just pass my work
> and as soon as I've left school I've got a job guaranteed but
> with my dad's business going downhill. . . I ended up in a bad
> situation really.
>
> (Male, aged 17)

'I wish I'd done my course work now.' Of course, it is easy to have regrets, especially if expectations are suddenly disappointed. Some would argue that these phases are inevitable, and that such a sense of a missed opportunity is inevitable. But the regrets are in the sense of missed opportunities. The fact that children tend to blame themselves, rather than the 'system' or others, is telling. They are children not looking for the chance to make complaints or cause trouble. Their wishing the circumstances had been different includes the sense of their own involvement, of not knowing at the time what the expectations were and of not knowing how to adapt to the implacable if unmysterious demands.

Regrets, personal and institutional

It might not seem, at first glance, surprising that there should be a sense of regret at not having worked harder – if this is associated with doing better. It is common to say 'if only I had made more of an effort', as if the person had the talent but had not bothered to apply it. This can be as much of an excuse for underachievement as anything. In an age of remorseless self-promotion the assertions of capacity will always replace those of achievement. These pupils do not hint that they wish they had done better in exams (which they would have done had they shown greater application) but they instead point out their personal failure to be more deeply engaged. This is an important, if subtle, distinction. Of course, hard work has outcomes, but the sense of being not fully involved, or not being really in tune with school, is pervasive. The result is lack of attention, of being distracted by all the other experiences of school. They know that at the heart of their problems is their 'attitude', which leads them to misbehave:

> I wish I could learn more instead of dossing about in lessons. No, I'm calming down now. Because I wasn't getting no work done. I was always getting done!
>
> (Male, Year 10)

There are periods of normlessness in all pupils' lives. The sense of hiatus, of not having a sense of direction, of being bored and passing the time through distraction, descends on all pupils for longer or shorter periods. Most assume that this will pass and that they will, this spate of childhood or adolescence done, return to the duties of application. For some the sense of estrangement gets steadily deeper; for most, there is a recognition that they have not been fully committed. Even if this is a phase it is recognized as a damaging one. The pupils are reflecting on the actual consequences of earlier failure, which will continue to affect them. Their disappointment with themselves reflects one of the consequences of the educational system.

Many pupils reflect on the amount of time they spent 'mucking about'. They realize that their energies were placed elsewhere, being directed at finding out how much they could get away with. The school became a different set of challenges: of learning how much misbehaviour a particular teacher would tolerate, or whether their lack of work would be noticed:

> I just wish I would have done more work in the first and second years. I regret that I was bad in the first and second years but now I've calmed down a bit. Not doing my work, messing about in class and all that, but most teachers say that I have calmed down a bit now, because it's got more serious, more close to GCSEs and all that.
>
> (Male, Year 10)

Like those who have reflected on how much time they have wasted, hindsight makes them realize what they have been doing (White with Brockington, 1983). The pressure of immediate exams helps to 'calm them down'. But the damage of messing about has been done:

> I just wish I'd. . . because sometimes I used to muck around in lessons. . . you know. . . my friends. But I'm leaving next week so I can't turn it back, can I? But I wish I just didn't mess around.
>
> (Female, Year 11)

It is clear that there were two sets of people to please, two different cultures to reflect. The 'friends' expected the 'mucking about' as clearly as the teachers assumed hard work. To be popular with some means being unpopular with others. For many pupils, it is a highly skilled art balancing the two.

Popularity is often won by challenging the academic norms but many pupils regret their own bad behaviour, and not just because of the consequences. The question is why they are driven to it. Will there always be those who believe in being part of a 'gang', and who will inevitably feel distanced from the demands of school, from the clear and alien expectations of the system? One of the reasons for seeking alternative approval is the pressure of the curriculum as it is presented:

Just that the work had been a bit easier and less pressure. Make you do work and if you don't bring it you get a punishment or something. They don't listen to the excuse that you've got. Sometimes people tell lies and they don't listen to anyone any more.

(Male, Year 10)

The sense of being alienated is very strong. Impossible or overzealous demands and a lack of sympathy for the point of view of the pupil lead to failure and the feeling of being earmarked as a troublemaker. This is the stronger for perceiving other more adept pupils 'getting away with it'. The sense of teachers 'not listening' and 'not wanting to know' is strong. The undercurrent of feeling is again of not being part of a system in which teachers are so fully a part.

One regret that pupils have concerns the attitudes of teachers and some of the teaching styles. We will note later how they regret not being able to realize that teachers have individual personalities and that they are people with whom pupils can talk. Partly because of the conditions of the classroom where the sheer number of people makes individual relationships impossible and partly because of the role that teachers have to play, there is little personal interaction. When it does happen, as on a school trip, it is something that pupils appreciate. It is odd to reflect on how little attention is paid to allowing the development of at least a few opportunities for individual relationships, beyond the stresses of the exams and the delivery of the curriculum. The regret for not knowing teachers better as people is paralleled by the experience of seeing teachers merely engaged in keeping order and imposing demands. In this, the National Curriculum does not help since there is even more pressure on teachers to 'get through' the syllabus (Galton *et al*, 1999). Teachers are there to make statements; they talk and pupils listen. The questions teachers ask, posed to the whole class, are mostly closed.

Such a picture of traditional classrooms, however encouraged by educational policies, is not in the best interests of children's emotional lives. There is a reflected longing for the missed opportunities of sharing jokes, of having some personal response from the teacher as an individual rather than as a role. The appreciation of humour, of a teacher sharing a joke, is well known. But this collective engagement with the class is not the same as the individual dialogue where the pupil is actually listened to. Such dialogue is normally restricted to a difficult incident, a confrontation. The pupil then, in a unique position of talking one to one, is on the defensive. Against such a strain the longing is for a natural everyday conversation with an adult – on any subject.

One regret, therefore, is that teachers could have been different:

> I sometimes wish the teachers were different. They should be able to explain better. Some teachers sometimes can't explain. So you're sometimes confused.
>
> (Male, Year 10)

The good 'explainer' is partly a matter of presentation; it is also a symbol of curiosity in the pupil's understanding (Cullingford, 1999b). The 'delivery' of a curriculum is not to be confused with teaching, let alone with learning. What is longed for is a different opportunity, or different conditions:

> Sometimes I'd prefer it if I had different lessons to what I'm doing, different teachers for different lessons.
>
> (Male, Year 10)

Certain teachers, for example in those subjects like art that allow it, can strike up a pattern of conversation that is less formal and less threatening. For most, however, the demands of their role and what they are expected to achieve put a great deal of pressure on all relationships. Teachers are, after all, perceived as beleaguered:

> I'd change the teachers to be more polite and to listen more and to help you when you really need it instead of just waiting around for someone to help you. To be more cheerful towards you as well; usually and mostly it's a sad face; they just walk around grumpy. They should be smiling and polite to the pupils instead of just being grumpy and horrible like they usually are.
>
> (Male, Year 10)

This strikes a note of sadness rather than anger. The lack of 'politeness' is a result of the stressful demands. Teachers could be expected to be ready to respond to an individual as they would in 'real' life. The picture of unhappiness, gloom and 'grumpiness' encapsulates the ethos of many a school. Teachers are depicted as separate, living their own unhappy lives of forced discontent. This image is a familiar one, the collective assumption about all teachers. It is also, and significantly, regretted. The lack of dialogue is an opportunity wasted.

The central part of life

Schooling takes up a significant proportion of people's lives. It dominates the most formative stage. There are all kinds of lessons being learnt, and attitudes to life developed in such a deep way they are difficult to detect. The facts that are learnt are for the most part forgotten; the set of emotional attitudes are not. What is learnt in school is essentially about society and culture, how people go about ordering their lives and how individual relationships affect understanding. On the one hand we see an almost monumental presentation of the demands of an impersonal system. On the other we witness the way in which individuals manipulate or suffer from the very system of which they are part. Beneath the surfaces at school are all the private analyses of experience:

> I think it's this girl 'F'. She's really brainy, but she doesn't really need to do. . . She doesn't really need to pay attention much, but I do. But we talk and she gets away with it and I don't.
>
> (Female, Year 10)

Unfairness is a far more complex notion than the misjudgements of teachers. It is the realization that some people can privately manipulate the public system, and that this can be done by a friend. One lesson learnt here is how poor this particular individual is at surviving as well as others: she knows, to her regret, that she does not possess the necessary skills.

The people pupils are with, much more than the school they are at, are often a matter of chance. Whilst there is an inevitability about the school attended, even a sameness in the experience of all, each school has its own ethos. It would always have been feasible, if not possible, to go elsewhere:

> If I could do it again, I'd like to do varied subjects, like at different high schools that some of my other friends go to. They do like photography and things. I'd find that really interesting, and drama. We don't really do anything like that here. Like in English, you hardly get any drama and when it is you don't do it properly.
>
> (Female, Year 10)

The awareness of other schools, like a realization of the limitations in pupils' own experience, remains strong. It is part of the curious arbitrariness of events. No one knows what the school will be like, but all depends on it. On the one hand is the ethos: the tone, the shared cultural assumptions, which could change. On the other are the personal chances, the friendships made and the influences allowed:

> If I could change I think I probably would have gone to another school. . . probably a school where they make you work harder and like. . . at this school I don't think they push you enough, because they've got a lot of like problem kids and they seem to concentrate more on those than on the brighter people and pushing them.
>
> (Female, Year 11)

The concentration on problem pupils and their actual exclusion from school has often been dealt with. Schools are judged by their ability to retain children as well as by their examination results. Less attention has been paid to those children who either psychologically exclude themselves (Pye, 1989) or who feel ignored by the system. Many pupils complain about the way in which teachers go about their routines, but these routines are often forced upon them by the need to keep order. There are many pupils who by their very compliance and their lack of trouble are ignored (Egan, 1997). In the disparity of levels of ability and the very tensions of endeavour in schools it is impossible to pay attention to everyone individually (Alexander, 2000). All expect to be 'pushed' but realize that teachers are either distracted or motivated not for the sake of pupils but for the sake of inspections. In such conditions (to which we will return in Chapter 8), it is very difficult to meet the needs of pupils. This is not to blame the teacher. Pupils also understand that the problem lies deeper than individuals, and if it lies in individuals it lies as much with them.

Happier days?

Without articulating it in so many words, pupils find their experience of school unsatisfactory. This does not mean that they are critical. They are taught to take school for granted. This is the way that society operates: with hierarchies of command, formal orders, private unanswered questions and tense hidden relationships. In these conditions pupils are unlikely to be asked about their experience, or put their sense of discontent into clearly argued analysis. This is where the concept of regret is so important. There is a reflective conclusion that for a number of reasons schooling was not the fulfilling experience that might have been expected. Whether it is from disengagement with part of the curriculum or distraction from pupils and teachers, or their own obscured distortions, there is a sense that it 'could have been better'.

One problem for schools is that to ask such fundamental cultural questions is against the norm. Schools are taken for granted in the ordering of the curriculum and in their structures of discipline. To question the system is not popular. Besides, it is argued, if schools do not give a satisfactory experience, why should we expect them to? Is not an unexamined assumption that schools are processes to which individuals must submit? The curriculum is generalized. The conditions in which teachers work are uniform. It all, then, depends on the pupils; and those who question are deemed recalcitrant.

The sense of regret in individuals is a reflection on the whole experience. By the end of schooling they will have imbibed just one official message about the purpose of what they have undergone. They should do well in exams so that their qualifications enable them to acquire good jobs. The end of schooling is, in every sense, the results. And all depends upon competition. The realization of these levels of meaning can often come too late:

> I wish I did not mess around or play outside so much. Now I have to pay for it because I'm working much harder and all that, although. . . but nights, like, I haven't got that much energy. I've been revising so much now. I'm so fed up with working, looking at books and my teachers will go to me. . . I look. . . add a bit more energy and you'll get a pass. But I just find it so difficult to carry on sometimes. Your brain wants to explode.
>
> (Female, Year 11)

The problem for so many pupils is that the demands of the school curriculum are monumental, general and, in the insistence on memory, iconoclastic. The distancing effect of such intractability cannot be underestimated. The relationship between the kinds of order imposed in discipline of movement and the order of the curriculum, 'broad and balanced', equally for everyone, is very close.

Beneath this monumental edifice are all the obscured or hidden emotions: almost a separate if parallel world to the discipline of classrooms. The personal experience of school is often marred by the pervasive nature of teasing: the formal humiliation of the classroom and the informal bullying in the interface:

It wasn't just other people. . . I was always being bullied so I didn't like it any more. I don't know. I didn't feel that the teachers were doing enough. I was really upset; this girl, I didn't want her anywhere near me. She was well known for it. She'd been expelled from about four schools and. . . took her in with open arms and I was like 'No' and she just started immediately. She did it to absolutely everybody. She had so many fights it was unbelievable. We had one incident where she was actually going to beat me up and I can't stand fighting, not when I know it can be resolved in some other way and I said, look, I don't want to go back to my lesson. It didn't seem like I was protected enough really and I just actually went home because I rang my mum and I said I'm not going back and she said, you know. . . Eventually so many people complained about this girl because their kids had come home with black eyes and every-thing that they got rid of her but it seemed to take a long time for them to actually do anything. She fired a lot of verbal abuse in front of the teachers and they just, like, don't do this, don't do this, and I was, like, I need a bit more than that. I feel really, really vulnerable here. It was awful.

(Female, Year 11)

This is the kind of incident that could be dismissed as unique, but it is cited at length since it is representative of so many such experiences. The mixture of personal pain and the anguish of seeing the system inactive and indifferent, for all kinds of 'political' reasons, reinforces all kinds of attitudes. School, therefore, embodies both the sense of personal frailty and disappointment with people's behaviour and the fact that the cultural system allows this to happen. The mixture of impersonal structures and their distance from the reality of the everyday, the tension between systems and people that schools so deeply demonstrate, make their mark on the formation of attitudes, a mark that many people subsequently deny.

What we learn from these witnesses is of a personal sense of disappointment. Their remorse is not angry, although they should have a right to feel anger. It is more a matter of realizing the difference between what happened and what might have been. There are enough signs of individual pleasures and understandings embedded in the experience of school to make it clear that there is a collective under-standing of what school might have been. The question remains whether the core of the curriculum, this mainstream drive of the school, is part of the pleasure or part of the disappointment.

5
The subject of the curriculum

The National Curriculum as a necessity

In the sparse justification given for the National Curriculum there are certain key phrases. The two most significant are those concerned with 'entitlement' and with the curriculum as 'broad and balanced'. Together, these phrases imply a vast body of knowledge that covers the whole spectrum of different subjects, facts and modes of thought. Whilst we should at least remind ourselves of the complexity of the relationship between a particular subject and its concomitant learning styles and skills – the bent of mind associated with a 'subject' or even imposed by it – most of the discussions of the National Curriculum pass such complexity by. This in itself expresses something of the nature of the curriculum as imposed and, whilst pupils are equally aware of the complicated nature of 'subjects', we will here deal with the idea of the curriculum in an almost monolithic way as the way in which it is presented in schools.

Putting aside for a moment all the 'hidden' curriculum of what actually *is* learnt in school, the formal curriculum is the body of knowledge that is supposed to be learnt. It is 'broad' in the sense that it covers a wide range of different 'disciplines', paying ostensible service to them all, in theory if not in fact. Its 'balance' lies in its attribute to concentrate on facts, on testable knowledge. This means that some particular excitement at new realms of thought will *not* take over, or skew, the general equitable tone of accumulation. The curriculum is assumed to be a whole, and the national version was introduced to prevent teachers ignoring some aspects of it, or, more potently, pursuing certain aspects that gave them greater satisfaction (Haviland, 1988). The 'balance' lay as much in prevention as in assuring pupils and parents that 'all' would be covered and nothing repeated.

The idea of a great and agreed body of knowledge that is somehow sacrosanct is conceptualized as an 'entitlement'. Rather like the concept of the hermeneutic school, the curriculum is something to which pupils have access, whatever their other forms of learning, and which they will either succeed in mastering or fail to master in differentiated degrees. Whatever the actual complexities of learning and the actual concepts learnt, the school system is conceptualized by those who administer the National Curriculum as the delivery of a centrally agreed body of knowledge. Whatever the preferences of teachers or pupils, all must take the 'table d'hôte' offered to all equally. In this sense 'entitlement' can mean either a refusal to allow any pupil to be deprived of knowledge, or it can mean absence of choice or personal preference.

The debate about a centralized curriculum, about entering these 'secret gardens' of learning, began with the notion of the 'core'. Despite the words 'broad' and 'balanced', this notion of a central, narrow essential still dominates. There are certain subjects, like mathematics and English, that have long been assumed to be at the heart of the curriculum. They are the ones that are supposed to provide those necessary learning skills that allow the other subjects to have their place. They are also seen as being of assumed importance in that numerate and literate students are seen as the natural product and justification of the education system. More recently, maths and English have been joined by science – perhaps envisaged as a technocratic subject, perhaps assumed to be dominated by information and communication technology. Science remains a more equivocal part of the core curriculum, as the pupils recognized. Nevertheless, the 'core' curriculum, that central necessity around which the rest must find their place, is now a triumvirate.

All this is about the official curriculum imposed on schools and centrally tested. The complexities beneath the surface hinted at already are more important for the pupils. Even at the formal level, the curriculum is complex. The distinction between the notion of a curriculum and of 'subjects' is important. It is the latter that pupils find significant. They have their favourites. Some satisfactions depend entirely on the teachers rather than the subject matter itself. Some subjects are associated with particular styles of learning, like constant writing. What is clear is that pupils do not conceptualize or recognize the curriculum in the same way as teachers (Ruddock, Harris and Wallace, 1994). What looks to the planners of the curriculum as coherent, well organized and balanced looks rather different for the pupils. For them the curriculum remains bitty as well as arbitrary, more likened to a pile of rubble than a clear structure. The whole relationship between subjects and skills, let alone 'transferable' skills, is troubled. Pupils feel very ambivalent about the very concept of 'key' skills, as will be explored later (Unwin and Wellington, 2001). Above all, the very concern with the idea of the 'subject' (*sic*) as opposed to the curriculum is itself significant.

Nevertheless there is a strong public line on the nature of the National Curriculum, its implementation and testing. Pupils understand what they are being measured against and what is expected from them. The question is what this experience means to them. The context of the questions is to ascertain what they think of the curriculum as given to them, without mentioning 'core' or any other of the defining phrases. The pupils were asked neutrally what they found were the main important subjects in school. Later they reflected on the utility of the curriculum and its relationship to their own lives, particularly their employment. Here they do not touch on what they particularly *like* but on what is presented to them, or they perceive, as the most significant.

The given core

The note that the pupils consistently struck gave the impression that the answer to what are the most important subjects is obvious. There is nothing equivocal about their response. Some might forget to add science but the core curriculum was clearly the centrepiece of the whole curriculum. When we analyse their consistent responses there are certain matters that go beyond the obvious. The core curriculum, maths, science and English, is important. But why? Usually these are not their favourite subjects. Only rarely are they deemed useful to them for their own personal futures. They are important because they are officially the core. They are important to the pupils because they are told they are important, and because, more significantly, they dominate the timetable both in timing and weight (Burgess, 1989).

At one level this might seem obvious. We are consistently reminded of the importance of the core curriculum. Government statements rippling through the media reiterate the centrality of those commercial skills that lie in reading and counting. This is the fact as given, and pupils accept that fact. There is no room for questioning. The distinction between the 'important' and the 'preferred' is readily made. Even the distinction between 'importance' and 'utility' is kept up. The core curriculum is important because that is the official and commonly assumed fact:

> English and maths and science. Because they're the main ones.
>
> (Female, Year 10)

> Probably maths and English, probably science. I don't know because to get into college, like maths and that's quite useful, aren't they?. . . I don't know really; they always sound as though, sort of like, and English are your main subjects and that.
>
> (Male, Year 10)

There are many interesting attempts to justify the core curriculum given by pupils, nearly all of which echo what they have heard about them. 'They always sound. . . as though they are quite useful, don't they?' In the place of inner conviction we witness the acceptance of the 'main ones' and then the more difficult part of justifying them.

The easiest justification is 'because I need them to go to college' (Male, Year 10). Increasingly entry requirements, especially those for learning part of a profession controlled by the government, like teaching, depend on passing tests in the core curriculum:

> Because maths, science and English are the major GCSE ones.
>
> (Male, Year 10)

> Maths and English and science will come in handy, because you need those qualifications for most jobs.
>
> (Female, Year 10)

> Maths and English. They're important. Science, but I'm not very good at it. If you want to get a good job and everything to go to university, you need maths and English; you need good grades in them to get what you want.
>
> (Female, Year 10)

It might be correct to concentrate on the centrality of the core curriculum, and it has certainly become the mantra for the pupils who undergo it. They recognize the way in which the system operates, and that the most important qualifications in exams, for the furtherance of their careers, are maths and English especially. The unquestioned assumption gives these subjects a particular status in themselves. They are pragmatic and necessary. Even if liked, they are burdened by their own necessity. They carry a weight of academic expectations.

The question then is whether the core curriculum is, in fact, a matter of knowledge, to be tested, or a matter of testable skills. The argument for maths and English is that they foster the ability to master particular applicable skills. But their actual utility is the entry they gave into college or university. They are most *necessary* qualifications – not as demonstrable skills but as passes. If the justification for them is the development of transferable skills, then this is undermined by the emphasis on them as qualifications:

> Well, with maths and English and science, them are the three
> main subjects what I'll take at college for my further career.

> (Male, Year 10)

> English, maths and science. I don't know. It depends what type
> of work you want to go into. . . because they're like your core
> subjects, aren't they? They carry you to get anywhere or owt.

> (Female, Year 10)

On the one hand we have the accepted importance of the core curriculum subjects. On the other hand the purpose implicit in their importance lies not in themselves but in their use as passports towards something else. They are taken both for their own sake and because they are enablers for something better. The curious fact is, however, that the implied justification for these 'skills' of numeracy and literacy lies not in their demonstration – more articulate and thoughtful beings – but in their utility as passes or qualifications. They are 'your core subjects, aren't they?' The same lack of explanation for wider issues of the curriculum naturally affects the pupils' perception of them.

The core curriculum subjects are, therefore, accepted as important because that is simply how things are. The reason for this lies partly in their being so much a central part of the structure of qualifications and because there must be explanations implicit in them:

> English will be one and I suppose maths would be like. . .
> maths, science; depends what I do after. They seem more
> important. In different jobs like, English would be writing a
> lot because most of them we do, it would be important. . . I
> don't know really.
>
> (Female, Year 10)

It should be noted that any centralized curriculum will be presented
as being the best possible, with more than a little propaganda. This
'propaganda' could be deemed by some to be part of the state's sense
of purpose. If the skills necessary for a competitive workforce are these,
then the core curriculum is in place to deliver them. If there is an
absence of a sense of the nature of the purpose of school in pupils,
then it is filled by the general unexamined political statements about
the skills, and the rising standards achieved by concentrating upon
them, as demonstrated by SAT results. These are all the measurements
as understood by the political world. They are accepted by pupils but
not in a way that explains their own circumstances to them.

Subjects and knowledge

The position of the core curriculum and its domination of the
National Curriculum has undergone some changes. For years there
were certain subjects that dominated. The Education Reform Act made
a curious attempt to spread some of that dominance to other subjects.
The spreading of the curriculum led inevitably to overload so that some
scaling down needed to be done (Coulby and Ward, 1996). The result
has been that the core curriculum has become dominant again, since
in key areas such as the statutory tests and teacher accountability *other*
subjects (however broad) have been 'scaled down'. The essential mental
set of the accepted significance of a 'core' remains.

Whilst there might be an official triumvirate, it is still maths and
English that dominate. Science is a subject that is having a difficult
time, when teachers suffer in particular from the domination of fact
rather than experiment. The sense of disappointment with it is strong
even in its supposed centrality (Siraz-Blatchford, 1996). The fact is that
it is still, as a subject rather than a skill, a less significant part of the
experience of school than the much more easily administered subjects
of mathematics and English:

English and maths are compulsory and that's what you need most.

(Male, Year 10)

Maths and English mostly, because when you get a job you mostly have to add things and stuff. English, you have to spell right and put your words in the right places and stuff. Well, maths and English, probably.

(Female, Year 10)

When it comes to the qualifications for a job, and for those skills that will equip them for employment, then the core curriculum is really just two.

The pupils' perspective on the emphasis in the formal curriculum on 'important' subjects is pragmatic in every sense. They recognize the significance given to the core, and the place of qualifications in the development of their careers. They have heard arguments about the necessary skills that employers might want. Indeed, the core curriculum is sometimes presented to them as a 'wish list' that future employers and present governments place upon them. Some might find this curriculum 'meaningless' (Dunne, 1999). Others might reflect on it as a cul-de-sac of 'curricular fundamentalism' (Slee, 1998). The way in which the pupils describe their experiences implies that they have a sense of acceptance (or submission) supported by all the received arguments based on utility. Many of the skills invoked by maths and English are seen as being important for their own sake rather than at the service of other subjects. They are not perceived as a means through which greater understanding can take place.

The result of such emphasis on utilitarian skills is that pupils have a necessarily pragmatic approach towards the formal curriculum. They connect what they have learnt in school naturally enough with what they might be doing afterwards but they reiterate that whatever they do there are just two subjects of importance. This is what they are consistently told. They see English and maths as the most 'useful' to their jobs in these terms. Other lessons do not make the same sense to them because these lessons are more peripheral. They have had it repeated to them countless times that they might *like* certain subjects but the only really important ones are maths and English. Whether this makes them better at these subjects is another matter.

The view of the curriculum generally is affected by the concentration on the core. It becomes utilitarian: acceptable if there is an immediate application, relished if there is personal satisfaction or pleasure, but not really taken too seriously. What matters first in terms of importance is the given core; afterwards, pupils find reasons to justify this:

> Some maths, but we do some maths; that's what you're not going to need at all in our school, like algebra, you're not going to need that. I don't know because I'm not quite sure what I want to do yet. Well, English is just everyday-to-day life, and maths, you've got to know somebody's given you the right change. But some of it is shaped.
>
> (Female, Year 10)

This view of utility is narrow and intense. Anything of doubtful value, in pragmatic terms, is deemed as 'useless' or 'stupid'. After all the messages that they have received about the curriculum it is not surprising that pupils should conclude that they perceive subjects that are:

> the practical ones, I suppose. The ones where you can put to me whatever job you're planning on doing.
>
> (Male, Year 10)

Usefulness and utility

Few would doubt that the curriculum is presented in utilitarian terms. There are few public statements about purpose beyond the necessary skills, standards and qualifications. The result is that pupils are equally pragmatic about their experiences. They submit to the status quo of the domination of the core curriculum. Whether this is an enlightening or successful state of affairs is often questioned. Some argue that the curriculum is itself a source of alienation and failure, especially in the later years and in inner cities (Kinder, 1997). Some suggest that the National Curriculum, particularly in science, has had the opposite effect to that intended (Hacker and Rose, 1998).

The weight of teacher evaluation, the overloading of the mandatory curriculum and the lack of resources have inevitably led to less interaction in the classroom and fewer scientific experiments. Even the theories of the original intentions appear more than doubtful. The 'broad and balanced' intentions of a curriculum have been replaced by the notion of 'standards and targets' (Davies and Edwards, 1999). The concept of 'entitlement' has become no more than a minimum legal requirement of whatever is on offer (Willan, 1998).

The research that surrounds the effects of the National Curriculum does not produce happy results (Cullingford and Oliver, 2001). The ways in which these pupils describe their experiences make one see why. One reason for the difficulty is the very attitudes towards subjects that have been encouraged in them. Some would say that the only acceptable purpose of schooling is to be pragmatic.

The problem is that if the only measure of the world of learning is practical utility there would not be much left:

> I just find them difficult but I don't think they're interesting. I can't see what learning about the structure of a molecule is going to do for me when I leave. I can't see myself going round the supermarket and saying, 'Well, that's made up of it.'

> (Female, Year 11)

There is, however, one aspect of the utilitarian that does begin to make personal sense to pupils. There are home skills that they feel will stand them in good stead in terms of a more positive attitude. Understanding the bill in supermarkets is one kind of usefulness, but there are other quite different ones that are formally involved. The core curriculum might be 'important' in a general way, but other things are more personally significant:

> I think the main ones are English, maths and science because a lot of people look at these. I think my performing arts as well because it shows how well I am at communicating with other people and it shows that I'm not scared to show my views and who help other people and people helping me.

> (Male, Year 11)

This is an alternative view of skills. The 'main ones' are opposed to the more subtle matters concerning learning in school, in fact the kinds of abilities, to get on with people, that employers might seek out. Pupils themselves on the one hand recognize what is officially 'important'. On the other they define what is really 'useful':

> Knowing where I'm going, knowing how to use things that I can communicate well now. I'm not shy. I used to be really shy. Speaking skills. I've got used to them skills now, just general skills.

> (Female, Year 11)

6
Skills learnt in school: for use or survival?

The monument of knowledge

For pupils, the curriculum is not a matter for debate. It is something given to them, in the hands of teachers and presented to them as a necessity, as facts about which they will be tested. For policy makers, on the contrary, the contents of the curriculum and its breadth are very significant. But even here the debate is surprisingly limited. The questions of depth and balance, of overload and proper respect to all the arts and sciences, are often invoked, as are the questions about modern languages or classics or the relationship between physical education and sport. These questions do not go deeply into the purpose of the curriculum. They are more a matter of keeping the different interest groups at bay.

When the National Curriculum was first promoted, a large number of subject panels was set up to suggest what should be contained within each of them. Each group gave justifications for their importance and, if they had been allowed to have their way completely, would each of them have taken over more than 50 per cent of all the time available in the school day. The way the National Curriculum was introduced suggests that the implications were not always understood (Black, 1997). What was revealed was the desperate set of passions around each subject. Sometimes these passions led to such quarrels that they did invite deeper debate on the nature and purpose of the curriculum as a whole. For example, the debate about history included the fiercely contested question of whether its study should centre on the celebration of national heritage (especially battles won) or on the understanding of a multicultural world, and whether chronology or themes might be the best means of organizing the delivery of the subject. The debate about the various subjects and interests that made up craft, design and technology led to the conclusion that technology should itself become the whole of the curriculum, or at least an organizing core. This conclusion about the centrality of a particular subject – a worthy advocacy – was unfortunately echoed by all the other subject panels justifying their own.

Most of the debates about the curriculum were not within subjects but between them, and centred on how much space each should have. This demonstrates at least one important truth. Each proposition for each subject believed that it was the most important of all, and that the proper understanding of, say, design technology would cover all matters and subsume the need for anything else. Whilst it is argued that any subject can be taught with intellectual respectability to any age (Bruner, 1967), the passion for each subject drew attention to something else. The argument for subjects is not so much a matter of the knowledge they convey but the ways in which they are applied and made use of. It is true that any subject is essentially about styles of thinking, the application of logic and the most efficient means of communication. Are these, then, the essential skills?

The 'core' curriculum is also centred on the notion of skills. The ability to write and count is assumed to be at the heart of all learning and these subjects are therefore, oddly, studied for their own sake rather than through their serving other subjects. The key skills tend to be assumed to be essential for all kinds of employment. They are so much taken for granted politically that pupils in schools are subtly influenced by the message. There are certain 'skills' that need to be learnt, and this is accepted by all.

The curriculum is something imposed upon the pupils and the pupils submit to this. The question remains whether the pupils are learning what they are supposed to and whether this learning consists of certain kinds of skills. Critical thinking skills, cognitive tools, philosophical logic and epistemology are none of them the kinds of skills promoted by the core curriculum: on the contrary. The skills involved are far more pragmatic and utilitarian. The skills learnt in the core are considered as applied, practical and mechanical, like competencies. Skills are to be used like tools, enabling pupils to carry out measurable tasks.

Skills are complex and the term can cover a wide range of cerebral activities as well as mundane tasks. What pupils learn in school is varied and includes the inadvertent as well as the formal. What then do pupils understand by skills? And, more pertinently, what kind of skills do they think they have learnt?

If the 'curriculum' still consists of the 'main' subjects, skills are seen as a series of drills that need to be perfected in readiness for employment (Dunne, 1999). Just as the most important qualifications are deemed to be maths and English, so the crucial skills are reduced to the fundamentals of reading, writing and maths (and a questionable amount of science). This is a pragmatic view, and pupils having accepted the 'core' might just as readily accept the centrality of these competencies. And yet, when they were asked about the skills that they thought they had learnt, there were a number of significant surprises.

What should be learnt?

Pupils are aware of what they are supposed to learn, and deeply conscious of those things they have failed to grasp. They are also aware of those things that they actually have learnt, so their responses to the question asking them to reflect on 'skills' were very interesting and thoughtful. Despite the emphasis on literacy and numeracy and despite the pupils' acceptance of their centrality, they were not considered useful in terms of 'skills'. Other matters learnt were far more important. One might have expected them to argue that their ability to use language and maths was essential, but they did not do so. This lack of connection between the core curriculum and skills might have been ascribed to the fact that they dissociated the core curriculum from skills, but this was not the case. The question was, after all, what was most *useful* to them. It was a perfect opportunity for them to consider the relationship between the mainstream of their experiences and the main justification for school. The fact that there was disjunction between the official, formal idea of significant skills and their own is significant. The most useful skills that pupils felt they had acquired at school, and that they felt would equip them for their futures, were a mixture of the pragmatic and the subtle, and nearly always learnt outside the central standard curriculum. Important subjects in the curriculum were one thing, useful skills another.

Acquired skills were often associated with certain learning styles and with things they enjoyed doing. They arose out of 'practical' work, on those matters that they could apply:

I like childcare because it is interesting. Geography: I don't know why I like it, and biology I've always really enjoyed doing stuff about plants and things and I really like it.

(Female, Year 10)

'Doing' things and 'enjoying' things are the prerequisite for acknowledging the usefulness of learning. So is the ability to work with others in small groups, so that there is time and space, and the chance to experiment – even to get things wrong. Having a change from the usual routines, or pursuing personal interests seemed to pupils 'useful' in themselves.

The working conditions when pursuing certain skills are themselves important. Skills, after all, consist of styles of working, the application of certain practical modes of thought to the task in hand. Having a 'change' and different approach to matters, replacing the familiar routines, is at once a challenge and a relief:

History is a small group because there's not many of us doing it and you like get on with your work. History is there and you just get on with your work and English like you do different tasks and that's good. So you get a change and things, so that's why I like English because you get a change in doing things and like sometimes you do things like London, soap operas and you get a change.

(Female, Year 10)

The very changes in styles of working are themselves important. The ability to adapt, as well as the variety of challenges, suggests the greater consciousness of the skills involved. Skills are either those definable competencies that can be measured or the more informed and carefully calculated intuitions that reflect the application of intelligence.

The working environment, with its particular demands and challenges, is an important context for the demonstration of skills:

I like English because I like writing stories and things like that, and CDT because it's fun and like designing stuff, and art because I like painting and stuff and we also get to listen to music whilst we are doing it and we can talk and stuff like this, mess about a bit because the teacher isn't really bothered about this; he does come over and help and that as long as you get your work done it's all right and your voice isn't too high

> and basically you do what you want and it gives you a chance
> to do your own work because you do your own projects and
> stuff like this.
>
> (Female, Year 10)

The ability to do 'your own projects', to work independently, is a skill
in itself. Learning has to be adaptable, and to concentrate on the task
in hand is a significant element in the demands of employment. The
working conditions are therefore closely associated with the pleasures,
the outcomes and the skills of work. The curriculum might be a dead
weight, but whatever is really being learnt is not as a fundamental
consequence of the imposition of someone else's will, and subsequent
testing, but as a freedom of personal manocuvrc: the inclusion of
'messing about' and getting 'your own work done'. Independent
learning is itself a skill, the application of personal interest.

This suggests a more complex and holistic idea of what a skill entails.
It is not necessarily something easily tested and quantified. It is an
approach to the subject that can be sustained and developed. In the
pupils' minds, therefore, there is a big gap at one level between those
skills that are officially defined as desirable and those that are more
personally recognized as useful. From the point of view of the system
as a whole, 'skills' are those practices that make an individual
employable:

> You've got a skill, haven't you, and if you can get fired you
> can go somewhere else and you've got that skill and you've
> nothing to worry about, and if you're good then you've nothing
> to worry about, have you?
>
> (Male, Year 10)

The transferability of ability is likened to the ease of moving from one
job to another. After all, one of the clichés of the time is the need for
flexible skills, on the grounds that no one will be able to stay in 'one
job for life', as if there were no longer any virtues in specialist
knowledge or becoming an expert.

Formal and personal skills

There is one link with the general policy on skills and the ways in which
pupils interpret them and this is in the application to jobs. Skills, more
than knowledge, are associated with employment. Skills, rather than

subject matter or even qualifications, are seen as the essential require-
ment of the job market:

> I've learnt skills. When I went to work experience I learnt a lot
> of skills there. I know about what it is, the world of work, and
> how we deal and I learnt a lot about science as well. So for a
> pharmacy I have to learn quite a lot of science too.
>
> (Male, Year 10)

Here we see two interrelated facts. Skills are invoked as something
both needed by, and central to, actual work experience. The 'world of
work' teaches the need for skills. It also triggers the reminder of the
fact that there are some subjects, a particular body of knowledge, that,
from the perspective of the subsequent job market, could be useful.
Only on reflection is the status of knowledge, of facts, enhanced. Given
a larger purpose, certain subjects come to life. The subjects by then
have played their part in allowing new and different experiences and
styles of work to flourish.

Until that realization of the applicability of skills, and the forms of
knowledge that inform them, the given curriculum can be very dry.
There are certain matters that pupils wish to be aware of:

> It's like your own life, own car, own home, living with your
> family. We're just kids now; we can't do anything; we have to
> listen to our parents, whatever they say. When we get a job we
> can go where we want: more independence.
>
> (Male, Year 11)

The perspective that pupils bring is strictly that of their own independent circumstances, with their own personal agendas. They are
looking for what is valuable to them both in the present circumstances
and in their future. The skills such an outlook warrant are not necessarily the same as those usually employed in the discussion of the
utilities of the curriculum. They do, however, give a significant insight
on the requirements, the personal desires and the needs that we
associate with school. Skills are ultimately to do with individual lives
and capacities.

Skills are matters that are so closely learnt that they remain when
everything formal is forgotten. They are deeply associated with styles
of working since they are not immediately testable. They are the
abilities to cope, to survive. They are therefore closely associated with
the home lives and the working lives of the present and the future:

Well, we've been learning computers and that and how to work
them and all that. In childcare, knowing all the things that we
need to know about looking after a child. I enjoy looking after
children and you can get involved with them and see what
they're doing.

(Female, Year 10)

'Key skills' are not just a matter of a core curriculum. They are the
abilities to bring some pragmatic knowledge to actual circumstances.
Looking after children and dealing with computers are the transactions
of daily life.

What are 'key' skills?

'Skills' are, therefore, a complex notion in the eyes of pupils. Skills
appear simple, even simplistic. They are invoked as the ability to make
use of what is learnt in the mechanistic way: reading, writing, mathematics and the application of rudimentary science. But pupils do not
interpret them in a simplistic way. There are certain significant skills
that they feel are important, that give a far deeper insight into the
experience of school. There is, in fact, a hierarchical list of what are
defined as skills that seems to pupils to be the core of what is learnt at
school. The most obvious level is associated with trades, work practices
and employability. The second is the ability to carry out those techno-
logical tasks that are consistently assumed to be in demand in communication technology. The third is the deepest, the most subtle and
the most revealing.

The first level of skills that are consciously acquired in schools
consists of those to do with potential employment. We should note
the word 'consciously'. If skills are defined narrowly, they are those
essential tools of learning, like reading, that enable other learning to
take place. If they are defined widely, there are all kinds of subconscious
acquisitions, of attitude and prejudices, of preferences and expectations,
that are slowly and mercilessly accumulated over the years of schooling. Pupils are at the same time aware of their own learning and aware
of the limitations (like the lack of usefulness or the irrelevance) of what
is taught. They are unaware of the means by which their attitudes are
formed. What is absorbed becomes so completely their own that there
cannot be conscious insight. And yet the pupils know that there are
such things as 'skills'. If these do not involve the core curriculum, they
are held in some esteem. There are certain useful values in what they
have acquired.

90

The first level of skill is associated with a trade. These are matters learnt, usually in conducive conditions, that can be applied. Skills are manipulative actions, rather than thoughts, that could prove useful outside school. They could be applied, even when untested within the school system:

> Like a trade, plastering, joinery: stuff like this. That's why I like CDT: it teaches me all about that – woodwork.
>
> (Male, Year 10)

Skills are applicable and clearly useful for the future. It is the 'life skills' and those matters like 'a trade' that appear to be most obviously useful. The skills acquired are to do with work experience. Whilst one would not question their utility, their very pragmatism and the very absence of any mention of thinking or critical skills either reveal something about the nature of school or reveal the narrow confines in which pupils have been taught to interpret experience.

Whatever the reason, the prevailing idea is that what has most usefully been learnt in school is what is most directly applicable:

> Yes, it's DT. Well, DT with graphics like drawing and that; you use a lot of technical drawing equipment and then sort of do bits on the computer and that, so yes, I've learnt quite a lot from this.
>
> (Male, Year 10)

> I think it's better to use your hands, you know, how to use is more.
>
> (Male, Year 10)

The practicalities, the sense that these are close to 'life skills' and those abilities that pupils can take away with them and present to other people: those are the 'skills' that matter. There is, of course, a connection with the qualifications desired by employers. It could be thought that 'skills' are a lower order than subjects. But subjects are what is necessary for the system; qualifications in them are terminal. Skills survive after school and are assumed to continue. Skills are also valued, however marginal some subjects that develop them, like woodwork, might appear to be:

> Like in one class a week we have supportive studies and we have done a lot about crime and police officers have come in

> and spoken to us. I think that helped us in a way. I can't say
> anything else that helped.
>
> (Female, Year 10)

No particular skills learnt? Nothing relevant? When pupils reflect on their experiences there appears to be a separation between school and the outside world. Sometimes they connect, but often not in terms that give definition or meaning to the lives of pupils.

Skills of schools and skills of living

There are few obvious links between the skills of living, including those involved in employment, and those matters learnt in school. Pupils have to think carefully about what might be applicable. On the one level the answer is obvious – the 'given' acceptance of the core curriculum. But that does not provide useful skills. Either its skills are to be taken for granted or they go so deep that they are no longer singled out or they are not seen to be directly relevant to employment. Skills are, instead, associated with styles of working that are directly transferable to other circumstances, from childcare to technology. The learning of skills is exceptional rather than mainstream. Skills are matters that are deemed useful:

> I've learnt to graphic-design. There's drawing lessons going
> on in life skills. Art is one of my best subjects and I'd like to do
> that for a job.
>
> (Male, Year 10)

'Life skills': it is interesting to note how little attention is paid formally to those matters of learning how to live in society, how to be a useful citizen or the economic matters of the day-to-day. These the pupils learn almost by the way. The formal part of the curriculum pushes such attention that is paid to them to a very small and insignificant edge. Nor does it engage in those questions of why society is as it is, and why human beings behave in the way they do, and why culture makes a difference, and why people are so different from each other yet carry similar traits. Pupils learn the rudimentary facts rather than question them. The level of 'skills' in living is more akin to that of competencies, those essential coping strategies that encourage a modicum of awareness for survival and which pupils learn about from each other. Skills therefore are seen as directly transferable abilities that pupils will take with them when they leave school.

Much of what is learnt is deemed irrelevant to the world outside school but there is one set of skills that pupils consider to be directly necessary as a tool to be applied in the rest of their lives. This is computing skills.

About computers in school, pupils have some very equivocal attitudes. They are often aware that the equipment they have at home is better than that provided at school (Cuthell, 2002). They believe they are often more knowledgeable about computers than their teachers (Crawford, 2002). They often find the lessons on computing boring (Pearson, 2000). Pupils do not, therefore, view this side of the technical curriculum as a large, exciting enterprise; they do not express that missionizing belief that at any moment the power of communication technology will transform their lives. (The National Grid for Learning is an example of the belief that providing schools with equipment and the means of communicating with each other will transform practice.) They do not feel that the introduction of computers has changed either the curriculum or the manner in which it is delivered (Underwood and Underwood, 1990). Nevertheless they acknowledge the use of computers as an essential skill:

> Computers. I've learnt about these, like how to use them. I like using equipment. I guess I'll be stressed but you get out of doing. . . I could be made redundant. Anything could happen really so I've no idea. . .
>
> (Male, Year 10)

Those pupils who come from more deprived socio-economic circumstances are more liable to rely on the school for their computing skills, but all recognize the economic necessity of keyboard abilities. Computers are accepted as central and the most important skills of manipulation, beyond the practical and vocational application of some subjects, lie in them:

> I've learnt how to use the computer. I've learnt how to use this sort of thing to do with the computer. You press buttons. . . I've learnt how to do that. I would like a computer.
>
> (Female, Year 10)

> Things like scientific calculators: all them buttons, all them protractors and set squares. That's about it.
>
> (Female, Year 10)

The ability to work a machine and the applied understanding of how it operates seem to them an essential skill. This links with the shared assumption that they will need the ability in many of the jobs that they might pursue. Some 'want to work on computers when I leave school' but all see the need to have an awareness of computers. This is also something that has been preached about for so long and so intently that it is a lesson deeply absorbed:

> How to load disks and fonts and all that on computers and how to make spreadsheets and how to do four-figure tank tables and loads of stuff. How to set paragraphs out and how to do my times tables and all this, which is pretty smart.
>
> (Male, Year 10)

The one technical skill that is recognized, more than woodwork and technical drawing, is the ability to work with the computer, not only word processing but the other more complex tasks. Computing (they do not usually refer to ICT in other terms) is recognized as a subject and a skill in its own right. It is not spoken of as a means of learning anything else. Pupils do not talk of the programs that enable the learning of history or science. Computing means learning skills, understanding the machinery itself. There are occasional overlaps since some subjects, like graphics, are dominated by computers:

> We use the computers in IT [*sic*]: they show you a lot of things like drawing junior impressions. . . the same in CDT that helps you with technical drawing, things like that.
>
> (Female, Year 10)

The ability to use computers is understood as an important skill as it is applicable to any form of employment. It is seen as something learnt in school that is directly transferable:

> I've learnt how to use computers. All I know about computers before I came here was like computer games and things like that. But now I've learnt all about work benches and programs and different stuff and I've got like really into them.
>
> (Male, Year 11)

One of the advantages of computers relates to their preferences for learning styles: learning can be approached in a different, more individual way. There are certain clearly understood outcomes. They learn skills that they can take with them:

> I've learnt about computers a lot more. I understand computers. I know how to do them, get into programs and things like that and that should help me, I think, when I leave school.
>
> (Male, Year 11)

The sense of mastery, of enthusiasm, can be found in pupils in some subjects outside the core curriculum, but this awareness of a central skill is particularly associated with programming. Whatever their experience of computer games at home, school makes them aware of the potential in computers not so much for learning as for work. That is why it is seen in terms of a transferable skill rather than a conduit of information.

Computing is, then, the second most important skill learnt at school. Its importance is clearly recognized and shared:

> If I'd worked more on computers and things. I don't think I know much about computers and I know when you get a job you need to. . . jobs is mostly about computer things. You work on computers and things. I haven't got much experience on computers because we don't get them much. . . it's only business studies sometimes.
>
> (Female, Year 11)

Even if they regret missing out on the opportunity, the skill is associated with jobs.

One of the pleasures associated with computers, and other practical subjects, is the style of learning. Individual tasks, small groups and unthreatening experiment, rather than humiliating failure or exposure, are related to the computer rooms. This sense of security is important:

> Computer skills, because we've got good computer rooms and as the teachers are right friendly, communication. I can talk to people. I'm quite confident.
>
> (Male, Year 11)

'Communication': we now come to what pupils deem to be the most important skill of all, 'I can talk to people.'

The most essential skill

Most of the skills that pupils are aware of learning at school are to do with behaviour they have learnt: to manipulate a machine, to carry out a task. These skills are often at the edge of the main concerns of school since a subject or skill like 'literacy' is not really associated by pupils with something active or useful. It is too closely embedded in testing, however important the core curriculum is. Literacy might be a qualification; skills are more to do with programming. But there is one perhaps surprising skill that pupils feel they have learnt. It does not fall within the formal mainstream endeavours of school. It is instead central to the hidden curriculum. It is how to deal with people, especially difficult people, including teachers.

From the pupils' point of view, if not that of the National Curriculum, social skills are at the centre of what they learn in schools. Schools are, in many ways, a perfect locus for observing the behaviour of people (Doyle, 1977). They are crowded. They are full of movement. They need control and discipline. They are dependent on good organization, both good crowd control and persuasion. They are also very hierarchical. There are many levels of command of which pupils are aware: the teachers with the heads of department, the heads of department under the head, the head controlled by governors, and all in the thrall of inspection (Cullingford, 1999a). Between the formal and informal hierarchies of school (Pollard, 1985) there are all kinds of tensions. Out of all this pupils acquire a complex lesson in different types of behaviour. They observe stress and its effects. They see the raw emotions of frustration, anger and humiliation. They experience the more secret pleasures of understanding and friendship, and they undergo the tensions of groups, favourites and outsiders.

It is, perhaps, not altogether surprising that the most important skill learnt at school is to do with social relationships. It is more surprising to find that pupils realize it. Of all things learnt this is the most important, especially how to deal with difficult people, including teachers. These are the 'life skills' that matter:

Meeting different people, interested in what I'm doing.

(Female, Year 10)

The ability to get along with other people is seen as a more significant ability in employment even than the skills of using a computer:

Learning to work with other people.

(Male, Year 10)

How to get on with other people and work in a group and things like that. Computers a little bit, but not much.

(Male, Year 10)

Just collaborating with other people and listening to others. In groups and outside, like gathering information from outside and things like that.

(Female, Year 10)

Despite all the emphasis on what should be learnt for the National Curriculum, and what can be tested, pupils realize that they are learning more complex things, like behaviour. They learn how to 'be polite'. They learn how to deal with other people, and how to learn in groups or by themselves. They are aware that they have learnt how to deal with teachers and with difficult fellow pupils, both of which points will be elaborated later. That they are aware of this as a 'skill' is, however, significant. Schools are seen as a social centre, as a small, perhaps symbolic, section of society. To this extent schools are indeed a preparation for life. What kind of vision they give of society is, of course, a different matter.

Social skills are an essential requirement for survival in school, if not with teachers then certainly with peers (Cullingford, 1999b). These skills include the positive ones of collaboration with others:

Yes, I think you learn the social skills because you have to work in groups sometimes. . . yes, we learnt to use quite a lot of science equipment and technical equipment, computers and that.

(Female, Year 10)

It is the social skills that come first. These skills are associated with positive learning rather than the social tensions that will be explored later. Collaboration, sharing and being able to work with others are seen as central:

Just to get on with adults and just to refer to them all the time.

(Male, Year 11)

Deeper than the formal curriculum of facts, as every teacher knows, are skills of relationships and learning how to learn. Many extensive programmes, like Headstart and Home School Early Learning Project, Leeds in 1995, have demonstrated that the most critical early learning lies in relationships (see also Bronfenbrenner, 1974). The pupils themselves, on reflecting on their experiences, are also aware of this – even if not conscious how deep it goes. Many of them believe that the skills learnt through experience, often in difficult circumstances, were more relevant than the formal curriculum (Barry, 2001). What pupils wanted was involvement and intellectual support, encouragement and a sense of 'respect'. To some extent they achieve these satisfactions in occasional subjects, like those that are so often marginalized. A number of the pupils cited drama as being one of the most significant subjects because it actually explored and delineated just those social relationships that were so crucial. Learning about themselves and about others was the most central of skills:

> Sort of how to stay calm. . . yeah. When teachers aggravate you. And how to communicate with others. And teachers that you don't like, stuff like that, yeah. Skills on the computer, which I would have, like, say, if I hadn't practised at the school, and just graphic skills.
>
> (Female, aged 16)

The mastering of herself is deemed a 'skill'. It is more important than the skill of computing, but nevertheless recognized as something learnt. This all suggests that what is actually being taught in schools is far deeper, more personal lessons than the formalities of subjects.

7
Experiencing school: learning about relationships

The essential learning

The most important skill learnt at school, as pupils keep pointing out, is that of dealing with other people. Relationships, both positive and destructive, are at the heart of the social experience of school. Behaviour is observed and closely structured. Every nuance of command and control, of disobedience and submissiveness, is part of the learning process. Teachers are judged and labelled by their abilities to keep control, or not, and all the complex social interactions of the hierarchies of school, including the most emotional displays of hurt and stress, are closely observed. Pupils keep a close eye on what is happening. They analyse the inner meanings and implications of all actions. That they react differently to different teachers is a truism so apparent that no one appears to think about it. The implications are, however, enormous. The school is the symbol of society, of ordered society at least, as a whole. There are certain people in command, with power, whose idiosyncrasies and weaknesses are centrally important to the pupils. Their own personal success or failure depends upon these.

Pupils, with informed instinct, detect weaknesses. The literature that surrounds their collective and individual ability to undermine authority is clear, especially from the teachers' experience. This gives them a deep-seated, some would say accurate, picture of society and its functions. They understand the command structures and how some can and others cannot function within them. They witness the daily powers of will that sometimes in a minor way and sometimes in a major way colour the experience of discipline in the classroom. They also witness the breakdown of people like teachers who, whatever the cause, can no longer cope. Every young teacher has only one major concern: to survive in the classroom, to keep control and to have the strategies that will prevent the risk of revolt.

Classrooms can be very intense. Who is going to be in control? Whose will prevails? The instinctive reaction to observed events is to find the most sensible and immediate collective norm: shall the teacher be responded to or ignored? That such conditions should be taken for granted is absurd. And yet it is the daily experience for many, if not all, teachers. What remains unexplored is the effect in the pupils' views. If they detect, or even seek out, weaknesses in individual teachers, and if they can psychologically smell teachers' trepidation, what do they then gather about those in authority?

The emotional centre of a school is in the way in which the people in it create their complex relationships. Teachers are clearly in the forefront of this. They deal with the individuals and the mass, they seek personal relationships for the sake of teaching and they are embodied with the power of command. The relationship with them is constantly analysed by pupils, seeing how far they can go to turn authority into something more accommodating, seeking out the levels of humanity in the rule of order (Pollard with Filer, 1995). The scrutiny of teachers, then, is an extremely important experience in school. Teachers' mannerisms and idiosyncrasies, their moods and their interests, are all observed and their reputations passed on from pupil to pupil.

No teacher would argue against this. They witness the way in which they are tested and hear about each other's reputations. The implications of such scrutiny for the forming of views of society are, however, rarely thought through. If learning how to deal with relationships, including handling teachers, is a central skill for pupils, then they are bound to have learnt a lot about human behaviour from their observations.

If teachers create certain kinds of relationships, what about the fellow pupils? The social world in the school is centred not on the rules and on discipline but on the daily intercourse between friends and enemies. Pupils learn from each other; they discuss their interests; they share their fears; they are rivals as well as helpers. In the competitive nature of school, through tests and exams, on the ability to answer questions, pupils are aware of their own standing. They are also aware of their own popularity or lack of it (Hartap, 1996; Berndt and Keefe, 1996). The volatility of children's friendships, with shifting patterns of allegiance and ostracism, is well known. Schools become something of a testing ground for relationships, bringing together unwilling and unusually disparate groups of young people who are forced to get along with each other. If relationships with teachers are complex, relationships between peer groups are even more so. Both kinds have to do with power and will. Both are about the organization of groups, as well as about individuals.

If there is one characteristic about the social nature of schools, it is the volatility, even the pain, that is associated with it. It is not only afterward that individuals confess their unhappiness or loneliness. At the time there are many critical incidents that cause bitter anguish. In the emotional traumas of childhood, friendships, or lack of them, are particularly significant. One of the most important experiences in schools is bullying.

The anti-social undercurrents of schools

Bullying, as a pervasive and widespread aspect of school life, is still not properly understood. This is partly because it is only grudgingly accepted as a fact, and partly because it tends to be defined in a very narrow way. It is subtle and often hidden.

The head teacher who says 'There is no bullying in my school' tends to be the one who most vigorously refuses to see what is actually going on, and in whose school bullying will be rife. The very same people who deny incidents of bullying will often themselves be experiencing it in their own lives, since stress and the causes of stress are inextricably linked to bullying, deliberate and inadvertent.

Bullying, defined as causing hurt in others, does not have to be physical, and nor does it have to be intentional. No service has been done to our understanding of the nature of school life by making clear definitions of bullies as being just those who deliberately target victims (Oliveus, 1993). If defined as those extreme cases of repeated victimization that sometimes lead to suicide, then bullying can be defined as affecting only a small proportion of the school populations. But if we listen to the voices of the pupils, and understand that even if they are not themselves victims they are observers of it then we must realize that bullying is rife. Bullying includes any form of behaviour that causes pain in others. It can take the form of teasing, or simply refusing to talk to someone. It can include humiliation in the class, or subtle and almost anonymous pushes in the corridors or in the playground.

There are some people who would argue that bullying is an everyday occurrence, that it is inevitable, a part of growing up or a means of preparing young people for what they should expect in adult life. It is nevertheless a core experience for pupils, and one that they resent. They themselves would not talk about it so vehemently if they did not feel that something should be done about it.

If bullying is a pervasive if unfortunate part of the reality of most schools, then it must be understood in the wider sense. The incidents that the pupils talk about are generally those outbreaks of physical violence that teachers are expected to be concerned about. The every-day experience of hurt is as much a formative influence on the thinking of pupils as the traumatic incidents where certain pupils are selected for victimization.

School life outside the classrooms is dominated by unacceptable behaviour. Studies of playgrounds in particular (Blatchford and Sharp, 1994) reveal the amount of fighting and general aggression that takes place, where the pushing and poking are so pervasive that it is difficult to make the distinction between rough play and deliberate aggression. Most of the time in schools is spent in classrooms, where bullying is easier to control, but where being 'picked on' is nevertheless rife. There are also significant amounts of time spent between periods, in morning and afternoon breaks and at lunchtime, when pupils are left largely to their own devices, to entertain and occupy themselves in any way they can. The opportunity to pass the time by acts of teasing and provocation is something pupils find difficult to resist. Being accepted by others is very important and this atavistic desire is also difficult to resist. Being rejected by peers is a very significant trauma that makes some unable to form normal social relationships (Boulton, 1995). Bullies are experts at seeing whom they can hurt with most effect (Whitney and Smith, 1993).

From the ways in which pupils talk about their experience of school it is clear that there are certain prevailing conditions, like 'waiting around', or being crowded into playgrounds, that give rise to incidents of bullying, which all have experienced. It is clear that there are many occasions in which pupils are hurt, whether it is intentional or not. There is no need to make too clear a distinction between physical and verbal violence, between bullying and teasing, or between the clear antipathies generated in some relationships and the more general volatility of personal connections. All of these issues form part of the learning experience. Views of human behaviour and perceptions of society are being steadily formed, whether this is a good thing or not.

Pupils are very clear about the social impact of school and the importance of the relationships in their own lives.

The social atmosphere of learning

The ethos of school is an important notion, if difficult to describe. Those who do describe it tend to concentrate on the relationships between staff, on the shared attitudes and values of those who are delivering the curriculum (Rutter *et al*, 1979). It is then assumed, perhaps correctly, that such an atmosphere directly affects the pupils. Pupils also generate amongst themselves an ethos; they have the power and influence to go against the expectations of the staff (Measor and Woods, 1984). The atmosphere of school might be a general shared emotional stance, with discipline and attention to detail, but ethos also prevails within classrooms, in particular lessons and, most pertinently, in particular groups. The general atmosphere of the school is important and quickly detected by pupils from their first day. It is also volatile and liable to change and there are many stories of the influence of some people, teachers or pupils, in dealing with, or ignoring, bullying.

Schools are small societies, which can easily be affected by the groups in them. At the most obvious level, there are demarcations of socio-economic circumstances and other distinctions of cultural origins:

> I don't like other students. I think they're horrible; they're cheeky; they're racist. There's lots of racism actually in this school. . . I've been to school with Asians now all my life but the Afro-Caribbeans come down and ever since then it didn't go well and there's been tension.
>
> (Male, Year 11)

Schools are formalized into classes, 'sets' and streams. They are also formed by groups: by 'gangs' of influential pupils. This has always been part of the fascination of school (Cullingford, 1991). Schools are places where young people, mostly inadvertently, learn about groups, whether minority ethnic groups or gender groups or groups based on other more subtle distinctions like cleverness or money or popularity. Racism is a form of bullying that is clearly common in some schools (consider the Stephen Lawrence enquiry). But racism is just one ostensible excuse for being 'cheeky' or 'horrible'. Other pupils are a source of distinction and antipathy, and, in certain conditions, excuses are sought for the unleashing of vitriol. Whilst racism is a particularly nasty and blatant form of trying to define enmities and attempting to hurt, it is the outcome of other complex insecurities. All the time there are the opportunities to discriminate.

There are many spaces in school where nothing much happens and where time needs to be filled in. Waiting for something to happen – to enter a classroom or some such instruction – is part of the prevailing ethos of school. Even the small pleasures like lunchtime involve queues:

> We have to be in this queue at lunchtime for dinners and then we only have a bit, 15 minutes or so, and sometimes you just walk around the school and break is the same. . . the queuing is not that good: you have to wait a long time.
>
> (Female, Year 10)

Waiting might be frustrating and take up time that could be spent on other things but in such circumstances there are all kinds of opportunity to fill the moment with petty disturbances, like physical expressions of frustration or boredom. The discipline of doing absolutely nothing at all is one that young people find particularly difficult:

> Everybody pushing in the line all the time and pushing around the corridors a lot.
>
> (Female, Year 10)

The general atmosphere is of sullen boredom, with the time filled in a desultory way. In these conditions, signs of disobedience or the assertion of individual choices can flourish:

> They should cut down on all these people smoking and everything.
>
> (Female, Year 10)

> When people smoke that really bugs me, like when they're hiding around the corners in the CDT area and everything, smoking. Like they must know about it and I think, and the only time they usually do it, say at break-time and dinner-time, maybe only sometimes at dinner-times, but why don't the teachers just happen to be walking past the area and catch them and punish them for it, but they don't.
>
> (Male, Year 10)

The telling point here is that there is an ambivalent attitude expressed by those in authority; and pupils learn that they can get away with behaviour that is against the law. No one reading that there are pupils smoking in obscure corners of the school will be surprised. It is part of being worldly-wise to know about this. Some would argue that there is nothing really wrong about smoking if people, whatever the age, want to. The ambivalent message to the pupils is that rules can be disobeyed, and there is a kind of amoral authority in asserting anti-social rights. When they 'get away with it', the very escape becomes a kind of primal sign of assertive independence.

Waiting for something to happen

If smoking prevails so does 'fighting'. This term is used to describe not the most vicious examples of bullying but the daily strife that is experienced in physical terms, from pushing to matters much more serious, when fighting is accepted as endemic in the school. Queuing gives the most obvious opportunity for provocation and it is those most frustrated by the vacuousness of wasted time who find the temptation to cause effects on others most difficult to resist:

> There's lots of fighting sometimes, just pupils. Boys. Sometimes the girls do it too. Older ones, it depends where they are; usually on the fields but they sometimes do it by the cars as well.
>
> (Female, Year 10)

The fighting is observed as a general condition. As war is supposed to be diplomacy by other means, so fighting is the physical expression of continuing personal antipathies:

> Fights. Boys. All years. Everywhere all over the school. Sometimes it's outside and sometimes it's inside. No, they just hardly do owt about it, but it's like people don't tell people who beat them up; they don't grass.
>
> (Male, Year 10)

Another social perception established is not to 'grass', to hide all the malicious behaviour from those who could (or should) do something about it. A great deal of what happens in school is hidden from authority. It is easily observed, but also the more easily ignored.

'Fighting' is a term that covers a whole range of matters. It is the outward manifestation of enmity, of sudden and soon past quarrels, or the outbreak of real personal animosity. Relationships can be seen in these terms: fighting for position or authority, or the assertion of personal rights. It becomes evident that the term 'beating up' is employed almost casually as a prevailing fact of school life.

Whilst the fact of fighting is forced upon pupils and accepted, it remains disliked. It is not as if the fact were endorsed as easily as it is taken for granted:

> There's a lot of fights. I don't like. But I think it seems to have been getting worse. A lot of the younger kids are really cheeky and always fighting. It seems to be getting a lot worse. When I was in the first and second year, everybody was like scared of the fifth year, but now they've got just no respect. They just think they can go round saying what they want when they like, to whoever they want. I don't like that.
>
> (Female, Year 11)

This refers not to specific incidents but to the general ethos, the spirit of a school. The phrase 'no respect' is itself telling. It refers not just to the individual's right to be assertive, but to the space given to other people. Once collective 'respect' for decent behaviour breaks down, the atmosphere becomes conducive to inflicting harm. This loss of 'respect' is considered pervasive. It might be associated with particular gangs, or a year group, but it creates a climate that is rough and unpleasant. And yet this is put up with as if that were the norm and complained about for the same reason. When pupils put the case so succinctly then it seems almost unbelievable that schools should harbour such social conditions. And yet I, like many others, was brought up as a teacher to learn to deal with such violent conditions – and be proud of it – as if to command and control the unwilling were an essential part of teaching.

The most important matter for a new teacher is to learn how to survive and how to cope in the classroom. This means discipline. And yet such a demand on the psychological strength of an individual must be seen as absurd. The battle of wills that schools exhibit cannot really be a good reflection of the social world (Crank, 1988). Pupils also realize the strain that teachers undergo, and why they prefer to ignore, rather than tackle, such conditions:

> I think the majority of them realize it's getting a lot more difficult to teach here because they just run riot during lessons and it's harder to learn to be honest because the kids just do what they want.
>
> (Female, Year 11)

The impression that pupils give, of gangs being able to do whatever they want, is a sign of the most obvious manifestation of a particular experience of school. 'Running riot' in lessons is unusual, but doing so between them, or in the playground, is common. The conditions for such behaviour are general neglect, a lack of supervision. There remain questions about the extent to which there should be, or need to be, constant monitoring and control of pupils. If there is the necessity for supervision, on the grounds that pupils would otherwise be rioting, that gives schools a distinct and repressive ethos.

All that remains unnoticed

Whether there is a need for a watchful and preventative presence or not, there are many periods of unsupervised and unstructured inactivity. At the psychological level, schooling includes large periods of waiting, for an instruction, for the sign that pupils can enter a classroom, before starting a set task or for the next bell. The amount of time spent in doing nothing more than desultorily brooding in a state of psychological anticipation for the next activity is significant. This might be part of the normal condition of those without set tasks or those who rely on constant deadlines or the stress of adrenalin and who do not know how to use the spaces of time creatively. It is also a sign of boredom, of the desultory nature of a lack of excitement.

Doing nothing much in particular, being bored, is a pervasive element in school. When pupils say there is nothing much to do, this is not so much blame for lack of stimulation as a description of what school is like. There might be psychological reasons for not being deeply engaged during lessons and therefore for feeling bored, but in the gaps of freedom, of time to mingle with friends, there is that same sense of a lack of stimulation from outside or motivation from within:

> It's a bit boring at times. There's nothing to do. Not enough at dinner-times. Nowhere to go or anything.
>
> (Female, Year 10)

> Well, nothing much. There's not really much to do; all you do
> is either go for something to eat in the dining hall or you can
> just wait outside for a bit until it's time for lessons. It's quite
> boring. There's nothing to do at break-times.
>
> (Male, Year 10)

The sense of waiting around with little to do reveals the compart-
mentalized nature of schools: of clear sets of activities in certain places,
of gaps between, or sudden demands, and the hiatus of finding things
to do for oneself. Playtimes or dinner-times are occasions where all
kinds of other social interactions can creep in.

Even in those unsupervised or 'free' moments, there are constraints,
places pupils are not allowed to go to. On the one hand we have a
structure of control. People are moved about, ordered, placed. As long
as all appears to be under control, as long as the people are moved
about correctly without obvious pushing and fighting, all is supposed
to be well. What happens within these structured movements is another
matter. The supervision or the ordering only goes so far:

> Not really good; there is nothing to do. There are certain areas
> where you're allowed and certain areas where you're not and
> there's nothing to keep you occupied. . . especially when you
> have the TV on in your classroom and we have MTV on school
> broadcasts; you are not allowed to watch in certain classrooms.
> I think most of the things that you see and hear go on in most
> schools.
>
> (Female, Year 10)

It is sometimes surprising to see which things are taken for granted,
which are accepted as generic and which cause surprise. The general
sense of waste is considered an incipient part of school. One might
have thought that having certain places used for particular activities
might be deemed reasonable. Yet that is questioned, as if most of the
decisions made about order and control were essentially arbitrary or
had been unexplained. Schools are considered to be there to 'keep you
occupied' in some way or another. They fill time, they are dependent
on the imposition of will and they are so hierarchical in their structure
that pupils are taught to await instructions, to submit to the next
forthcoming demand.

In such an outlook there are bound to be tracts of emptiness where
'there is not really much to do. Most of the time is spent just hanging
around' (Female, Year 10). The problem lies not necessarily with the

inability of pupils to know what to do with their time but the assumption that the only tasks worth doing are those they are told to do. Schools set up clear distinctions between work and play. Work is what you are told to do; it is the fulfilment of the teacher's will. Play is what is done nefariously in those gaps that are left. There are overlaps. Pupils 'play' secretly in lessons. Play is 'freedom of choice'. Play is nevertheless distinct. It is associated with self-indulgence, with passing the time. Both work and play conjure up in the minds of pupils the occupation of time, the distraction of the mind by some kind of imposition, the demand for formal task or outcome, or the filling of the gaps:

> We should have more facilities to do some things. Like at break-times we usually don't really have anything to do except go to the common room and play pool but the balls have been thieved so we can't do this; then we have to bring our own cards in; that's all we do.
>
> (Male, Year 11)

It has been argued that the sense of boredom, of having nothing to do, is a result of a lack of facilities, a lack of provision. It could also be argued that the sense of boredom is a symptom of expecting to be distracted or entertained, or waiting for some privilege that is imposed rather than creating something for oneself. Schools actually generate passivity. They demand that what pupils do is not their own choice but given to them. Even ostensible entertainment comes in this category. The result is an urge to find something to fill the time, and the most immediate ways of doing this are anti-social. Being at a loss, in a crowd, brings about the perfect conditions for 'messing around', for challenging the rules of private and nefarious excitements:

> The people my age just. . . they're not going anywhere, quite a lot of them. They know that, so they are just messing around and dragging other people down, whatever. They just don't do their work and mess about in lessons. I mean, they do things, I mean inside jobs for the break-ins and things like that.
>
> (Male, Year 11)

The seeking of challenges

Once there is an atmosphere and an expectation that it is important to be occupied, then the occupations will, if self-created, tend to be arbitrary and personally directed. The most primitive form of social interaction is challenge; it might appear in terms of teasing, where the members of the same crowd carry each other, or it could be a collective will to behave badly against the forms of social constraint, but it is always some kind of outbreak against the norm:

> Everybody crowds in there and then you get people throwing food and stuff and you just want to get out. And you get kicked out at dinner-time. I'd better like if we could all walk around or something inside when it's cold especially.
>
> (Female, Year 11)

Rules are one side of the conditions; on the other side lie the challenges. It is as if some kind of confrontation is expected. The pupils are seen at once as a mass, a collective whole, but also as a seething group of individuals, looking for an opportunity to unleash their energy. The sense of boredom and the will to misbehave go together. There are crowds of pupils who are waiting for order to be imposed, like a crowd of demonstrators against a police presence. The differences are that the constraints are less manifest and the demonstrations are a general sense of protest rather than a rallying to a particular cause. The sense of demarcation lines and being on opposite sides in a potential confrontation is clear:

> At break-times it used to be really, really like loads of people, like they get pushed around and all this and especially at dinners, right, there's really big queues to get a dinner. I really hate that. I really hate waiting.
>
> (Male, Year 11)

Crowds with nothing to do: these are the conditions that are rife for bullying. Of all social relationships in school, what weighs most heavily on pupils is the undercurrent of fear that derives from the deliberate or undeliberate hurt that they experience. There are so many potential problems that can lead to trauma that, for some, the wonder is that they do not experience more of it. Many unkindnesses are deliberate and the more culpable for that, but the experience of individuals is that bullying is so endemic, so pervasive, that it almost does not matter where it comes from. It can be anonymous or inadvertent. It can be sudden and immediate, or long-term and subtle. It is part of the condition of school and part of the conditioning is the way that pupils accept it, almost laconically, as a fact of life.

Bullying is witnessed by all and, more to the point, felt to be both pervasive and ignored:

> I don't see somebody doing anything about it.
>
> (Female, Year 11)

> There's always things happening like people beating up first years and things like that. And I don't like it but I go along with it like a laugh. But it's like if I don't laugh at it like, they start picking on me. It's like just being with a crowd. It's like all just being mates. And I don't like it when. . . like if I, like a teacher, and then like other person's slagging her off and I don't like it but I still go along with it. . . for other people, 'cos they just like make fun of me. . . I wouldn't go so far as I would actually do so but I don't feel good with myself.
>
> (Male, Year 11)

There are many misunderstandings, probably deliberate, about the nature of bullying. This illuminative analysis encapsulates some of the facts on bullying that are so easily put to the side. The first misunderstanding is about the extent. There is 'always' a general sense that bullying is in the air. It could be described as taking place for a particular percentage of time. Some commentators try to parcel bullying into particular amounts – the number of incidents or the number of perpetrators or victims. Bullying is not like this. To obtain figures you need to have clear definitions, boundaries and distinctions between different acts, hard to define even in the most closely observed incidents. From the point of view of those who suffer from bullying, such definitions, of the degree of intent or the time spent on planning, are meaningless. Bullying is an irrational and pervasive act. All are 'victims'. There is no typology that labels one person as purely responsible.

The half-hidden malaise of school

Bullies feel themselves as much under threat as others. They are vulnerable and easily provoked and it is in their inadequacies that their threat lies. This is not an instant psychological explanation of bullies but suggests recognition of their manic expressions of vulnerability. There are clearly cases of certain gang leaders deliberately inflicting pain but there are many more of individuals reacting regularly to perceived or real provocation. The crucial point is not the typology of individual bully or victim but the 'going along with it'. The pressure on conforming is so strong that people will do those things that they know even at the time are wrong, and that they do not like. Think of all the levels of peer pressure. It is part of being in a 'crowd', of being with 'mates'. All that sounds positive, but there is also the urgency of the threat. Conformity is being 'in'; the alternative is to be 'picked on'. This is the nature of bullying: the crowd or the mob or the majority, however defined, prevails over individuality. There are some who can escape this but most do not wish to 'stand up'.

Such an experience of conformity is not rare, nor the shameful ambivalence of its confession. Pupils learn to behave in school as they will subsequently do in the workplace. That sense of not 'feeling good' with oneself is important. It does not, however, prevent playing along with the system. Those who are under the most unseemly pressure feel prevailed upon to join in. Others are more fortunate. They witness the same things but are allowed to remain aloof. Some bystanders join in. Some give encouragement by their witness and their passivity. Others condone by turning away:

> Sometimes there's bits of bullying and things like that but it's never affected me. Luckily, you see it, and I think it happens in every school really. I don't think it's too bad. I just see the boys, usually the same group and that. But I just ignore them.

> (Male, Year 10)

All the means possible to distance himself from the consequences of bullying are involved in this. The victims are not mentioned. It did not affect him personally, since he can ignore it. Given that, the fact of bullying is 'not too bad' from his point of view. It is also 'not too bad' in a judicious sense, given other prevailing norms. Other schools might be even worse. What is significant is the assumption of its presence.

Some might go along with bullying or be sucked into it. Others might observe it mentally. Others experience it far more personally:

> Being picked on all the time because of your size and stuff like that... anybody. They just start calling you names and because you're small they think they can start beating you... my parents have told me to tell the teachers because it doesn't stop them, so I do. Most of them don't, no; I used to go to Mr C; he didn't do anything.

> (Male, Year 10)

The crucial fact is that the idea of being singled out, of not conforming, is all part of the prevailing tone of schools; the formal demands of the curriculum are echoed by the social undercurrents. Being 'picked on' is not an isolated incident but something almost casual in the way 'they start beating you'. It is clearly too common an occurrence for the teachers to deal with.

Examples abound. Each one is slightly different and yet familiar. There are certain patterns, like the flexing of muscles by the strong over the weak – but the strong can be so because of number as much as individual power. There are those who cannot stand provocation and cannot cope with it, and that in itself makes them vulnerable. Such patterns lead some to argue that these tendencies to hurt are atavistic, so deeply seated that they are inevitable and therefore allowable. The evidence suggests that they are an unnatural occurrence because of the conditions prevailing in school on the one hand and the primitive genetic and social assumptions on the other. I am tempted to say that if people think that bullying is inevitable then we have the societies and consequences we deserve, let alone the schools. From the point of view of the pupils, however, the prevalence of bullying is never associated with its inevitability:

> I thought I was going to get slapped on, and I feel I would have got picked on. They were chasing me. They just caught me and my mates told them to leave me alone. I don't like bullies; they get me mad.
>
> (Male, Year 10)

This was a consequence of 'stepping in' to avoid someone else being bullied.

Culpable witness

The individual or collective act of taking bullying seriously and attempting to control it is considered rare amongst pupils and teachers alike. In the normal conditions, bullying is such an everyday occurrence that it is easy to ignore. Some feel that there is so little to be done that it is best to ignore it, lest the very stepping in should provoke more trouble:

> Well, there is a bit of bullying when you walk past, you either see a fourth year bullying a first year or something like that. Like this guy in the school who's always being battered. He's

shy; he's in the third year but he's just a chicken. He's always going 'Leave me alone' and all that but they're always bullying him. You all have to tell them to leave him alone when you walk past. He's always running away from people.

(Female, Year 10)

One can picture here the prevailing conditions, the almost daily ritual of an individual being chased. There are two unquestioned assumptions that arise from this acceptance of a 'bit' of bullying. One is the sense of the inevitable victim – 'He's just a chicken' – as if it were to some extent his fault. The other is the sense of a norm: he is 'always' being bullied. It is as if that is what he is for. The stronger will always hurt the weak. The view of society as the battle of wills with those who survive and those who do not is a bleak one.

It has been argued that school is a rite of passage that has little to do with subsequent experiences of society, as if nothing that has been experienced (or learnt) will survive. And yet all pupils are witnesses to personal acts such as aggression and animosity, and, more significantly, the acceptance of, or at best indifference to, this fact. The most troublesome part of the world of bullying is the silent witness:

When people fight in the playground everybody gathers round. There's a lot of bullying going round. . . mostly boys over something they do in classroom or pens and stuff. What people steal from each other.

(Female, Year 10)

When bullying is accepted as part of a culture, as a way of dealing with personal matters in a public way, it pervades the ways in which communities and society as a whole are viewed. All the time we see the breaking down of those theoretical distinctions between people who wilfully inflict pain on the rest and people who look upon what is happening, between those who feel themselves unfairly picked on or blamed and those who at the same time realize that their guilt or innocence makes little difference in the prevailing social atmosphere:

Because I sometimes mess around. . . They pick on me. When I don't mess around I still get picked on. When I'm in. . . you see everybody listen to me and if I do something they do something and whenever I don't do something they still say do it; I shall get in trouble for it.

(Male, Year 11)

There are various elements in the culture of bullying. This does not imply that there is any excuse for those who perpetrate acts of cruelty, any more than there is for those who bully in large organizations. Nevertheless it is the prevailing culture that allows individuals to abuse the normal understandings and courtesies of personal interaction. People get embroiled in the assumptions that others make. They 'pick on me', I 'sometimes mess around', which means picking on other people. This pupil is the centre of attention, which he relishes, the ringleader, the one most cajoled into acting badly. At the same time he is in trouble for it, 'picked on' by the teachers. He does not know whether to be proud or ashamed of his notoriety. The significance here, however, is the way in which he is by some collective will manipulated into the position. The shared culture of school, ineffable but inevitable, prevails. Without the ambiguity and complexities of all these interactions, individual acts of kindness or nastiness would be noticed far more.

Such a culture of rebellion, of standing out against the prevailing norm whilst fitting in to the expectations of others, is juxtaposed against the prevalence of rules. Schools are places where the imposition of will, of force, is paramount. One cannot assert that there would be less bullying if there were fewer rules since that is a correlation that is beside the point. One can say that the imposition of discipline and the strength of reaction against it go together; the more so when there is a clear demarcation line:

> Rules that they're made. Like they say this place is out of bounds and all the stuff and like they made is as if it's a prison or something because then they're like a little area and then like mostly we can't go on the field down there and that's where the sun shines anyway. . . it's a bit boring there.

> (Female, Year 10)

'They' make the rules. The rest adhere to them or choose not to. They certainly question them. If the rules seem arbitrary they are so, because they are imposed by an implacable will, sometimes anonymous and sometimes embodied in a particular person. The analogy with prison, with being incarcerated against their will, is again telling:

> I just want to get away. It's like a prison; it's so depressing in here; it's horrible. There's people standing over you all the time, watching what you're going to do and you can't do what you want.

> (Female, Year 11)

The sense of antipathy, of having some will against which to react, is part of the fact of school. Teachers make rules and pupils follow them. When the latter question, then a battle of wills occurs. The equitable balance might not be difficult to achieve in some circumstances but in others the whole notion of such a balance of power is questionable. In regimes of force the outbreak of bullying tends to be greater. Again, we are not suggesting that the pure lack of any order at all is the answer. This would be a far cry from the hopes and aspirations of pupils who like discipline and order, but it is the pupils who need to be involved in the conditions of school and have their learning about personal relationships and anti-social behaviour recognized.

The discipline of authority is imposed by teachers and this is often seen as something oppressive. It is inevitable and accepted as such, but the way it is conducted causes concern:

> He's one of those types that say, if you say something he sends you out, he sends you on call. You go to Mr A and you do stuff for Mr A and it gets put down in a little book. If you get sent out on call for two times, you get sent home. If you get sent out three or four times you'll get sent home, but Mr C sending people mostly all the time and if you come late he makes you stand outside.
>
> (Male, Year 10)

The arcane rules of teachers are utterly understandable. Teachers need to survive. They must prevail. But the rules are different since no human actions can be demarcated in such a quantitative way. Teachers do their best; the pupils submit and, at the same time, question the very imposition of will. Looking at this from the outside, not at the justifications but the inner reality of the facts, is there not more than a hint of the absurd?

Is the job of teachers to improve discipline? Is it to make people obey rules? Is that what teaching is really concerned with? The question remains open. I used to get the better of the most recalcitrant pupils in East London. I was proud of it. I still am. But is that what teachers are supposed to do?

8
Pupils' relationship with teachers

The role of teachers

The criticism of teachers has a long history. Perhaps this criticism derives from the fear or suspicion of being beholden to anybody or owing personal success to others. There is a deep-seated tradition of depicting teachers as those who 'cannot do' anything worth while, as if 'doing' were defined as anything pursued for personal profit. From the portrayal of 'the schoolmaster' in Dickens's *Our Mutual Friend* to the more formalized disparagement by successive government ministers, teachers, for all their dedication and untraceable influence, are an easy target for attack. They devote themselves to the success of others. They give away their knowledge freely. Their actions are driven essentially by missionary instincts. In this mercenary age, formed by a culture of selfishness and instant self-gratification, teachers are easy to despise.

There is something about the role of teachers that has always attracted criticism. The need to impose control on recalcitrant pupils gives them the kind of forced authority that lends little dignity to their actions. I used to be proud of being able to impose my will on severely unruly disaffected boys in the slums of London. Reflecting on this afterwards, I realize that the task that I was carrying out was more than faintly absurd. Knowing how to control such anger and opposition might have been heroic and certainly took some moral courage, but the absurdity of being in such a position still weighs on me. This is at the heart of the dilemma of being a teacher. When pupils wish to learn then teaching is a joy, and yet it is an act associated with opposition, with reluctance and even with hate.

I touch on a personal note of my own experience in order to declare not only my understanding of what it is like to be a teacher but my admiration for, as well as sympathy for, the tasks they carry out. What follows, from the experience of pupils, is largely critical, since this is the deepest effect that they recall. Of course there are many exceptions. There is not one pupil, however disaffected, who does not remember individual teachers with affection (Cullingford, 1999b). Yet there is an underlying relationship with the role of teachers that is negative, dispiriting and disappointing.

It is essential to acknowledge the distinction between the role and the personality. We are here analysing the 'teachers' not as a particular individual associated with a subject, but as someone in authority over a class and someone who is, with his or her colleagues, seen as the central *raison d'être* of the school. Some pupils find it very hard to dissociate the necessary role of the teacher in imposing discipline from the personal animosity that singles out the individual. This is why the phrase 'picked on' is so important. For all children, it is the role of the teacher, the generalized anonymous actions that they understand, that is oppressive. Whilst acknowledging that each school is different and that there are many examples of harmonious well-being, usually in the less socially and economically deprived areas, there is something about the role of the teacher that is distinctive and generalized.

Whilst the job of the teacher is far more difficult in certain places than others, and at certain times than others, that note of disparagement about the very idea of the role, that sense of superciliousness with which it is held, goes back a long way, certainly to the introduction of a universal state education, and, again judging by writers like Dickens, a long time before that. Whilst individuals can always remember their favourite teacher and some outstanding lessons, the general sense of teachers in a school is that of imposed will, of often arbitrary judgements and of presenting information on which pupils will be tested. The essential relationship is that of a group of young people trying to work out what the teacher wants them to do, to guess what it is and fulfil whatever is expected. The critical testing of teachers is part of the strategy of guessing (Pollard, 1985). All questions in school are interpreted as 'closed' (Barnes, Britton and Rosen, 1969) even if the teacher is genuinely attempting to elicit information. The art, from the pupils' point of view, is to anticipate whatever it is the teacher wants, and the assumption they make is that it is something that essentially remains hidden from them in its purpose, and part of the power of authority.

This point of view of pupils feeling, after a time, both disenfranchised and suspicious is well researched and has been established a long time. This needs to be said because we live at a time that is particularly difficult for teachers in most of the anglophonic world (Alexander, 2000). Teachers are constantly criticized by the very politicians and civil servants who are trying to recruit them. They are notoriously 'named and shamed' in reports, and public statements by the Office for Standards in Education. This is inevitably so in a cultural climate that is based on a system of measuring school effectiveness against targets (Mortimore *et al*, 1979). The school improvement industry, triggered by the research of Rutter and his colleagues in 1979, is based not only on the assumption that there are measurable outcomes to detect signs of weakness and strength, from standard attainment test results to incidences of truancy, but that these outcomes are the responsibility of teachers.

The result of critical inspections and accountability is that teachers are exposed to scrutiny, not only from outside but from their own pupils. This is often forgotten. That teachers are disillusioned and demoralized is well documented (Jeffrey and Woods, 1996). The demands placed upon them, the constant inspection and the deprofessionalization of the task of teaching all play their part. The central problem is the changing emphasis on their role as 'delivering' someone else's curriculum in a way that is also dictated from outside. They no longer have the freedom to teach what they think best and in a way that they feel is most conducive to learning. Pupils detect this. When they see teachers cajoling them into working harder they assume that this is happening because the teachers are afraid of what inspectors will say if the results are not good enough (Cullingford and Oliver, 2001). The culture of blame and criticism imposed by inspection is naturally shared by pupils (Slee, 1998).

The task of teaching has always been difficult partly because of the way in which society sees teachers and partly because of the nature of schools and their organization. There are many pupils who find schools oppressive and alienating, partly because of the imposition of certain kinds of language and expectation (see, for example, Hargreaves, 1967; Willis, 1977). Given the reluctance of many pupils to learn, teachers are very easy to undermine. They have always cherished sensitive support and a school ethos matched to pupils' needs (Charlton, Jones and Ogilvie, 1989). They find these less and less available. Inspection and the way in which the National Curriculum works put particular pressures on teachers that are widely recognized as undermining (Campbell, 1998; Croll and Hastings, 1996).

Teachers are supposed to do a 'job' rather than have a 'way of life'. They are 'mechanical' rather than artists. If the pupils are also critical of teachers and their motivations, this is an additional result of the public abuse that teachers receive. Pupils' dissatisfactions, however, go deeper than this. Certain aspects of the teachers' role have not changed. When the Oracle project was first reported, based on more liberal and open primary schools, it was discovered how much of the time was spent by teachers talking and expounding (Galton, Simon and Croll, 1980). When the research was later replicated it was seen that teaching is still a matter of teachers talking and children listening (Galton *et al*, 1999). The National Curriculum might have made this far more necessary and widespread, since the task of 'getting through' the material is so incessant (Chandler, Fritz and Hala, 1989), but there has always been an assumption that school is like this.

This role of delivering the curriculum come what may is assumed by pupils to affect all teachers. For all the individual differences there are certain things that all teachers do. The very fact that pupils miss the opportunity to get to know teachers personally, and that they cherish those very few occasions when they can strike up a more intimate, friendly relationship, underlines how much of the time teachers are simply carrying out their role. Teachers also feel torn by the tensions between the demands of their job and the potential of closer, more complex relationships with pupils (Butroyd, 2001). The daily routine of a school, shuffling numbers of pupils from place to place and racing through the syllabus, makes any escape from the role of discipline keeper both difficult and potentially dangerous.

Both pupils and teachers are oppressed by the ambivalence between the needs of personal relationships and the demands of the professional role. Pupils respect those who keep discipline and display strictness. They accept the need for order and the imposition of it in an impersonal, disinterested and fair way. At the same time they look for cracks in the façade of authority, a sense of humour, a shared observation. Some teachers are clearly more respected and rated more highly than others, depending on both their ability to order the classroom as a whole and their prowess at 'explaining' the subjects (Cullingford, 1991). Clarity of exposition is a professional matter that affects pupils individually; it is to that extent a personal matter. This is why teachers are so closely associated with subjects and why some subjects are liked because of the personality of the teacher. Teachers are seen both as experts of their subjects, full of knowledge, and as constrained by the syllabus, prevented from making the most of their own personal rich experience.

Pupils spend a large amount of time in school simply observing teachers. They need to understand not only what is expected of them, but what many of the hidden signals mean. Pupils are in the power of teachers. On the one hand they can find teachers simply boring or incomprehensible, going through the subject matter too fast or too slowly. On the other hand they can experience teachers in terms of personal animosity, through being humiliated or by being ignored. The complaint that teachers ignore bullying is echoed in the sense that teachers in the classroom ignore individual differences. In the constraints of school, how could it be otherwise?

The dominance of being taught

Whatever our sympathy with the lot of teachers, the pupils' attitudes towards them, and their general status, is generally bleak. Whatever the individual exceptions, and the fact that they are exceptional and prized as such is significant, the experience of teachers is likened to an oppressive regime. Of course the picture that emerges is complex as well as consistent, since there are so many influences that teachers bring to bear, but there are some clear indications about the way in which teachers, in their power, are central to the experiences of school. When teachers cannot be tolerated the only escape is exclusions or truancy (Cullingford, 1991). Teachers are there to help. They are also there to be obeyed:

> Now the teachers say that we should have respect for them teaching us and we should be listening to them. I don't really like that idea, because sometimes I thought the teachers don't be really nice to us and they usually boss us around and when we do ask for help they don't tend to give you the help that you need. I mean if I go to assemblies now every day. . . you always say, a teacher, 'We're here to help you.' But when we go there and ask for help they don't seem to have time for you and even though you do ask for help they only give a small amount of help. So I don't like that concept. Just the way they are. They say that we're going to be the next generation; they always seem to say that to us. But when it comes down they tend to help us, they just say, 'When you go out in the whole world, you'll be alone.' That's all they say; I know it by heart.

> (Female, Year 11)

Teachers obviously mean well. Their intentions are never in doubt. The fact that they do not deliver is the fault of the system in which they operate. This causes tensions for pupils and teachers. The rhetoric does not match the reality. Pupils understand that such inability to deliver what is needed is, like stress, imposed on teachers by managerial demands, but that does not alleviate their dissatisfaction.

Teachers wish to have 'respect', which, when they use this term, means obedience. The roles observed here are quite clear; we 'should be listening to them'. This leads to being bossed around, so that 'respect' is only a one-way process rather than a mutual understanding. The most disappointing part of the mismatch between rhetoric and reality is between the desire for individual help and the inability to give it. Teachers say one thing but, when the help offered is asked for, they don't tend to give what pupils need. It is a matter of 'not having time'. But that is a fact of life; it is 'the way they are'. Pupils assume that there is a culture of indifference, that really they are not expected to ask for help. They interpret this as not only indifference but a deliberate stance, since 'you are on your own'. Like the rallying cry of 'Get on with your work', the message is understood as indifference.

The most worrying concern of pupils is that all oppression or lack of support stems from the feeling that teachers are indifferent, that they do not care personally:

> I can understand the point of view that they can't be bothered with it any more because like I say most of the people were just turning up at school because they had to; they didn't have to do any work when they were there. Teachers basically weren't there to teach them, they were just to look after them basically. It's rather pointless if you are doing this. . . other teachers just give up. It was a lost cause.

> (Male, aged 18)

The root of the problem for such a pupil is the shared indifference to learning. Once the main purpose of the school is lost, as it so often is, then all that is left is the need for oppression, for discipline, for the insistence on obedience. This is one reason why schools are so often likened to prisons. Parents have a statutory duty to ensure pupils attend school, and one of the measurements of the success or failure of a school is its ability to keep pupils incarcerated. The teacher's role descends into 'looking after' pupils rather than anything more creative, struggling to control rather than teach.

The psychological absence of teachers

If teachers are resented for their control, they are even more resented when they cannot be 'bothered' to control. The expectation of the disciplinary powers of teachers is extraordinarily high, as if pupils assumed that the onus for order is entirely on the teachers and that the duty of pupils is virtually to test their capacity. Those teachers who cannot cope are despised:

> I wish the teachers were better. Some of them can't even control the class and you know. . . one teacher was actually frightened of this boy. Yes, he was. The teacher just like. . . 'All right, do whatever you want.'
>
> (Female, Year 11)

This is part of the curious culture of some schools that accepts that it is unsurprising if some pupils do not wish to learn or wish to 'mess about':

> I think the majority of them realize it's getting a lot more difficult to teach here because they just riot during lessons and it's harder to learn, to be honest, because the kids just do what they want.
>
> (Female, Year 11)

The absurdity of the circumstances is clear, but it is a result of the estrangement of pupils from schools. Schools are such collective places that all are affected by the actions of the few. The difficulties of teaching centre more and more on discipline, on 'coping strategies', than on the intricacies of the subject matter or the complexities of pedagogy:

> If there is people messing about we have to be cruel; in other schools there aren't any teachers like them. I can only find four or five teachers who are. . . if people mess about they tell them off. But I have seen many teachers just sitting and let them mess about. One teacher that I think is really good is Mr –. They don't mess about with people; if you mess about they chuck you out. They are like relaxed; you just have to relax with them. But other teachers you just sit down and can't do anything else, listen to other boys who mess about. That's it.
>
> (Male, Year 11)

123

Some teachers, who are respected for it, are able to deal with difficult pupils. One can understand why others simply cease to be engaged in that battle of wills. Those who have mastered the art of discipline can 'relax' since not only their reputation but their very manner exudes that confidence of command, and pupils, like Cornwall recognizing King Lear as an authority by his manner, can see at once if they cannot get away with 'messing about'. At the same time pupils do not respect some of the weapons that teachers resort to in order to keep discipline.

Pupils like strictness and general rules but not being singled out. They do not like the personalization of discipline. They accept overall authority but resent it when it affects them personally:

> I still do all the work but I don't like the teachers. Sometimes I get sent out. Mr – sends you out for no reason whatsoever. If you walk in he just tells you to get out. It happens to most people. It's just that he thinks he knows everything but he doesn't.
>
> (Male, Year 10)

Some of the relationships with teachers are constantly troubled:

> I don't like the teacher and she doesn't like me. . . I don't get on with the teachers. It's from the past when my dad was in the school. My dad had a go at her and she doesn't like that.
>
> (Female, Year 10)

There are all kinds of judgements that are formed, from previous experience, that result in certain pupils being singled out, or sent out in anticipation that something might happen. Discipline then becomes a personal matter:

> Mr –, because he's one of those types that say if you say something he sends you out, or sends you on call. . . if you get sent out on call for two times you get sent home. . . Mr – sending people out mostly all the time and if you come late he makes you stand outside.
>
> (Male, Year 10)

One of the problems for schools is that individual teachers have their own standards of discipline. There is little consistency observed. Some teachers have 'given up' and have become indifferent. Others will not tolerate even the hint of disobedience:

The teacher. Just too strict. You can't really talk socially to your friends in class. You can't even talk really; he just makes you do your work. He tells you to shut up.

(Male, Year 10)

They're always shouting and going on about stuff. They send you out for nowt.

(Male, Year 10)

The teachers might well have their reasons, but each one is different. A special layer of subservience to the whims of individuals is learning their particular expectations. It is like guessing, in a repressive regime, which person has the most power and how to please him. Being 'picked on' without reason, 'for nowt', is a by-product of the failure initially to adapt to a new classroom or a new collective ethos. The variable approaches of teachers make pupils learn how to control their behaviour and vary it. This is part of their learning about 'relationships'.

Some pupils are particularly vulnerable to the strict demands of teachers, especially when under the influence of their peers:

She always gets me done for anything I don't do. . . He moved me around all the classroom and I didn't do owt. Well, there's this guy who sits next to me, he's always like getting me done and I'm always moving and getting into trouble.

(Male, Year 10)

Fairness and unfairness

We have already witnessed the ability of fellow pupils to cause problems, but a particular satisfaction seems to be derived from placing peers and acquaintances in the path of the least patient and most angry of teachers. Being 'picked on' is often the result of a previous reputation that derives from relationships with peers rather than deserved responses to bad behaviour. Each class is different, and teachers are observed to treat pupils differently.

Unfairness is resented, even when it arises out of good intentions:

People used to get picked on all the time. . . Supposedly people do a good piece of work and they get a commendation slip, which is sort of like. . . I don't know how to say it, commends

125

them for their work. . . but lately people have just been going into lesson behaving for say nine of them and disrupting the rest of the year and because they have behaved for those nine the teachers see it as a surprise and they commend them with commendation slips.

(Male, Year 10)

The rejoicing over 'one sinner that repenteth' does not necessarily appeal to the others. Those who draw attention to themselves might receive a great deal of punishment but they also have their rewards. Any system of rewards and punishment cannot always be seen to be fair. Positive discrimination can also be resented:

Some kids are cheeky and what I really don't like about school is once we were in French and half her class were misbehaving and all of us got detention apart from a disabled person and a deaf person. All of us even though half of us weren't doing anything. He did report it to the headmaster and he didn't do anything about it. That happens often. We had some exams and the disabled person got much longer than what we did and it's all meant to be equal and stuff. In wheelchairs and stuff like that; you know they haven't got writing problems. . . but they still get longer.

(Female, Year 10)

Unfairness is one of the central concerns in the social world of school. Sometimes it is made into a policy, like discriminating in favour of some or rewarding others. The arbitrariness of punishments, meted out to those who have the misfortune to be caught rather than those who are more responsible, is also resented. The unevenness of expectations and classroom routines is, however, evident. Teachers vary in their demands and in their ability to be interesting. They have different standards of behaviour and ability. Some lessons are felt to be particularly oppressive compared to the others:

I hate German. I don't like him. The teacher. He's just arrogant. You have to work in silence for a whole hour and 10 minutes and I can't shut up. I'm always getting into trouble. We still get told to shut up and get on with it.

(Female, Year 10)

It is very easy for pupils to feel oppressed in some lessons when they are allowed to talk in others; variations of style lead to some lessons (and some teachers therefore) being associated with boredom:

> She just keeps on talking and talking; you don't do work. It's just so boring in there.
>
> (Female, Year 10)

Teachers vary in their approach to discipline; they are also felt to be indifferent to the individual needs of pupils. Often the two are associated. Whilst all pupils can reflect on particular moments of pleasure, they all share a sense of the majority of lessons being both 'boring and pointless'. The two go together. Anything will be dull if it has no sensible purpose. This has a great deal to do with the teaching style:

> Depends which teachers as well. Some teachers don't cater for the needs of all students. . . he don't cater for the needs for me; he finds and moves on to the special, which I don't really like. The teaching method I think is too boring. It doesn't get you involved. It's just like here's your work, do it, and people do it; they might get it but it doesn't catch your interest. It makes you lose interest; that doesn't encourage people to work. . . there isn't so much teaching methods. I'm not blaming the school but that's the way it is, and if you're like me I get bored really quickly so I don't really like it.
>
> (Male, Year 11)

Every teacher knows the difficulty of catering for the needs of a wide variety of pupils, differentiated by their attitudes and learning styles as well as their abilities. Pupils also feel they are not catered for, especially those who are above or below the mean levels of performance since they are the ones who stand out. We have a sense of teachers delivering the curriculum, of handing out tasks, of keeping pupils occupied, even if their motivation is to reach the higher standards.

Pupils can learn by themselves rather than through listening to the teachers talking but what they seek is not only clear explanations but a motivation to learn. Boredom derives from losing all sense of purpose in a subject:

> I think it were history because it just bored me. Really did bore me. . . And I weren't that good at maths either. It were like. . . I

can add up and I'm not stupid but it were just doing sums and stuff like that, that I couldn't do. And it were like the teacher just did us, they didn't seem to teach it, like it, like it were just 'Sit down; get on with it.' They couldn't be bothered; we couldn't be bothered.

(Female, aged 16)

We see the loss of confidence in the teacher. The recurring phrase is about 'not bothering', or putting the onus on the pupils to learn without showing them how. 'It's up to you' is the phrase of commands and exhortations without support. As in any poorly run organization there is an imbalance between responsibility and the means to fulfil it.

The inner curriculum of teaching

Teachers have a lot of subtle power. They can discriminate between pupils. They can 'pick out' some and ignore others:

I don't like how they teach. When you ask them questions and they go to someone else and they just ignore you.

(Male, Year 10)

It is very easy for pupils to feel, in such a large crowd of them, ignored and even humiliated:

Sometimes if they're busy then they won't help you until they're free. . . it's really difficult for me because I used to have hearing problems in the first year and I couldn't understand nothing of it and I lost track and I still can't understand a lot of it.

(Male, Year 10)

Falling behind the expectations and the pace of the class can be an effective way of learning to dislike a particular subject:

Well, the teacher, she was. . . she went at the pace of like the better ones in the group. She didn't slow down for the less able ones. . . and that makes you dislike the subject.

(Female, aged 15)

The slower pupils are always cautious of themselves and can easily be humiliated:

> 'Cos my teacher was horrid to me. He used to embarrass me in front of the class. He thought he was really funny but nobody else did. He used to make me stand there and he used to laugh at my homework 'cos it wasn't right.
>
> (Female, aged 17)

Unfortunately, stories of being exposed as 'stupid' are many, although there are many more inadvertent incidents than ones in which the teacher derives some malicious satisfaction from hurting the pride of individuals. It is also part of being 'picked on', or being exposed for what the teachers see as deviancy.

The power that teachers have is clear, even if it is not absolute. Some of this power is directed towards discipline, where teachers make and, more ambivalently, interpret the rules (Wilson and Cowell, 1990). It is, however, based on the fact that teachers are there to enforce learning: the real power lies in what they do in the classroom. When dealing with discipline, they can punish and seek out offenders; they might equally well be indifferent to acts of bullying and there are many instances when they choose not to assert their authority. Even when indiscipline affects their own teaching they can be indifferent to it. There are those who create a regime that pupils find oppressive: this is based on the demands being made. Some pupils react against the ambition of teachers:

> I don't like any teachers because she pushes you too hard. She's all right but she says that if you get under this certain mark you get detention even if you're not really brainy. She like punishes you even if you've tried your best. It makes you not want to do anything. It makes me feel I used to like it at first, but now I just don't want to do any more. I have to though.
>
> (Female, Year 10)

There are few choices in school, in action or in thought, at least on the surface. You 'have to' go to school and 'have to' learn. Teachers are observed as desiring high standards of output and of application. This is considered worthy but it is oppressive if assumed to be a sign of their own success. It can feel oppressive as part of the unintentional discipline system of the school. Work is often seen as punishment. Indeed, every week, extra homework is commonly used as punishment. Making pupils learn something leads to being forced to do more of it because it is a tool of control. However much the pupils do, they have to demonstrate even greater success, like schools hitting even more demanding targets and, if they do not do so, being inevitably accused of marking time or having too low standards. 'Doing your best' is not good enough. There are targets and tests. The results often are that pupils do not 'want to do anything'; all the pleasures of motivation are lost. Homework becomes a chore and all work an oppression:

> I don't like the teacher either. . . she explains things pretty well but she's too strict. You know in normal classrooms you can lean over to your mate and go all right and all this and talk to them. But it's got to be total silence in her classroom.

> (Male, Year 10)

The sense of oppression associated with teachers is not just a matter of discipline, of being overstrict. It is a question of demands, of attention to the details of work as well as behaviour. It is important for pupils to feel comfortable with learning but there are many classrooms where there is a sense of unease. The pupils are being forced to learn, as if they had no natural desire to do so. They are scrutinized for signs of misbehaviour as if without such a watch chaos would ensue. The unease can be created in a number of ways. One is a sense of disagreeing with the teacher, but being made to feel there is no right to do so:

> It's the teacher. I don't like the teacher. She's a bit overpowering. I don't know. She doesn't buy lottery tickets and things. I'm not against being with your religion like, but she's like, it's just her opinion counts. I can't say anything else. She doesn't want anybody else to buy lottery tickets and things. She thinks it's gambling and things like that.

> (Female, Year 10)

Teachers' opinions 'count' in such a way that allows no argument. The teacher deals in correct facts, in certainties. It is, therefore 'overpowering' if the same certainty is applied to matters on which the pupils also have ideas.

Teachers are assumed to have the power of what they teach. They demand that pupils pay attention to them as the controllers and organizers of the curriculum, even if they, in their turn, are controlled by others. This makes the ability to explain this subject the more important. Conversely, such necessary reliance on teachers can lead to problems:

Maths is just so difficult. I've had three teachers now and I don't understand none of them. I mean they just sit there and they give you all these equations and you know you just look at them and you can't figure them out and the difficult part is all three of the teachers explain it in a different way. I mean you can't understand it. I mean you get into an exam and, you know, I don't understand what they are saying. I'm going to get an 'E' in maths anyway. I've failed maths, I know. So I just said after we sit in now we went to like a course work type, so I don't have to sit the exam because it's too difficult. I've tried the paper and I've failed bad ways. You know Mr –? He came in, right, and scared the daylights out of me.

(Female, Year 11)

This might be a student impossible to teach or deemed innumerate. It could also be that every attempt to explain meets the deep-seated lack of self-belief that prevents any cerebral movement. But the sense of failure is palpable as well as typical and the sense of a lack of self-belief very undermining. It is a real feeling and is shared at some moment or other, in at least one subject, by all. From the learning of reading onwards there are moments when something is presented that has no obvious meaning at all, for example a reading book.

Teacher dependency

In the experience of school, often kept private, the need for a teacher to understand, let alone explain, is paramount. When it does not happen it can be for lack of time, lack of noticing or lack of concern. It could also be a deliberate methodology:

The teacher that we've got, he's an all-right person, but he's got unusual teaching methods which he doesn't actually teach. He expects you to find out from books. He's given you a book and that and I'm not really good at that kind of learning just from a textbook and I've done quite badly in it. Like he sends you off at the beginning. . . right, you go to him; you say, 'Can I have a pass to go to the IT room or the library?' and he just gives it you and then I used to end up in the library just talking about doing work.

(Male, Year 11)

The variations in approaches to teaching are characterized not just by the particular extremes of method, but from the pupils' point of view, by contrasts of expectation. Research on teachers in the classroom looks at the way they dominate lessons by talking, the way they set work for pupils to carry out by themselves or by the use of groups, and the layout of the classroom (see the Oracle project: Galton and Simon, 1980). From the point of view of pupils, the variations between teachers are significant at a different level. It is the intensity or the quality of the relationship that matters, however they go about teaching. When an 'unusual' teaching method is introduced, like sending pupils off to find out for themselves, the real question is whether this is being done in the pupils' interests or for the convenience of the teacher.

When teachers appear not to be carrying out their duties this can be a matter of their indifference or inability:

> He knows a lot about the subject. He's a good teacher but he just doesn't know the way to teach people, just like when he's talking about something they just start making noises and he doesn't like it when they mess around, but people just mess around in that certain lesson. In other lessons they're all right.

> (Male, Year 11)

There is a note of sadness here. Even the 'good teacher', erudite and probably interesting, is in turn oppressed by the difficulty in handling pupils who detect weakness. Just as pupils are often humiliated for their lack of understanding so teachers are humiliated by the difficulty in maintaining order. It is an absurd situation. Some teachers spend all their time in matters of discipline, when little academic work is done, and others have their discipline undermined when even less is achieved. Either way the pupils rely heavily on the teachers. They look to teachers for the lead. Teachers, and not what is learnt, are the central concern.

The fact that teachers have such power is a matter of concern, especially for the teachers. The 'power' is not a question of automatic command but of centrality, of being seen as the mainstay of learning. They replace the subject as a centre of attention. They create or destroy different subjects through their relationship with the pupils:

> I find their subjects pretty hard and the teachers don't get it across so much and it just seems so difficult. Just mainly teachers. It's like I'm not really bothered about what I'm doing, it's just different teachers I have. Like history. I enjoyed that in the first and second years but when I got a different teacher I

didn't like it 'cos like I didn't like the teacher at all. But I'd like to have a good teacher but in the long run I would prefer a hard teacher because she gets you, it gets you working. In the end she's giving you a detention and then you do the work. But I had French and she was so easy you just didn't have to work all lesson and then I got really low grades.

(Male, Year 11)

The central experience of school is relationships, with teachers as well as peers. This fact is often misunderstood, as if schools were just academic places devoted wholly to the gaining of knowledge. Subjects are not important for their own sake, for the acquisition of wisdom or the pursuit of knowledge, but for the experiences they give, through teachers, and the preparation for tests.

Teachers as roles, teachers as people

The concentration on the social relationships of school means that all kinds of understandings and opinions about the world are being acquired at a level far beyond the ostensible hierarchies of learning. The distinction between the subject and the way it is taught is fully understood. The ability to make people do things in a way they might not wish to, the bullying, the indifference and the constant battle for power all give insights into a society 'red in tooth and claw'. Schools give opportunities for the sense of unfairness:

I'm not too keen on the teachers; he always picks on people. I used to have another teacher but they put us into top sets and bottom sets. I'm in the top set now and the teacher just picks on people and he expects too much of you.

(Female, Year 10)

Being 'picked on' is a reflection of demand, of cajoling, as well as bullying. In the crowded and impersonal world of the mass, the most terrifying as well as the most satisfying moments are those of being recognized. Most pupils strive for anonymity and most attain it (Pye, 1989). It is most convenient that way, for all involved. And yet one cannot help questioning if such an ethos is really what schools should be trying to achieve. Is not the essential aim the fulfilment of the individual? Most pupils feel schools are about conformity, about not being 'different', whether in behaviour or standards.

133

The experience of school is focused on teachers. This sounds both bland and obvious. Teachers do what they need to do; they convey knowledge. The way it is reinterpreted by pupils, however, suggests something different. They feel disenfranchised. The very means of organizing their learning and the very acceptance of their recalcitrance makes them feel marginalized. The fact that teachers themselves are under pressure and demoralized makes this worse. There is something strange that takes place in schools.

The surprising fact is that all these profound problems and difficulties are mostly overcome. Despite all, there are achievements and successes. Pupils scrutinize teachers closely and are generally critical. They see the deficiencies, the variability of expectations and the indifference. These limitations also reveal what the possibilities could be, the shared learning, the clear explanations and time for a real personal relationship. Teachers are also appreciated; whilst those who stand out are individual and exceptional, their virtues are as generalized as the problem:

> Some of my relationships with some of the teachers and they generally go out of their way for you. They help you with your work; if you're not sure on something you can stay behind and they'll help you. They seem to enjoy teaching: not all of them, but some of them.
>
> (Female, Year 11)

'Going out of their way to help' is a pursuit of a personal understanding. It suggests a curiosity in the pupils and their development. It takes up time. But it is centrally linked to that insight into the effective teacher: 'They seem to enjoy teaching.' Even if some might think that is against the law, it is still the crucial point.

Good teaching should not be a matter of command but a matter of response:

> You can just go to a teacher and just ask them what you want and when you want and nobody's going to say, 'No, I can't deal with it at the moment; just go away.' And whoever you go to just find time for, even if it's for a few seconds, they just find time and ask you what's wrong.
>
> (Male, Year 11)

There is no need to dwell on the centrality of civilized courtesy and on its effects. The relationships symbolized here are quite different from the managerial concerns with command structures and measurable outcomes. The conditions in which teachers work make such responsiveness difficult but, even in the circumstances of schooling, it is this shared vision of learning that makes a difference to the pupils' lives. Social relationships are at the centre. If they are right, then all else follows.

9
The learning styles of pupils

Teaching styles and learning styles

The research on teachers' styles of teaching is abundant if not always subtle. Long before school effectiveness research became so prominent there were constant attempts to discover and disseminate information about those precise actions that will have the most immediate impact on pupils. At certain levels this managerial approach to successful teaching can be quite crude. Distinctions between 'formal' and 'informal', or between the 'inductive' and 'traditional' approaches, between whole class teaching and group work, make teachers sound like mechanics learning a trade. Whether in the imposition of the instructions about 'literacy hours' or in the formulation of how to teach presented by the government through the 'three wise men' (Alexander, Rose and Wood-head, 1992), there are many assumptions made about teaching based on the essential belief that what is taught is what is learnt, or that what is learnt depends on the success and efficiency or the teacher's style of delivery. This makes teachers seem as if they were without different personalities, as if pupils did not react differently according to their personal characteristics. Exploring pupils' perceptions of teachers demonstrates that there are some essential ground rules that are successful, but these are rather different from and more subtle than distinctions between, say, ostensibly 'formal' and 'informal' approaches.

Even in the rather more sophisticated attempts to isolate the principles of good teaching practice (Bennett *et al*, 1984; Turner-Bisset, 2001) it is clear that, in such complex circumstances, to isolate particular and generalizable skills is difficult, if not impossible. So many things are happening in so many ways to so many people in one classroom that even a minute could be analysed in a thousand different ways (Doyle, 1977; Bourdieu, 1990). At the same time it is abundantly clear that some teachers are more successful than others, and that recognizing them through observation is not a difficult task. If this is so then why cannot good practice be disseminated and emulated? We can see why the formulation of a set of actions, like rules, has become a holy grail of educational research.

The reasons why such simple formulae cannot be so easily operationalized is understandable. The character of the individual teacher, the knowledge and personality, cannot be reduced to a series of labels or 'competencies'. The history, motivation and attitudes of each individual pupil cannot be dismissed as if a pupil is a mere *tabula rasa*. Above all it is those who are most capable of having insight into what makes a 'good', successful teacher who are less happy with a single formula. The irony is that the more the observer realizes how complex is the phenomenon of good teaching, the clearer he or she is about it when it is made manifest, and the less happy he or she is with simple lists of competencies.

There have been some more sophisticated attempts to describe different teachers in operation, showing some of the parameters of behaviour that make for success or failure. The work of Bennett *et al* (1984) gave many interesting, if depressing, insights into the relationships between teacher behaviour and approaches and their pupils, typically at primary level where the research has been far more extensive (Galton, Simon and Croll, 1980). They were, of course, concerned with actions rather than personalities, but what made their approach more sophisticated is that they had to take into account the behaviours of pupils as well as teachers. This was developed not just in terms of measurable outcomes but in the ways in which pupils interacted with each other, the 'time on task' they displayed and the ways in which they appeared to imbibe knowledge. Certain styles of approach have definite impacts. Even if what occurs inside the minds of individuals is something else again, these approaches to understanding teaching show, if nothing else, the inappropriateness of crude distinctions like 'formal' and 'informal', as if fierce discipline, rows of pupils and lengthy lectures were one approach, and friendly, individual relationships and chaos were the other.

There are clear practices that are successful, even if the individual personality varies. These are to do with a whole complex of cultural, ecological factors, from the purpose of the lesson, the amount of talk and the quality of the dialogue to matters of time and pace (Alexander,

2000). Many of these observations, strengthened by international research and comparisons as in Alexander's work, are also being made constantly by the pupils themselves. If we really wanted to know what makes some teachers more effective than others, we could not do better than listen to what the pupils say. The pupils, after all, are being made to respond in a variety of ways to different teachers with their varying demands. Pupils know when a teacher means what she says, however informal it sounds, and understand the expected norms of personal responsibility, whatever the layout of the classroom.

The Oracle report (see Galton, Simon and Croll, 1980) looked at the experiences of pupils in the classroom, the interactions between them and the ways in which they were organized, working as individuals and as groups. The great challenge is to discover the distinction between those occasions when the pupils are ostensibly learning and the occasions when they actually are. It is easy to observe the different friendship patterns amongst groups of children but more difficult to uncover their meaning. It is relatively simple to note the extent to which pupils appear to be working – 'time on task' – but less so to discover the extent to which they are actually thinking or understanding the work that they are undertaking. The mind is so complex, with so many layers of inattention, that even when concentrating intently on one task for a few minutes there will be multiple cerebral connections being made, associated images and self-consciousness. 'Day-dreams' can be deliberate or inadvertent but they are a powerful layer of the mind, seeking connections, placing new understanding in the context of the old. 'On task' is therefore only the starting point for research.

The normal and preferred condition of the classroom is supposed to be a quiet working atmosphere in which all pupils are strenuously working at their individual or collective tasks. This condition is always one that can be challenged by 'messing about', sometimes in a spectacular, sometimes in a subtle, way. The real challenge to work lies at a deeper level. Whilst pupils might look as if they are applying themselves assiduously, this does not mean that they are doing so. The demands that classrooms make are long periods of unbroken and unassisted concentration. These demands are difficult to meet. The desire to discuss, to share ideas, is always present in the minds of pupils. It is at the individual level that some pupils turn away from the demands of the task, by simply not concentrating or by doing the minimum. Some know just how little they can get away with (Pye, 1989). Others are estranged from any demand, and feel psychologically excluded (Cullingford, 1999b). All pupils understand the realities of working on a task, the ebb and flow of concentration, the distraction of acquiring the right pencil and paper, the superimposed voice of the teacher, and the dialogues with others.

Pupils will want to talk to each other. The great question for teachers is the extent to which they can use this fact to their advantage. The study of classroom interactions is only partly that of the interactions between the teachers and the rest. The relationships between pupils are not just a distraction but part of the learning process (for example, the Oracle project). Opinion and attitudes are formed more in discussion with fellow pupils than at the demand of the teacher. The formal and precise facts read in a textbook do not have the same subtle penetrative effect as the overheard remark.

Groups, gangs and tribes

The experience of schooling includes the ways in which large groups are herded around, and how small groups are made to work together. Many of the groups are based on friendship and are private and personal. However, many others are part of the repertoire of teaching, with pupils made to work on a set task with each other according to judgements made about their ability, the convenience of the teacher or the availability of equipment.

There is a great deal of work that has been carried out about group work, even if it is has been more concerned with the social rather than the cognitive aspects (Galton and Williamson, 1995). The crucial point about group work is the distinction between the convenience of having a number of children working on the same task, individually, and cooperative learning. What is so often described as 'group work' is not really that but no more than collections of children who happen to be sitting together when doing their own work (Bennett and Dunne, 1992). The question of whether they work individually or cooperatively is, like that of 'open' or 'closed' questions, at the heart of pupils' academic experience. The two go together because the real dilemma for pupils is the extent to which they need to guess what is wanted and to fulfil the demands of the curriculum, and the extent to which they can, to some extent at least, think for themselves and, more realistically, find out for themselves.

Pupils are always aware of abilities and, whatever the teacher says, they know about ability groups (King, 1989). They hold themselves back if they go too far ahead of their peers. They judge their pace carefully. They also know that they can learn a lot from each other, but this causes difficulties as well as pleasures. There can be distractions or competitions. There can be jealousies or rivalries. The possibility of cooperation however does afford a glimpse into the pleasures of learning (Ghaye, 1986). This is because the real secret of learning is its independence, not from everyone else, but from the demands of assessment. Independent learning is not the same as individual learning. Independence means the ownership of learning. It is not carried out only at the behest of the teacher or because of the demands of the curriculum. It is that sense of personal worth and achievement that is based on pupils learning something for themselves. If the definition of a teaching style as a competency that has an immediate and measurable effect on pupils' achievements is the 'holy grail' of official educational research, so the sense of personal learning – just the opposite – is the goal for pupils. Even those who resent being taught have a desire to learn.

Studies of pupils' group work tend to conclude that, the more the onus is placed on pupils to learn from each other and to find alternative sources of information, the more successful the pupils are (Bennett *et al*, 1984). The problem with this is the fact that it goes against the prevailing notion of the all-powerful class teachers delivering the set tasks (Cullingford and Oliver, 2001). As Bennett pointed out, making pupils learn by themselves has two effects: the pupils learn more but the teachers feel guilty. It is not an easy task to say to a pupil, 'Go away and find out for yourself' – the sense of discomfort is symbolized by the fact that such a technique is described in vulgar terms (BOFO: 'Bugger off and find out' – or worse). The sense of unease that pupils learn despite the teacher is deep.

The possibilities of using pupils as a source of knowledge and a means of enquiring are infinite, but very rarely used, especially in the current educational climate. To use groups successfully takes some psychological courage. It is more subtle to arrange, since it is a matter of enabling pupils to become each other's teachers as well as learners (Slavin, 1978, 1983). There are small distinctions between successful and unsuccessful groups: one 'brighter' pupil with two 'slower' pupils work better than the alternative balance where the one 'slower' pupil will be left out (Bennett and Cass, 1988). The faster learners will always do well, unless they are undermined by competing against each other. One of the additional attractions of group work for pupils is that it allows greater possibilities of practical work, of actually carrying out a task, as well as collaborating (Galton and Williamson, 1995). A real 'task', something practical like a scientific experiment, allows the making of mistakes and encourages discussion, the sharing of opinions and ideas.

The social ambience of the school in all its volatility spills over into the classroom. In the classroom the prevailing atmosphere appears to be more subdued, but the personal tensions – the interactions, comparisons and rivalries – continue. After all, each pupil, like each school in a league table, is in competition. This gives the idea of collaboration a particularly difficult edge. As we will see, many pupils know that their preferred style of learning runs counter to the ethos and the expectations of school. However they are organized, in groups or classes, they are there to work for themselves, to manage their own individual work. 'You are on your own' is a teacher's phrase that reverberates in their minds. In this complexity of demands, what do the pupils themselves think?

Learning to survive

The pupils were asked about their favourite or their most preferred style of learning. They were not asked to define their least liked ways of learning, since that is well documented and comes across clearly: the whole class lecture, the demands on the teacher, the imposition of tests and the constant stream of closed questions followed by interminable writing. The boredom of school comes across very clearly, the sense of carrying out meaningless tasks for the sake of keeping pupils busy. The positive nature of this question is emphasized because the pupils' answers show a subtlety of understanding that reveals their insight into the nature of schools. In the tensions they reveal between individuals and group learning they delineate that the question of what they are learning *for* is a very complex one. 'It all depends.' It depends on the implicit purpose and the nature of the outcome. They cannot forget the difference between their own desires and the imposed will. They might prefer to do certain things but they know that they are expected to do others. They realize that the demands of school and the concomitant exams are in place, not so much to fit them for the future as to fit them to the system. They are in competition, and they need to 'get through' the tasks. They must learn certain subjects and they are expected to acquire particular skills. To this extent they have little choice. They might long for closer personal relationships with teachers out of 'role' but the functioning of school makes that very difficult if not impossible. On the one hand they like cooperative learning. On the other they realize that they are being judged in competition. Whatever might be useful in their futures, they think that the school system demands something different from collaboration.

Working in groups can be enjoyable. At one level it is pupils' preferred learning style. It does, however, carry with it certain temptations that they point out. Any escape from the anonymous monotony of the whole class can be welcomed but, as they point out, this can be for a variety of reasons:

> I like doing equipment and I like working in a group as well. . .
> you feel as though you're doing more. . . all the work or maybe
> copying off a friend, something like that. . . sometimes I prefer
> playing around.
>
> (Female, Year 10)

'Doing equipment', carrying out a task without the close attention of the teacher, is always popular. It is practical and carries with it a sense of independence. Group work can be very productive, but it can also entail taking short cuts, and the extreme of escape is to 'play around'.

'It all depends.' Pupils are aware of their limitations and the need to adapt to the circumstances:

> Well, it depends. If I were in a group with friends, that's OK,
> but if it's like some other people that are not right then I don't
> like it but it's OK in a group. I do, but by myself I will but I'll
> only have my own ideas but I want someone else to give me
> ideas. I can work hard but I can't, well, I can concentrate but
> when I feel I like to work then I work. . . it depends on the
> subject though. Like in games and all that stuff you have to be
> challenged and like with mostly like in my group they all get
> good marks, results and I'm quite in the middle but I'm not
> happy with the teacher.
>
> (Female, Year 10)

Group work means either working with friends or working with fellow pupils placed together because of comparative abilities. Being 'in the middle' can be a judgement on academic prowess but it is also applicable to friendships. The question is the extent to which she feels 'challenged' and the extent to which she can 'concentrate'. As in the distinction between the arrangements of pupils into small collective round tables and the academic prerogative of getting them to work properly, the real question is the extent to which pupils feel they are being aided in bringing out their best. They long for challenges and deserve the ability to display concentration. They know that some group work aids this, and that other experiences actually undermine the way they approach what they are set to do:

I enjoy it when we do like experiments in science and things like that. I like working in groups but like for different subjects because sometimes I think it can pull you back a bit working in groups. In English I think it's quite a good thing but in maths like we've done it once or twice where we worked in groups; for that, it didn't work at all.

(Male, Year 10)

It all depends on the nature of the task and the demands being made. Experiments are always appreciated, but some group work can 'pull you back a bit'.

Working together or in competition

Working together brings temptations to talk, undermining the purpose of school. Nevertheless, group work is appreciated for all the other learning that it brings with it. It is only when working with other pupils that there appears to be a sense of open questions and answers and being allowed personal opinions:

In a group, because you can discuss it and because you get different opinions of what you're doing, don't you, and stuff about when you're doing and you learn then, don't you?

(Male, Year 10)

Discussions and opinions are associated with real learning, with personal engagement. Collaboration is seen to have immediate benefits:

I like working in a group. You can help others and they can help you and you get more work done and faster.

(Female, Year 10)

Working with others symbolizes the concentration on learning rather than on being taught. It leads to more creative and open experiences of discussion, of practical activities:

I like working in groups and using my hands a lot. It's more interesting when you're working with friends and that.

(Female, Year 10)

> We usually work in a group, yes, in discussion, because you
> can hear what everybody else says and that you take that in
> and you can give your own opinions and things like that.

> (Male, Year 10)

The forming of opinions and giving consideration to what other people
say make for interesting discussions. In a sense that is the real purpose
of schooling, of learning: to collaborate and to accept differences of
opinion, to recognize that there are many different sources of knowledge and that so much of what is of value depends on a point of view.
The myth of a vast monolith of knowledge, which is rigid and immut-
able, is mitigated by the experience of discussion. Group work is
therefore associated with the forming of opinions. It is the slight
recognition that the ways in which personal understandings are formed
are an individual and private matter and not necessarily the same as
all that is tested.

For many pupils, working in groups is also efficient. If there is
something to be done it is much easier to do it in collaboration with
others. Whilst this goes against the norms of a competitive examination
system, it makes sense to pupils who are, for the rest of their lives,
going to work collaboratively. Other people can help, by spreading
the information base and distributing tasks, and much more can be
achieved. There is also a sense of control in this:

> I work good in groups. Sometimes I don't work good on my
> own. It depends what lesson it is really. There are times when
> I just think to myself I'm going to work hard for this lesson
> and I work hard but it can't be done all the time.

> (Male, Year 10)

> I like working in a group, because when you work in a group
> you don't have to do it all by yourself. If you're working in
> threes a person can do the other thing and you can get it done
> quicker.
>
> (Female, Year 10)

Some pupils depend upon learning from each other. This can be a
limitation as well as a strength. They can rely too heavily on others to
do the work for them, rather than think it through for themselves. At
the same time, others can help them overcome the mental block of
retreating from the demands put upon them rather than engaging with

the demands. Sharing work can also be pragmatic. Tasks are shared, and the results communicated to each other as well as to the teacher:

> I like working in a group. I can work on my own but if I'm working in a group I feel better, more comfortable. If I'm on my own I'm rushing and trying to get it done by myself but if I'm in a group we can share the work out.
>
> (Female, Year 10)

Groups are supportive as well as challenging. The comfort zone of discussion and opinion mitigates the relentless concentration on fact. The personal pressure of having to learn something, of being forced to deliver the answers demanded, is lightened by sharing:

> When you're by yourself you're just trying to work it all out in one go, but if there's loads of you then different people can make different things out.
>
> (Male, Year 10)

The comfort factor is also practical. Useful tasks are not just the remembrance of facts but 'working things out'. They can be a matter of opinion (as in English) rather than finding the right answer (as in maths), but having a sense of collective wisdom and shared endeavour takes some of the pressure off having to 'work things out' individually:

> If I'm working in a group I like to do a little practical work just to get an idea of what we're doing and like everybody gets the feel of it. I also like sitting down and working when there is revision to do or if we've got a test, just to get the things I need to know in mind. And group work I like because it lets other people show their views to you so you can change things for the better.
>
> (Male, Year 11)

The contrast between the advantages of group work and the need to work individually is clear. Tests, revision and internalizing answers 'in the mind' can only be done by oneself. A stage towards that is the 'feel' of it, sharing views and doing practical activities. It is emblematic that it is through discussing different views, rather than tests, that one can 'change things for the better'.

The temptations of groups

The pleasure of group work is clear, as are the temptations that go with it:

> No, I'm not the practical type. I like working in a group. I prefer it in a group. In some cases people just use it as a time to talk but whereas me and my friends like, all right, got to be true, right, we do talk a little but we always produce the results at the end of it as well.
>
> (Male, Year 10)

Working in groups can be creative and can also be a distraction from the set tasks. It is a question of the best means of 'producing the results'. If the self-indulgence of talking undermines the application to a particular task then other people, particularly those who 'mess about', can be a fatal distraction. For this reason, and because school is so competitive, the greater academic emphasis is upon the rights of working individually.

Working by oneself is the standard expectation of school, whether organized in classes, groups or seminars, in the library or at the computer. The collective results, like a play or game, are seen to depend on the prowess of the individual. The ethos of school amongst pupils, if not necessarily amongst teachers, is of individuality, at least in most Western countries (Bronfenbrenner, 1978; Alexander, 2000). This is part of the cult of the individual as the basis of success. It might not be taken altogether seriously by children, given their sense of the relative and their ontological modesty and realism, but it is inculcated by the social system of competition and differentiated outcomes.

At one point or another the onus is on the individual:

> By myself. I get a lot more done. If the work's like normal. But if the work is too easy, then I'm just not interested, and if it's too hard, I'm interested.
>
> (Male, Year 10)

The personal challenge is important. Self-motivation is difficult to impose, but it is really what school should be fostering: that pleasure in the satisfying of curiosity that is the seeking of knowledge. Working individually can be a reward as well as a means of attaining the highest levels of success:

She lets us go off by ourselves into the library. There's like a final group of us who are a bit better at maths and can understand it more so we go to the library and do our own research and stuff like that. I like working by myself and using my hands. I prefer working by myself because you don't have to think about everyone else and make sure everyone else is doing and coming up to scratch and doing the same amount as you can, also so I don't lag behind and slope off everyone else.

(Female, Year 10)

Collaboration entails doing good, in helping others and being responsible for success. Conversely, being able to go off to do 'research' is at once a joint activity, contributing to 'collective knowledge', but also one in which the individual is only concerned with her own needs. This is the condition in which demands for standards can best be met.

Avoiding routines

What is most prized in terms of learning style is variety. There are bound to be equivocal reactions to an incessant stream of group work or an unalleviated amount of working solidly without interaction with others. Real work, after all, combines all kinds of strategies, and is flexible and complex. Working with others can be distracting as easily as it can be supportive:

Well, um, if I work in a group I used to get distracted and don't used to do any work but if I work on my own I do get work done but I can't concentrate on it and I always have to break off, which I think that's going to be a problem when I leave. I can't really work hard for a long time, like say I have to take breaks every. . . often I can't get started as well.

(Male, Year 11)

It could be argued that there are some pupils who will always find it hard to concentrate and to finish things off. For such pupils, working with others could be the one creative solution. Being able to work steadily on a particular task, without distractions, is a rare commodity. Even writers can do it only for so long. The usual condition of work is to lapse into other things, actions or thoughts, as part of the pattern of work. It is well known that the 'attention span' of those who listen to a lecture is limited, but even this is a somewhat naïve or simplistic interpretation of 'attention', as if it were a single matter of steady, impervious concentration. The lapses of attention are as much to do with a sense of failure, of disbelief in one's own abilities, and in the association of hard work with humiliation, as with the desire to be distracted. The conditions of schooling, including the constraint due to accountability of 'naming and shaming', make the demands of work the more complicated. Concentration at best is full of lapses, of breaks into half-connected or disconnected thoughts. A lack of interest or desire undermines any chance of paying close attention.

Academic work is always a mixture of personal endeavour and collaboration:

> I prefer to work on my own because I find I can make my own decisions and things like that and where I'm not arguing with other people and that, but I do like working in groups in other things like in sport and English and subjects where I'm not too strong. I work in groups and it helps me get along with the subjects better. But another thing like graphics where you have to use tools and things like that I prefer to work on my own because I know what I'm doing best myself.
>
> (Male, Year 11)

All the equivocation of the tension between individual and group learning is pointed up by the tension between making 'one's own decisions' and the support for those subjects where pupils lack the confidence to make their own decisions. Pupils want to be able to work by themselves, to be competent in what they do. When they know what they are doing they prefer to work on their own as they know what they are 'doing best themselves'. It is their uncertainties in some subjects that make them appreciate the advantages of collaboration, as well as the pleasure in exchanging opinions. They learn from each other as well as from the teacher.

The styles of working, and the levels of application, depend upon the kinds of demands that are being made. This is not just a matter of response to a teacher or the subjects but a sign of the difficulty in keeping up the intensity of close cerebral energy all the time. Learning styles will vary not just between pupils but also for individual pupils. They adapt to the particular needs of the moment:

I work good in groups. Sometimes I don't work good on my own; it depends what lesson it is really. There are times when I just think to myself I'm going to work hard for this lesson and I work hard, but it can't be done all the time.

(Male, Year 10)

Hard work is associated with working alone. This cannot be 'done all the time' and yet so many assumptions about the literacy hours are based on the significance of the imposition of a syllabus, based on the steady accumulation of material, approached steadily in the same way. Pupils differ all the time. 'It depends' on the lesson as well as the subject, the mood as well as the context. From pure concentration, pupils seek some relief:

I like groups, and equipment. That type of thing. 'Cos it's like. . . I don't know. . . it doesn't seem as challenging in groups. I think it takes a load off in groups. If you're in the top group and things like that, you get, you know, not pushed but you've got to do stuff to keep in that group.

(Female, Year 10)

Groups are supportive and less of a challenge than the exposure of personal achievement. At the same time groups are academic havens, and used as a means of avoiding personal challenge. In academic streaming, groups are often chosen carefully by putting pupils into carefully graded abilities. Groups are then a comfort in a different sense, avoiding too high a level of expectation or avoiding any scrutiny at all. Teachers might protest that it is they who organize the academic level, but we know it is as much the calculation of the pupils, and the manipulation by them of results, as any external act.

Working hard is always difficult to sustain if there is no pleasure in it:

I don't particularly like being stuck in a classroom behind a desk. I like to do things, get out. But I mean I don't mind working on me own or in a group; it doesn't matter. Depends what it is. If I'm enjoying it then I'll work hard at it, but if I don't enjoy it then maybe don't work as hard as I need to work harder at it so. . .

(Male, Year 11)

The pleasures of collaboration

Collaborative learning takes away some of the pressure of being forced to work, or being 'stuck' with the demands of the syllabus. It can give a different, more subtle pleasure to the state of learning. It is, of course, always a surprise to rediscover the fact that learning can be a chore. For adults, learning is an essential definition of life, a celebration. And yet it is often made an oppression of school. For this reason alone, the need for variety, for the chance to manifest different styles of learning, is considered very important. Pupils do not mind working alone or with others, as long as they have some freedom of choice:

> I like working in a group, mostly, but it doesn't bother me about working on my own. Because there's a lot more people there and you can find out other things from what they're doing and things like that.
>
> (Female, Year 10)

> I like working in groups sometimes and I like working on computer as well. You get more ideas, tell other people what you feel and they can tell you what they feel. Sometimes when you are by yourself you can get on with your own work. Sometimes when you are in groups you start thinking and yet get held back.
>
> (Male, Year 10)

Working with others means discovery and discussion. It is associated with finding out, both facts and what other people feel and think. It is centred on learning about the nature of relationships, of collaboration or mutual interests. It is ironic that this creative endeavour is contrasted in the minds of pupils with the necessity of being 'on task', with getting on with their own individual work. 'More ideas' derive from other people, but the demand of the system is for them to make all ideas seem like their own.

There is one central territory in the emplacements of work where pupils are supposed to collaborate, to work together and yet remain individual. 'Experiments', working with equipment, doing things and talking about the actions, are very much appreciated. It seems to pupils to be a wholly different dimension of learning, a collaborative and creative act:

I like sometimes if we've got a lot on with work. I like just get on with it by myself and get it out of the way, but I really enjoy like in English when we work in groups and things like that and with equipment like experiments in chemistry, biology and physics. . . I don't think anybody enjoys working really hard but I don't mind it if it has to be done. . . so I make the best of it.

(Female, Year 10)

Between the submission to what has to be done, putting up with things, getting on with it and all the other phrases of necessary imposition, there is real pleasure in working with others, on 'equipment'. It is easy to understand how different a style of learning is afforded by experiments, where all minds are individually attuned to one observation, something shared. That mutual concern with one task transforms the group into collaboration and mutual curiosity without distraction:

I prefer it in a group with lots of equipment. So we can co-operate together instead of. . . if you're on your own you might get stuck if you've got no one to turn to. If you're in a group and everyone's together you can help each other. In science we've got some really good equipment. We'll always be doing an experiment like, after every two lessons there might be a lesson of chemistry and whatever, with chemicals involved and stuff like that.

(Male, Year 10)

The demands on the individual are balanced by the experience of co-operation, of people 'helping each other'. The place where learning is most associated with the most creative of circumstances appears to be those lessons where some kind of practical activity and mutual curiosity can best be displayed, be it in science, CDT or art. One of the defining significances of such learning is that all, including the teacher, are sharing the same curiosity. They are all involved, on one side, rather than confronting each other. As with all real relationships, it is in the sharing of points of view about something outside both parties that most matters. In these moments of the scientific experiment, the observers are all learners, and they show the same curiosity. It might last a short time but it is symbolic of what learning could be. It also relates to that often-neglected need of young children, to share in an intellectually creative relationship (Dunn, 1988; Cullingford, 1990).

The learning styles that pupils prefer are those that include flexibility, variety and attention to individual needs. They are also rooted in the desire to *share* experiences and ideas rather than be confronted by them. This implies a strong rapport with the teacher, as if both were learning together, rather than the imposition of a series of learnt competencies, however well delivered. Whatever the surfaces of the lessons, pupils have their private thoughts, their moods and their boredom. They might not want to be distracted but they do appreciate excitements. If these are not provided with the lesson, they can always be super-imposed by the pupils themselves.

Constant levels of concentration are impossible, so that what is felt as variety is interpreted as the necessary breaking of tension rather than gimmicks:

> It depends on my moods most. I can't. . . because sometimes if I'm active I want to get up and do things and sometimes, if I just want to rest and just do my work quietly, I just tend to sit down and rest.
>
> (Female, Year 10)

A firm reaction to this might be that it is impossible to accommodate any pupils like this amongst so many. The need is to enforce self-discipline. Such 'moods', periods of intense stimulation and times of ostensible 'rest', are a shared pattern of all pupils learning. They do not want to do the same thing in the same way all the time:

> Each lesson's different. But I don't, um, I prefer it if you don't have to be silent and you can talk but sometimes I don't always do my work if that is that's what you're allowed to do. If I'm feeling tired I just don't do anything.
>
> (Male, Year 11)

The demands of constant mental activity on pupils are strong. Whether they are realistic or 'sustainable' is another matter.

Pupils learn a great deal from the discipline of having to work together, and from the seeking out of information for themselves. Once the pressure on teachers to 'deliver' is less, and the expectation on pupils to learn, in their own way, is greater, all kinds of things can be achieved. When this subtle change of emphasis takes place it is not easily detected. Indeed it could be argued that it is against all that Ofsted stands for, and would be rooted out by inspectors if it did not remain hidden. Pupils are actually learning all kinds of matters in school that have little to do with the curriculum. They learn about personal relationships and about collaboration. Their preferred learning styles reflect this:

> Working as part of a team. Definitely. Also leadership skills and things. Like what qualities are requested. Learning to take the things that aren't that good along with the good. You've got to take the good with the bad or vice versa.

> (Female, aged 18)

Conclusions

It could be argued that pupils are in school to learn how to submit to the discipline imposed, to accept the requirements of the curriculum and to learn whatever it is that the 'deliverers' and the teachers wish them to. This could also sound like an oppressive regime with clear command structures imposing such requirements on the pupils that they are taught not to question, not to think and not to be independent. Alternatively these two extremes point up the complexity of the reality of the everyday complex negotiations that involve well-meaning teachers attempting to ameliorate the system, and strongly motivated pupils intent on surviving it. All the time we are reminded that the inner realities of schooling, in all its complexity, are quite different from the models superimposed upon it in a theoretical, or political, way.

If pupils were really listened to, would there still be a debate about the skills that teachers need? If learners were allowed to say what they would find most helpful, there would be no need to debate what teachers should do. This is not, in fact, as difficult to put into practice as one might think. The central point is putting the onus of learning on the pupils, sharing the desire and allowing them to learn in a variety of ways.

The problem for the teachers is that, bland as that sounds, and surely obvious, the reality, with the imposition of the curriculum, with the syllabus, with tests, appears impossible. It 'appears' impossible, but the most creative teachers actually employ those principles in their own way, despite the threat of inspection.

Classroom relationships are awkward in the context of the system of schooling that we generally promote. Attention is diverted from what really happens to what is supposed to happen so it is hard to conduct a debate about such matters at an academic level. It is important to try to recognize the actuality of power relationships in the classroom, the tendency to confront rather than collaborate. This has become a cultural matter, resting on the assumption that pupils are incorrigibly anti-intellectual and do not wish to learn. The mantra is that it is only by targets and assistance that standards will be raised, at least for some. The result is a strong sense of conflict. All questions, however inclusive, become 'closed', as if power were entirely on one side and 'empower-ment' taken from the other (Manke, 2001). The ability to discuss real inner thoughts is severely limited (Pointon and Kershaw, 2001).

Nowhere is the issue of pupils learning, and teachers attempting to help, more poignantly ambivalent than in the political issue of class size. Clearly the factor of class size compared to other variables is not the most important one (Jamieson, Johnson and Dickson, 1998). But the psychological impact of class size, on the teachers and pupils, far more subtle, is another matter. No wonder the research on class size as a variable is unclear (Blatchford and Mortimore, 1993), since the other intervening factors, like people, are more important. The crucial matter with the classroom is clearly the morale, stress and enthusiasm of those involved within it (Blatchford and Martin, 1998). Normally one would link such a statement with the personal and professional lives of teachers. Should it not include the pupils? Pupils long for individual attention, and they desire the opportunities to collaborate. They would love to share ideas with teachers and to that end would accept any 'style' that made it possible. It is not the class size as such that prevents this, although large classes are far harder to handle, as all teachers know, but the class mentality. This is not the product of teachers' desire but of the prevailing cultural assumptions of schooling. The quality of teaching depends upon the quality of pupils' learning experiences (Bennett *et al*, 1984), to turn it upside down. Pupils' learning styles require a different level of attention. That this is impossible in the present circumstances is shown in some cross-cultural studies (Alexander, 2000). When parents have the luxury of choosing schools, they go for those where the sizes of class are small and the pupils are guaranteed some individual attention. This is what all pupils would also choose (Dalin *et al*, 1994).

10
School and life beyond

Rites of passage

Schools are an introduction into the adult world. They can be seen as some vast initiation ceremony, preparing young people for the life to come. In the ways in which they are organized, with tiers of examinations as formalized rites of passage, this remains true. Success at school is measured by the outcome, by the entry into the next stage, and rarely as something worth while in its own right. The 'top-down' barriers dictated by universities, another rite of passage, or by more direct entry into the world of work, create an enclosure, a limitation around the experience of school. Even from an early age, pupils understand schooling as a preparation for something else (Cullingford, 1991). It is seen as an interim stage, like growing up. Its meaning depends upon whatever happens later.

If schools are both explicitly and implicitly a preparation for something else then they ask to be judged by that. This is not the same judgement as that made by league tables, where academic success is the one accolade, but is the sense of purpose given by the school. It is after all no surprise that those schools that produce the most successful results, in terms of examinations and subsequent careers, have certain advantages, like Eton. League tables simply reflect privilege. The question that is raised here goes deeper. If schools are preparing pupils for their subsequent lives, then what exactly are pupils learning? Do they feel fully equipped? Are they prepared? Do schools provide those supposedly essential skills for survival?

Raising the question about what schools are preparing pupils for also raises an automatic response: they are there to equip pupils for employment and for qualifications, so that they can be subsequently even better employed. This might be a reasonable reaction, but it does miss out all the other 'life skills' that could be valuable, like the personal relationships that pupils rate so highly. In the formal curriculum there are periods devoted to citizenship, to parenting and to personal social education. Even religion still has its slot. And yet the amount of time given to these is so small that they make almost no impression on pupils in terms of value, weight or significance. The 'core' subjects predominate because they are supposed to equip pupils for the subsequent world of employment.

To that extent the 'initiation' of the Western tradition of schooling is a very narrow one. Perhaps it is assumed that formal values and meanings will be learnt elsewhere. Perhaps these values are not deemed to be significant. Perhaps they are assumed to be a matter of other influences than those of the formal educational system. Whatever the reason, the result is that schools look to the 'world of work' as the one connection they have with the lives of pupils after they have left. Virtually all the research that has taken place on the relationship between what has taken place in school and what has happened subsequently is about employment. This might be natural. Both are concerned with the formal, public skills that are supposedly taught. The rest is private and personal. And yet, we know that pupils learn a vision of society as a whole, and of their place in it, that is far more deep, far more subtle, than those competencies for which schools can be held accountable.

The underlying question is whether pupils feel themselves to be prepared for their future lives and whether they would recognize the fact if they are not. The more obvious question is whether they feel prepared for the future as defined by the meaning of school, for work, for jobs, for the acquisition of money, for pulling their weight in the collective economy. Those studies that have tried to understand the subsequent meanings of school have concentrated on the perspective of work (White with Brockington, 1983). From that point of view alone the limitations of the curriculum in terms of irrelevance are apparent. The other skills, of understanding the social system, surviving the demands of social pressure and taking part in the duties of economic life, are left out altogether. These skills are deemed to be personal or a natural consequence of the rules of the state, of employers and of social security.

From the beginning of school the connection between the experience of the time, and what would happen subsequently, has been of great significance. If the only point of school is implicitly the terminal results of examinations, that casts a great shadow over everything else that takes place. Whether it is the ultimate end of a distinct period or the initiation into a more meaningful, permanent one, the outcome of schooling, except for those who wish to avoid it, is the world of work. This gives schools their *raison d'être* and their ostensible shape. Schools are not just an experience, but a temporary preparation. The focus on preparation is always in the minds of children. That this means preparation for employment is implicit in the fact that all other experiences of their subsequent lives – homes, families, urban centres, politics, news and international affairs – are already a central part of their daily experience. There is nothing except paid work that is saved up for the future.

The fact that young children are not hidden or removed from the realities of adult life is sometimes forgotten or deliberately ignored. There is very little in the way of experience that is not pictured to them on television, and many illicit pleasures, those that politicians would ban, are thrust at them, as in magazines purposefully aimed at titillation. This public world is not part of the curriculum of school. There are moments when certain aspects are touched upon, like health education or the study of the media, but the real issues of the world, controversial or challenging, are not a central part of the official curriculum. There is the token subject of citizenship, but the standard fare offered in schools is very rarely about the world as children witness it. Even history, which could be so relevant to contemporary understanding, does not use the present circumstances as a starting point for understanding. The curriculum is formal, content-based and prescribed, and the philosophy that drives seems to be far more to do with testing than with understanding.

As a result of this vacuum at the heart of school, two strands of understanding emerge. One is the hidden curriculum of private conversations, of discussions outside classrooms of what is seen on television or other semi-public interests. The other is the realization that the one connection schools have with the future lives of pupils is with the world of employment. Even if teachers do not lay stress on it, the very raft of qualifications that pupils are made to take is based on the notion that it will enable them to acquire good jobs. Qualifications might not equip them for jobs, but they are seen as a necessary prerequisite.

In the minds of pupils there is a strong connection between adult life and employment. All the other pleasures or difficulties of adult life are well known, including the effects of having money and the necessity to have enough of it. Work enables the acquisition of money, and the consequent pleasures of spending. For young people the threat of the future lies in having to do without, and the consequences for the very poor are completely clear. If employment is an important theme for pupils this could be because the connection between school and work is the one sense of purpose that is clearly expressed by politicians. It is the one *raison d'être* of schools generally agreed, and it is certainly the focus of most of the research on the relationship between the experience in school and that of the days after school (Tight, 1995). Work and adult life are seen to go together.

If there is one way in which the future and the present in school are brought together it is through the promotion of the skills necessary for employment. There have been many initiatives designed to promote understanding of industry and capital, including sending teachers into private enterprise and arranging visits to factories. 'Work experience', whilst usually limited to those who will not go on to university, is seen as a way for pupils to gain an understanding of what their future lives will be like. More often than not, work-related provision has little impact since it is not fully integrated into the curriculum (Saunders, Stoney and Weston, 1997). Since work-related studies do not relate to the overall purpose of school, they have little impact on the very pupils for whom they were designed – the low attainers and the disaffected. That glimpse into the 'world of work' that consists of knowledge, of career possibilities, rarely enters into the realms of motivation and personal commitment.

The 'world of work' is a much-used phrase that suggests something about the high esteem in which employment is held, from the point of view of schooling. Given that it is seen as a whole 'world', it is not surprising that work experience is considered important, and less surprising that the implicit purpose of school, like skills, is directed towards employment. From the point of view of pupils, however, work experience is considered less important than schoolwork, and not rated as being worth while (Petherbridge, 1997). One problem is that work experience is neither mainstream in the school curriculum nor does it reproduce the perceived 'needs' of industry. The subject work is raised in school as a means of transition, of preparing pupils for their future lives. It is a subject in which a critical stance is taken. There are few serious discussions about the economy and about the meaning of the way that trade is organized. The whole social context of work, or rights and responsibilities, appears to be peripheral. Whilst employment is considered important, some of its concomitant moralities and contracts are rarely looked at closely. 'Transition' to work is supposed to be smooth and as untroubled as possible.

From the school's point of view, the transition between it and the next experience, whether further study or employment, is supposed to be made as easy as possible. The goal of schools is, after all, supposed to be preparation for work, for the next stage. As even the youngest children perceive it, the purpose of schools is jobs. In fact, the transition is rarely smooth, and never smooth for those who are not academically successful. There is a marked contrast between the experiences of school and what happens afterwards. Most of the research on this conflict is based on the views of those who have left. Naturally enough, the reflections on what has happened are given a sharp focus with hindsight, although this study reveals that pupils can anticipate the mixture of disappointment and bewilderment that surrounds the thoughts of those who have left.

Do schools connect?

Reflecting on the experience of school after they have left, the unemployed or the estranged all regret the lack of purpose, the irrelevance, of their experience of school from their subsequent point of view (White with Brockington, 1983). If school is an induction into the adult world, defined in terms of employment, then for many it is a very poor one. From the circumstances of those who have not found jobs, the sense of disappointment is naturally deep, but the bewilderment that surrounds it – a feeling that the whole experience of school was strange and unhappy as well as purposeless – is even more telling. Whilst at school, pupils are kept going by being told that it all makes sense in acquiring jobs. When that promise is not fulfilled, the whole nature of schools is brought into question.

The disillusionment of those who struggle to find jobs is well recorded, and there are a number of clearly defined difficulties that they had within school, whatever country they were in. Those who feel estranged from school never developed a sense of inclusion even at this time, and never developed a relationship with teachers. They found the formal curriculum dreary and irrelevant (Attenbrough, Engel and Martin, 1995). The school leavers are fearful about what awaits them outside school but believe that it cannot be worse than staying in school. They might want to leave school from economic necessity but more often because of their sense of isolation from their peers, bullying and the sense of mistreatment by teachers (Hollingshead, 1975).

Those who have the most difficulty in school clearly have this problem reflected in their subsequent experience. It could be argued that those who have subsequent problems tend to lay the blame for their experience on school. It is also often argued that there are some socio-economically deprived pupils for whom difficulties in school will be evidence. But the fact that such subsequent problems are predictable lays stress on the power of the experience of school, and the difficulty of shedding some of its effects. Most pupils want to devise a strong meaning for working, whether in school or paid employment, but can find it undermined (Cress, 1992). Some pupils find there is a great deal of conflict between their jobs and their academic achievement; they are the ones who in both phases are less motivated and more cynical (Stern *et al*, 1990). The influence of the family background remains very strong, whatever the role of school (Peters, 2000). Indeed, given the orientation of school towards preparation for employment or for 'transition', it is surprising how little influence it has. This cannot simply be laid on the influence of the early years or the responsibility of parents. Those most economically deprived have every motivation to do something about it: aspiration in the disadvantaged is well documented. But these aspirations often remain unfulfilled, as if the motivation was not nurtured by school.

There was a time when schooling was a refuge from the exploitation of work. It is now generally accepted, without particular scrutiny, that the role of school is preparation for work. Far from being a protection for children, it is a matter of them having the necessary skills. The public justification for schools includes ' childminding' so parents can continue to be employed, and it might include the imposition of the necessary social disciplines, whilst the parents are busy (Cullingford, 1986). In all accepted definitions, schools are a preparation for some other life, meaning the workplace in one form or another. The study of what this might mean, measured in different disciplines, from sociology to law, from philosophy to economics, is normally left until later, in the post-compulsory years, as if that essential problem were only then of great significance, as if the individual is only a fully fledged member of society when he or she is allowed to vote. Until then, little in the general experience of society or politics is essentially questioned. It is as if this were indeed a separate world.

Those who have left school, particularly the unemployed, are very critical of their experiences. But what of those who are still there, and whose futures remain open and full of ostensible promise? How do they perceive the experience of school in the light of what might happen next? The pupils all had some experience of work, whether arranged by the school or not. They talked about employment, or unemployment, at some length, with their parents if not their teachers. They were clearly focused on their future and gave a very clear picture of the place of school in the context of their lives as a whole, embracing the future as well as the present.

School as employment

The experience of schooling is a mixture of sudden, dramatic, even traumatic, moments and a seemingly endless series of monotonous routines. The same thing happens day after day, structured by timetables and adhering to the implacable expectations of group behaviours. Within this sameness of routine there are certain changes in the rites of passage that leave a mark. The most obvious one is the first day in the new school, the sense of dislocation and anonymity when confronted by the unfamiliar world that already belongs so superciliously to others. Within the experience of school there are those sudden dramas like an outbreak of violence either between pupils or with teachers. And within these conflagrations there is the more private, unending trauma of the thought of an ending. What happens next? The real disturbance of school is the impending threat of the hereafter. For some, this is something to be looked forward to, as a genuine rite of passage to the next stage. To others it means the confrontation with a world less protective and less understanding. For them school is clung to as a safe if temporary haven. The majority, for all their uncertainties, look forward to leaving school as longingly as to an escape from prison. Whatever the uncertainties they have, they feel that the 'independence of working on my own', as well as earning money, is greatly to be preferred.

The reward for leaving school is, of course, financial. Although there are many who take part-time jobs, and although school life is associated with the financial protections of home, the sense of independence implies both practical and philosophical freedom:

> I'll be glad to get out of schoolwork. You will be able to meet like new people; you'll be able to be doing what you've been working to all your life sort of thing. So I am looking forward to that.
>
> (Female, Year 10)

Leaving school is 'what you have been working to'. That is obvious, but it also gives a sense of the release, the ultimate end of the purpose of school. It might be a release, but it is also a goal. The aim of school is to leave it. Leaving it might entail a type of 'graduating', a sign of approval that a stage has been duly met, but it can also imply a rejection. Pupils leave whether they have received the expected accolades or not. The terminal exams mark the fitness for the next stage, but pupils always leave before the results. This is more than significant. Pupils have to move on, and there is little sense in many countries of a sense of great achievement.

Moving on means the opportunity to leave certain matters aside, including the people:

> getting away from all the people you don't like. I mean you don't have to see them whenever. . . mainly pupils. Half of lads, anyway.
>
> (Male, Year 10)

One of the most significant experiences of escape is the release associated with getting away from other people, both fellow pupils and teachers, as if the society of school were not only too contained but involved the more difficult sides of human relationships. Whilst pupils might feel that they have learnt a great deal about how to deal with other people – the greatest skill – they also feel that the most oppressive side of school is the regime. Work is no such problem. The way in which other people behave is:

> Not having to put up with teachers I don't like. Not taking orders from them. . . general things like that.
>
> (Male, Year 10)

At one level no one wants to be ordered around. At another, pupils are expected to submit. It is this anomaly that makes schools difficult. The sense that 'I can't wait to get out' is a common one. With the best intentions, like examination results, the school has to make demands. There is not just cajoling but coercions. The school's sense of standards is clear and inflexible. This can be interpreted as an oppression by pupils, as in lack of 'respect' for them and their own purposes.

Some people could argue, even if anecdotally, that a sense of oppression exaggerates the ethos of school. There are, after all, plenty of lighter moments, and a series of routines that could easily be negotiated. School might be dull, they would argue, but if there really is a sense of oppression it is not deliberate. Whatever the term used, school depends on the enforcing of rules, the insistence on learning and the control of pleasures. Rules and discipline are imposed and, even in those regimes that try to include the voice and the participation of pupils, there is an assumption by the majority that real power nevertheless remains with the teachers, that 'they' impose the rules (Cullingford, 1986). Oppression may not describe the regime but it does sum up the feelings of pupils. That sense of unease or lack of ownership, of being forced to do things, pervades the emotions and lives of pupils.

The ambivalent security of school

Attendance at school is not voluntary. Being allowed to leave school is like the ending of a sentence. It is a sign of liberation, of greater autonomy, of being taken seriously as an individual. School has provided many of the answers to social questions, of how to behave, what is expected and how to conduct oneself in a large mass of people. School to this extent has replaced personal responsibility with rules, a sense of personal accountability with discipline. This is a form of oppression but it is also a type of security.

Many pupils look forward to release from school, but there are some who also see the end of the compulsory years as frightening. The safety of school as well as its control lies in the certainty of its rules and in a strong sense of security, which might be missed:

> I will, because you will feel less secure. At school you feel that teachers are watching out for you but at college you'll feel that the teachers will only want you to do the work and they don't really care about you.
>
> (Female, Year 11)

Whilst some relish the thought of 'not being bossed about', there are others who feel that this meticulous attention was also a particular form of interest, that 'watching out for you' means that a certain amount of responsibility was being taken by someone else:

> I'm scared of growing up really. That sounds a bit sort of. . . the idea of having to work sort of full time and be responsible scares me a bit. . . I would like to go to university but the idea of being in debt scares me a lot as well. . . I mean, the idea of

having to carry around this much debt with me for a long time really freaks me out.

(Female, aged 18)

It is an interesting observation that keeps being reiterated by pupils that all kinds of decisions are not in their hands, but in the hands of teachers. Those who wish to remain invisible and anonymous, and those who do not really like the burden of decision making find in that fact a kind of security, rather than an oppression from which to escape. The question of whether pupils feel fully prepared for life outside school is raised yet again. Whatever skills were learnt in school, there remains a great deal of uncertainty about the future. The sense of insecurity is such that pupils see the school as a type of cocoon from which they must break out in the natural course of events, but which had its own wadding of comfort.

The prospects of life after school are varied, but rest on the simple patterns of earning money and gaining useful qualifications in order to do so:

I'll probably go to tech, some kind of tech, here; after that I'll just go out and see if I can get a job or something. . . because it brings in some money for me and it's probably better than schools. If I can get a job then I'm not bothered. If I get a job that pleases me that will be even better.

(Male, Year 10)

'Getting started' is seen as being quite hard. As in entering the school for the first time, there is a sense of apprehension and uncertainty about what the expectations should be:

I don't know – it's just that there'll be nothing to do apart from going to college to get a job. There'll be nothing to do from like. . . after you've finished your exams. . . if you go to college you're all right, but if you can't get into college you go looking for a job.

(Female, Year 10)

'Getting a job' is what the pupils will do if they do not gain the necessary qualifications in order to acquire a better job. College is an extension of school, at least in the sense of postponing the next phase.

Getting a job means earning money. It might be better to enjoy the job, but there is a clear will to seek employment for its mercenary rewards as well as the more subtle matter of job satisfaction:

> I don't know yet, just try and get a job, see if anything else comes up. Whatever I can do. I'd prefer to be at home but it can't be done so I'd get a job if I could find one. I'll probably be always on the lookout for better jobs. If I find a job I really like I'll stick to it.
>
> (Male, Year 10)

Finding a job is seen as a matter of chance, of opportunity, rather than a result of determination or will. Even if a job is found it does not have to be permanent. It all depends on what will happen, and that uncertainty is as true of the jobs as of the examinations. The uncertainty arises from the sense of being alone in the world, without any imposed structure:

> I don't know what I'm going to do. I don't know if I'll be able to go to college. I don't know if I'll get the grades. I'll be skint. I've nobody to tell me what to do.
>
> (Female, Year 10)

The exposure to the job market

Having a job – any job – is seen as an achievement. Those who do not consider themselves or who are not considered as academically gifted feel very apprehensive about their immediate future. They would like to be employed but express little idea about how to go about it, as if it were a decision to be left for the time being as too demanding to face. The difficulties are always apparent:

> I'd love to have a job. Just nobody wants to give me one because I'm either too young or I ain't got my experience, but they don't understand somebody has to give you a job in the first place to get experience before you can have any.
>
> (Female, aged 17)

Whatever the good intentions and the willingness to try anything, as long as it pays, pupils share the perception that jobs are hard to come by. They hear of unemployment at both first and second hand:

> Because loads of other people I know, my mum and dad know,
> they haven't been able to get a job at all. Some friends who left
> school they have been having trouble so I don't think it will be
> easy at all. . . it might depend on the job really.

(Female, Year 10)

It is a perception widely shared that 'finding a job' is never easy,
sometimes because pupils lack the necessary qualifications, skills or
experience, and sometimes because of the competition. There are not
enough jobs available for all. There are 'not that many jobs around at
the moment', so to find one is 'difficult':

> I've been told no because the world's getting smaller. There's
> more companies going bankrupt so there's less jobs and when
> they put more things up there's less money for the other
> companies.

(Male, Year 10)

Whatever the reasons there is an assumption that there are not enough
jobs and that not even the best equipped or prepared will find what
suits them. There is no simple correlation given between jobs and
qualifications:

> 'Cos you can be overqualified and you can be underqualified.
> And there lots of people nowadays without a job so and they'll
> probably leave school, leave college and be a lot more out of
> jobs.

(Female, Year 10)

If schooling is supposed to be a preparation for employment, the fact
that the lack of jobs figures so significantly in pupils' thinking suggests
that there is an unacknowledged undermining in the sense of purpose
in schools. There is no certainty of a job, and even uncertainties for
those who have a job, a sense of general insecurity. If the whole purpose
of education is employment, then the prospect of being without one
or insecure is the most difficult to accept, and undermines the very
experience of school:

> Most people of my age think they might get a job.

(Female, Year 10)

It depends like if you get into a good firm or establishment then you might have a secure job but if it's not like say a well-known one maybe then, I don't know, you might have to, I don't know, you might be chucked out or whatever.

(Male, Year 10)

There are many political messages that are constantly paraded about the future of employment, including the necessity for the appropriate technical skills, like computing, or the need for basic qualifications, as in grammar and arithmetic. Another well-orchestrated message about school is the assumption that no job is permanent and that the notion that the acquisition of the necessarily complex skills associated with one profession leads automatically to the security of permanent employment is out of order and out of date. Whilst the excitement of the entrepreneur constantly seeking new opportunities and the main chance and adapting to whatever is offered with speed and panache might have been the intended message, the unforeseen consequence of this social advertising in the young is a strong sense of insecurity and impermanence. This muddled version of a future of uncertain and short-term employment has a strong effect on the thinking of pupils about to leave school:

Well, right, I think I'll stop because the nurses don't get paid that much. Some of them do get redundant. So it depends on what technology comes into nursing; technology and equipment using and. . . I might have to do a course or I might have to drop out because they don't take that much. . . they tend to be much younger so they're active. But I don't think I'll have a job always. Because there's so many people are unemployed. There are so many people unemployed and people out there want qualifications. So it's better to stay in education than be unemployed. At least you get to go into training; at least you get money and everything. But if you do have a family that's going to be a bit difficult. . . they just want qualifications and active in technology.

(Female, Year 11)

This typifies the interpretations given to the currencies of generalized social thought: the vulnerabilities of work to the impact of new technologies and, conversely, the need to adapt to the new technologies; the need for qualifications and the fact that gaining them could well be a postponement of the time of unemployment. Contradictions prevail in the arguments, but not as deeply as the sense of insecurity, uncertainty and bewilderment. So many people are observed to be unemployed. Schooling, as it was a hundred years earlier, is a period of protection against such unemployment. And yet schools are not those places of natural calm and fruitful endeavour if their essential justification is their preparation for the future. There are other social issues as well that are raised but the underlying sense is that equivocal and ambivalent attitude towards the hope and threat of the new technology.

Leaving school can be feared. Pupils are entering a certain degree of uncertainty. Being on their own, however, can be associated with the lonely challenges of the proffered work, unknown and essentially untried. Many pupils have had experiences of working, like paper rounds and glimpses into offices and factories as part of the oddly titled 'work experience' as if what took place in school was not work in the real sense. These experiences have not given deep insights into employment, so that the general images that surround jobs remain very important. For some pupils the opportunity to escape from the closed world of school is to be relished. It is an escape to freedom, of being released from being told what to do. Schools are constraining, and compulsion is at the heart of the legislation that supports them. There is one small freedom from school that is surprisingly cherished, and that is not having to get out of bed so early in the morning. Clearly those who see this as a particular virtue have not yet confronted the realization of working practices:

> No more school in the morning; it's different, isn't it? I don't have to wake up at 7 o'clock in the morning to catch the bus.
>
> (Male, Year 10)

> Not being bossed by teachers any more and not having to get up at a certain time and come in.
>
> (Male, Year 10)

> Not having to wake up on a morning and good about leaving, I don't know, like a weight off your shoulders to think I don't have to go to school.
>
> (Female, Year 10)

There is no guarantee that, after the period of relief, like a holiday, there will be no more early mornings. What is revealing, however, is the sense of reluctance: there is no choice but to attend, and this is at the behest of the teachers and the system and not a shared agreement. If school includes that sense of being 'bossed around' it is also telling that leaving school is like having 'weight off your shoulders'.

Schools are not inevitably such burdens, but the language and tone of the pupils do suggest a sense of being forced to do things, informing the kind of explanation that emerges from the dialogue. School is compulsory. The very phrase indicates the burden that has to be accepted.

Conclusions

The relationship between schooling and what happens afterwards is complicated. With hindsight all kinds of changes to the memories of school are made, with certain realities highlighted because of the power of hindsight. Even with the passage of time it is interesting how many of the most significant memories of school are dark and traumatic. Even teachers say they are often driven to take up their profession because of their bad memories of school (Cullingford, 1986). School is a rite of passage and, as such, can indicate initiations that are unpleasant as well as useful. Schools, by their peculiar mixtures of different people with different outlooks and motivations, are bound to be challenging. The question remains whether the challenges should be so distant from the needs of the pupils.

If schools are a rite of passage and if their function as training for citizenship and personal identity is constantly undermined, then all that we are left with is the purpose of employment (Egan, 1997). They are supposed to develop the skills and attitudes needed for a world of paid work. Schools are supposed to enable those who leave them to feel confident of their abilities. This is difficult if there is a perception that there are no further securities in work. Security is sought after: the desire for a 'steady job' goes deep. In the face of this, the information that pupils receive about the world of manufacturing and service industry is an undermining one, or the solution to this fear is to revert to what is most interesting personally and see what happens, hoping that something will work out:

> My mother was always saying to me, oh, why don't you become an engineer or a technician like your dad, and I'm thinking that a lot of thing on the news like coal mines being closed down and everything and loads of engineering firms that my dad knows have closed down as well so it's a bit

worrying to think, oh well, I've got a steady job here, but will it last long? So I thought I'll go for the original one like being an actor and see where that goes.

(Male, Year 11)

11
The social context of school

There are many different levels of engagement within schools. It is the most personal and individual level that affects all pupils. We know that, whatever the surface matter relating to the lesson, there are all kinds of disconnected thoughts that are taking place, sometimes in addition to, sometimes as an alternative to, the matter in hand. Even whilst someone is trying to concentrate, the mind will occasionally stray, into images and associations and a critical scrutiny of what is taking place. There will also be moments of almost deliberate abstraction, of day-dreams or a series of thoughts that have little to do with what is formally taking place. And then there are the other distractions, the disturbances, the other social life of the school.

The distinction between the formal curriculum and the broader social life is clear. They overlap and intertwine, but for many pupils it is the hidden curriculum that is more important. Feeling socially excluded from the demands of the school, pupils' sense of meaning is given a social framework by the discussion with friends, their ideas and appearances, and the intensity of changing relationships. The school is not just a series of formal inputs carefully imbibed but full of gaps, between lessons, in breaks and at lunchtime. These 'gaps', which provide so much of the more intense emotional engagement, will often spill over into the lessons. There is no immediate or sudden break. When we study closely the way in which pupils work, the question of a 'time on task' is immediately changed from the ostensible involvement with what the teacher demands and the actual distractions either visible or invisible. The visible distractions are talking with other people, spending time finding the right book or a sharp pencil, or simply waiting. Visible distractions are also sulking in silence, looking at a sheet of paper that remains blank but for the title of what is never even understood, and doing nothing. The invisible distractions are all those heterogeneous thoughts that are always engaging the mind. Even without these, the obvious distractions from work take up a considerable amount of time. Allowing for all the break-times, the minutes of preparation in lessons and waiting for something to happen, the time spent actually 'on task' in school is a small proportion. Some estimate it at 20 per cent. (This is to quote a generous figure, even if it is assumed that pupils are concentrating fully when they are sitting with a pen in their hand. In the careful survey carried out by the author, allowing for the time spent in breaks, getting pencils and talking to others, the time spent on working was more like 7 per cent of the school day.)

All this needs reiterating because there is a collective and almost atavistic myth that schools can be judged only on the formal curriculum and that they are hermetically sealed from the outside world. The real influence of school lies in all the messages the pupils receive, from each other as well as through their observation of teachers' behaviour. The subject matter presented to them to imbibe does not in itself form their minds or influence their behaviour. The learning styles and ways of thinking are formulated by the pupils individually. They adapt in their own way to different subjects and different teachers. As they acknowledge, the skills that are useful to them are more subtle than the ability to recite erudite facts.

Even more significantly, a school cannot be sealed off from its surrounding community. It might be the wish of Ofsted inspectors to judge a school purely on the quality of inputs and outputs, as if these symbolic gates successfully barred the outside world. The irony is that the more that schools are judged by the criteria of natural accountability the more the influence of socio-economic circumstances can be seen. The creation of league tables reveals, without a blush, that those schools whose pupils are provided by the better off are all top of the league, and those whose pupils are poor are at the bottom. This is no surprise; but the league tables continue on blandly as before, for all the rhetoric about other forms of measurement like value-added. The Prime Minister, who created this mantra, 'location, location, location', was absolutely correct. Yet there is still a significant gap between the general political thinking, 'political' in the sense of including journalists, and the more studied research evidence, which suggests that schools, whilst making a difference, account for only a small percentage of explaining the life chances and development of their pupils.

Within schools are small societies; outside lie all the influences of parents and neighbourhoods. What, then, are the thoughts of those pupils sitting in the classroom, ostensibly working? To an extent these thoughts have to do, even if obliquely, with the subject they are undergoing. At the same time the associations that the mind makes will keep hinting, at least, at other matters and, if allowed to, enable it to stray to fantasy and to all the other matters of interest that are the stuff of everyday conversation, like the latest episode of a television programme or the latest film. There are two strands of thought that clearly emerge and deserve exploration. One, which is the particular subject here, is to do with pupils' own personal circumstances: their own contexts and their own futures. We are reminded that the kinds of choices these young people make can be sophisticated as well as complex (Hodkinson, Sparkes and Hodkinson, 1996). Dropping out of school can be a more creative act than simply failing. From the point of view of the system it is only what officially takes place that counts. Anything that takes place in the 'gaps', outside formal lessons, is dismissed. For young people the choices of what to do with their lives and how to deal with them are both more demanding and more sophisticated (Hodkinson, Sparkes and Hodkinson, 1996).

Pupils also bring with them a whole range of other facts and influences that are part of their larger social lives. At one level are all the private interests, their tastes and entertainments. At another are their reflections on the world in which they live, from their homes to the world as a whole. We sometimes prefer to forget how knowledge-able young people are. They see the news and are aware of what is going on. More importantly, they have a keen understanding of the political issues involved (Jeffrey, 2001). They are not immune from all the political events that surround every school, from the impact of governmental policy to the different locations of power. The critical observations of teachers' behaviour, the management systems and the fear of inspection all add to their broader social understanding. Pupils also talk to each other and influence each other's thinking. The school is affected by the intake, by the very encouragement, or lack of it, that pupils bring to schools, but they are also influenced by the attitudes and thoughts of parents and others. For each individual pupil, school is only part of the overall context of life. This conclusion is, in a sense, so obvious it should not need repeating but, like so many matters seemingly obvious, it is often ignored.

The attitudes that pupils bring with them into school clearly make a deep impression. Their motivations and their belief in themselves are formed by their sense of parental interest or pressure. There are some cases where parents are clearly undermining, where a father, for example, casts nothing but scorn on the whole idea of education (Cullingford, 1999b). The interest that parents have in their children's work and, at a more subtle level, the belief they have in their children's ability are a strong influence.

Rather than being asked directly about the role of their parents in their schooling, the pupils here were asked who influenced them in their choice of career and in decisions like staying on and going to university, or leaving school as soon as possible. The influences are clearly many but it is parents (and never teachers) who are cited as the most significant. The experience of home connects in their minds with their futures, sometimes as if nothing that took place at school made any difference. For many pupils school appears as a peripheral, a temporary, matter when the normal flow of life continues.

From the teachers' point of view, home life is normally kept as much as possible at a distance. This is because when it does intrude it tends to do so in a troublesome way. A pupil may be in trouble so the parent has to be brought in, a parent may come to complain (Holden and Cullingford, in press) or a family may have such a reputation that teachers warn each other about the offspring of that family. Rarely is the matter of the most salience to pupils – where they live and their relationships with their parents – discussed, in however sensitive a manner, with teachers. Occasionally, in the early years, the extremity of the difficulties in the home will force attention to be paid to them, but usually such matters are considered private, as there is simply no time to pursue a dialogue.

In the circumstances of pupils' complete lives, schooling is a short part designed to shape their future but not necessarily influence it. The choices that need to be made are more likely to be formed by parents and siblings, as well as peers, than by the formal structures provided by school. Whatever the hours spent in school, more time is spent at home and in a way this is significant. Generally attitudes can be traced back:

> When I told my mum about wanting to be a caterer or an instructor, she thought it was quite a good idea because like when she's really busy on a Sunday I do all the dinners and everyone enjoys it so she thought it would be a good idea to get a catering job.
>
> (Male, Year 10)

It's like my dad is always busy or something or tired and I help mum a lot and when we go to bed I'll sit on mum's bed and talk to her.

(Female, Year 10)

The practical experiences and the acknowledgement of skills pervade the pupils' attitudes towards their own careers. The observation of their parents' experiences and varying degrees of satisfaction with their jobs is a powerful influence. Support and encouragement from a parent are duly noted, as is the lack of them, the *laissez-faire* indifference or the excuses that prevent any distinct personal curiosity – being 'busy' or 'tired'. The significance of parental detachment has already been noted (Cullingford, 1999b). Nothing undermines pupils more than indifference, not even those moments of humiliation at school. Parents' attitudes are not occasional and cannot be escaped. They are the foundations on which all else depends:

No, I can't really talk to them. I can't find it easy to talk to them or anything. I don't think they can. I know I shouldn't say that but I don't think they have much interest, so. . . Dad's glad when I get good marks but he's not upset when I do bad. He says as long as you've tried your best. My mum she hasn't got no confidence in me at all. She just, I don't know, she's always down on me.

(Female, Year 10)

There are many occasions in school when pupils' confidence can be undermined. Every test, every wrong answer, every misunderstanding is an opportunity for humiliation. These can be overcome if there is support at home. The ontological confidence comes from the belief in their ability. What pupils find hard is either the overbearing demands of an over-authoritative parent or the more subtly destructive effects of indifference – 'Do whatever you want.' This *laissez-faire* attitude has its ostensible attractions – 'As long as you're happy' – and sounds far kinder, but it is not necessarily interpreted, or meant, as palpable support. Children can detect real concern in their parents, when it is there, and the difference between saying emollient phrases that are the psychobabble of encouragement and the real engagement of interest.

Sometimes the sense of personal responsibility seems so strong that the influence of parents is only revealed in a more subtle way. Pupils would not always wish to acknowledge where the formative influences are:

> I've just decided myself. I haven't really took much notice of
> what my mum and dad have really said; but I suppose really,
> growing up, my dad and my brother, with them being in the
> army, and that's what I want to do as well, and with them being
> engineers I'd like to do that.
>
> (Male, aged 17)

Despite taking no notice of what parents say, what they demonstrate
remains significant. The advice that parents give, or do not give, also
derives from a specific context. Are they saying, 'Do better than me' or
'Do as well as me'? Do they say 'emulate' or 'avoid'? It does not need
much explanation to give children a clear indication about whether
their parents are happy or not. Attitudes to business, the professions
and other jobs are formed by such observation.

The influence of the home life on school is pervasive. It is not a
separate entity but informs the whole approach to learning. We see
glimpses of this in many of the revelations pupils make. Sometimes
the pressure of responsibility can clearly affect the whole experience
of school:

> I get the feeling. . . in like they're going to get old. Sometimes
> it worries me that my dad and my mum are going to get old
> and I'm going to have to look after them. I've got experience
> of looking after old people and I can get upset that they might
> die one day and I'm going to have to look after them. Some-
> times I think I don't want to get into a job, I'm fed up with
> working. I'm fed up with learning things but then I have to
> think like who's going to get the money in because it will take
> my brother five years to be where he wants to be and it may
> take me more time than him and just have to get some income
> in. So I can't back down now. I've come too far. Sometimes I
> do feel I want to back down and it's like, if I'm fed up with
> work like. I've got to get some science investigations handed
> in now, and I get fed up of working on my own and keeping
> reading and reading books and sometimes the information
> doesn't go into your brain. I mean you sit there for an hour or
> two hours or a whole day trying to get some information like
> and then you fall back and then you look and go, 'I've only
> learnt textiles today', and you've got so much to do. It's
> unbelievable.
>
> (Female, Year 11)

There are layers of pressures and motivations. The sense of oppression and the lack of real meaning in the tasks – 'It's unbelievable' – are clear. There is difficulty in imbibing all the information and self-consciousness about the inability to do all that is demanded, so that self-criticism adds to the undermining. All this is the result of the perception of pressure – working on her own, 'having' to get work handed in and constantly reading. This sense of pressure clearly derives from the fact that she 'wants' to back down, to drop out, but she can't. This is not because of any personal motivation but because of the needs of her family. She is going through all this because of the fear of the future, because the family will need money. She feels responsible for her parents, and this is reinforced by work experience that takes her to old people's homes. She is fed up with working, and fed up with 'learning things'. But she cannot back down. It is as if, like Macbeth, she finds herself having gone so far that to return would be as tedious as to continue. The possibility of 'backing down' is always there, which makes the parental pressure, however subtle, the more, not less, significant.

The pressures that parents exert can be powerful. Pupils expect some kind of concern, but sometimes the hopes and expectations are very clear:

> They wanted me to be a doctor. I don't think I'll be a doctor because I took single science. I'm no good at science. I've told them that and they would let. . . just try as hard as I can and be what you want to. I don't know, because no one's been a doctor in the family. There's been a solicitor, things like that, but not a doctor. They want me to be a doctor but I don't think that I will. My dad owns a business and my mum's a housewife; she stays at home. My dad he goes 'to get good grades, get a good report' and everything. My mum's bothered too but my dad reads the report most of the time.
>
> (Female, Year 10)

There are different kinds of expectations: the more general ones of wanting the children to do well, reading the reports and giving the impression of saying 'Come on', and the more specific earmarking of a particular job (Bettelheim, 1987). This latter idea appears often and has a strong potential for future disappointment – 'I wish you had been a doctor.' For pupils, finding their own interests and predilections, having particular jobs thrust at them causes equivocal reactions:

> My dad wants me to go into the Navy, and my mum, well my mum's a bit, she'd like me to go into the Navy but I think she'd prefer me to stay at home really but my dad definitely wants me to do it. He thinks it would be good for me.
>
> (Male, Year 10)

The Navy would 'do him good', presumably more than school. Whatever he thinks about this idea, it puts the purpose of school into a different perspective. It is a reminder of school as an enabling institution, fitting pupils for the next stage, even if the pupils themselves know they are unlikely to obtain the qualifications:

> They want me to be a doctor but I know I won't get the qualifications for it, so I changed my mind to computers. My mum wants me to do computers.
>
> (Male, Year 10)

Sometimes the pupils talk in terms of the 'pressure' to do well, which is felt in the home as well as at school. Naturally the parents want their children to have the 'best jobs in the world' but they also have a clear idea of what kinds of jobs those might be:

> My dad, he's always giving me lectures about that you should always be looking ahead and all this. He's always been telling me to get my own business; it will be better than working for someone.
>
> (Male, Year 10)

'Giving lectures' and 'always telling me' are not only examples of the language of parental cajoling but echo the one message given out at school. There is a purpose; there is a pragmatic outcome at the end of the educational experience to which the pupils are supposed to be devoted. It is supposed to make everything worth while. There are therefore specific pressures to make the right career choices and bend the experience of school in that direction:

> And my parents have always been saying if you're good at maths then accountancy's in demand and that's the best job for you and basically from there, and then coming to school and asking. . . but I've heard that accountancy can be pretty boring. My dad was always good at college but he had loads of health problems and it forced him to quit education and it's

why he always wants me to fulfil his ambitions like. I'm his only son. I think it's because of the pressure that I'm doing well actually.

(Male, Year 10)

There is, then, something to be said for the assertive interest of parents. The problem lies in keeping the balance between concern and over-authoritarianism: the coercions of school should be balanced by a different energy from home. There is also a balance between what people 'ought to do' and the actualities of experience, as well as a relationship between the subjects studied and the outcomes. If a pupil is good at maths, or science, does this inevitably mean a certain kind of career? It might not mean accountancy. Pupils often connect what gives them personal pleasure, like childminding, and the utility of certain subjects, joining them together in a possible career.

Many parents present an inadvertent pressure in wishing their children to do well, to make up for their own disappointments. Children fulfil their parents' ambitions. It is those parents who were especially disappointed in their own educational experiences, whether for health reasons or not, who sometimes overtly place their hopes in their children's educational success:

'Cos my dad he started working and then went back and did it so it took him longer and he says that it is best to get them all out of the way. Get it done and then you've got them for the rest of your life.

(Male, Year 11)

Children are shaped by their parents' experience in all kinds of ways. The very way they approach school is deeply affected by it, not only in the early years. The relationship between most parents and school is an awkward one, in so far as they have put their trust in what the school is doing and cannot really interfere with the day-to-day experiences of their children's schools (Cullingford, 1996). Parents are at a further remove than the peer groups, but they nevertheless go through with their children some of the emotional excitements and disappointments of the educational experience. Their reactions help to shape pupils' attitudes, just as pupils react to what they call their teachers' 'moods'.

On one matter teachers and parents are united, and that is doing well in exams:

> My mum said about a week ago that if I get good grades she'd give me a tenner for every good grade so I said I don't like that stuff like that so. . . she's eased off a bit. Don't like heavy pressures and stuff like that.
>
> (Male, Year 11)

There are less overt ways of putting expectations on children, but the parental pressure is easily detected even if disguised. Pupils know if it is 'for their own good' as well as making up for their parents' own sense of disappointment. The effects of too much pressure can be to make the pupils rebel against it:

> I've got a younger one; he's really brainy, you see; he's sort of like when he was in Year 8 he had the Year 10 standard working, and he's always getting the best reports in his year and everything and my dad's always putting me down because of him. I just can't be bothered. It's like when somebody keeps telling you to do something and you can't do it, you just don't do it, you want to fail at it to get him sad like, so he hasn't got no control over you, so it's like putting yourself into control. My mum has supported me. Well, my dad has supported me too but I decided he wanted me to do, to become a solicitor, talk to him. I told him, then he goes, 'Oh, OK, I'll stick with you because. . .' I told him no, I want to become this. . . so he just gave up.
>
> (Male, Year 11)

This is a typical reaction *against* pressure of a kind that takes place in school every day, but not so often at home. It is pressure that, like tests for some, has the opposite effect to that intended. Instead of finding it beneficial, there is a reaction against it, tellingly out of a desire to be 'in control'. Personal autonomy reacts against external pressure, especially if it comes from the parental equivalent of SATs and league tables – comparisons with siblings. Too much forceful cajoling can lead to a desire to fail. Any escape from it is sought, but unfortunately also a kind of revenge.

The balance between the right kind of support and personal interest, and the inadvertent effects of a more direct and charged expectation is a difficult one, since no interest at all or encouragement of whatever the child is doing can be interpreted as indifference. Sometimes all kinds of different levels of emotional expectations come together:

Well, it's beautician is what I want to do and my dad says a pharmacist because that's quite similar to beautician because you use chemicals and everything and he goes it's quite similar, so my dad's trying to tell me to do pharmacy but I'm more interested in beautician. He's not forcing me; he just tries to give me a choice. He just goes like, 'You'll have your own job and that; you won't be going in and out and travelling places or something.' He goes, 'You can have your own pharmacy or something. It's quite a good business as well.' No, he doesn't put pressure on me. He goes, 'Do whatever you want. Just be happy whatever you do.'

(Female, Year 10)

Whilst there is 'no pressure' put upon her, clearly the father cannot quite let go, at least of what he sees as the rational arguments that suggest that one career is better than another. Being a beautician is what she wants to 'do'. 'He's not forcing me; he just tries to give me a choice.'

The last phrase – 'Do whatever you want' – is telling. It has many resonances. It can mean anything from a general encouragement – 'whatever you're good at' or 'whatever makes you happy' – through to a benign lack of interference, to a complete indifference. It is a phrase or an attitude that keeps recurring:

She doesn't mind what I take as long as I'm happy with it and I've always wanted to do this.

(Female, Year 10)

They would like me to do anything that I'm happy with. They don't want me to be particularly anything. They don't force me into doing something that I don't want to do.

(Male, Year 10)

'As long as they are happy' can be the kind of support these pupils need at school. It is not the same as:

They're not bothered really. They just said that it's up to me what I want to do.

(Female, Year 10)

> I don't think they're really bothered what I do just as long as I
> get a job and I can keep up with it and I'm doing OK as is.
>
> (Male, Year 11)

One of the results of the amount of time spent in schools is the creation
of the sense of independence. It is up to the pupils themselves to make
choices, to work hard, to gain success:

> Well, my mum: she talks about business. . . my dad he just gives
> me 'It's up to you now. It's up to you now. I've done my job;
> it's up to you.'
>
> (Male, Year 11)

'It's up to you' is a phrase that again echoes the cajoling of teachers.
There is an obvious and unhelpful echo in the use of this phrase in the
school, where the responsibility for success lies not in independence
but in following the dictates of the curriculum. In school it is up to the
pupils to conform, to submit to the exigencies of the examination and
testing system. This is not really independence in the way that parents
mean it. The phrase of the pushing parents – 'Come on' – is balanced
by the concern to let children get on with whatever they want to do.

   The idea of qualifications for better employment and more money
is the one line that parents take up. They also talk of the significance
of contentment, also 'up to you':

> My mum wants me to be a plumber. . . He says do stuff that
> you enjoy; go for the one that you enjoy, because if you don't
> then you may regret it and you may get something that you
> don't like and you'll just keep on changing it all the time. Like
> he says don't go for second best; if you want to do it, you go
> for it.
>
> (Male, Year 11)

There are many ambiguities in the passing of responsibility, and in
personal choice and individual autonomy. There are latent messages,
hopes of success, of making up for other disappointments. The views
of parents and others are often of great significance for pupils, whatever
the messages are. They are frameworks in which the pupils operate. It
is up to the individual to do well, be happy or work hard. All these
might be pressures but they can also be a symbol of a withdrawal of

interest. Unfortunately or otherwise, what parents (or their equivalents) symbolize is a sense of security, a support that goes deeper than that of school:

> My dad's dead and I don't know where my mum is. . . They [her sister and sister's husband] just said they'd be there for me whatever I decide to do.
>
> (Female, Year 10)

Whilst the early influence of parents, and the relationships formed at home, is slowly being recognized, it is easy to forget the continuing presence of home, or the alternative and more individually orientated circumstances of young people. The subject matter and the interest of school are separate from the experience of home, and, just as the more subtle matters of teachers' behaviour, like their enthusiasm, have a more profound effect on attitudes than the subjects they profess, so are many opinions and styles of thought developed at home. It is, of course, much easier to demonstrate what is learnt in school. It can be tested. The type of language, the tone of voice and the mental gestures that are developed at home are both more individual and more long-lasting than some of the academic matters of school. Certain assumptions are imbibed rather than taught.

If the influence of parents can be tested by observation and by personal experiences, it is less easy to demonstrate the self-awareness of being oneself or to trace the particular influences that form character-istics. The most significant insights into learning, into those subtle influences that cannot be intellectually dismissed, are harder to prove. It is in general attitudes that we detect how significant are the influences of parents' outlooks on life. They might cajole or they might encourage; they might be indifferent or they might be careless; but the general social attitudes of parents come through clearly. This is one reason why so many pupils follow a similar path in employment to that taken by their parents. Naturally, they would wish to do better. Naturally, their parents wish them subliminally to rectify their own mistakes, but the outlook expressed by parents remains effective:

> My parents want me to go to university. . . somewhere like. . . I was interested in business studies because my dad has his own business so I know how much money you can make out of your business. I started getting interested when I was 10. They would like me to do anything that I'm happy with. They

> don't want me to do particularly anything. They don't want to force me into doing something that I didn't want to do.
>
> (Male, Year 10)

For all the demurring about pressure the expectations are clear. There is nothing obviously forceful about influence. There are few instances of following a particular course of action in a preordained manner. The rewards of business are experienced as well as advertised. Knowing how much money can be made is linked naturally with the opportunity to go to university.

The influence of the parents and the desire to make money can take many forms. From the same school we see a connection being made both similar to, and different from, that of 'business':

> Well, it was basically that my dad does a sort of trade – joinery. I've seen what he does and I thought, I like that. I like outside work. Basically the wage, I'm interested in the money side. They haven't really noticed. It's up to me what I want to do really.
>
> (Male, Year 10)

The one contrast lies in the under-expressed high expectations of one set of parents and the others 'not even' noticing. The influence, however, is as deep and as taken for granted.

Those who have long been less than happy at school tend to be those who have thought about alternatives for a long time, just as they leave earlier. Some parents do not approve of their children expressing a dislike of school but have a clear idea that it can be left as soon as is feasible:

> No, they go mad [if I'm not at school]... My mum wants me to be a mechanic as well. My dad does as well... and my granddad and brother-in-law.
>
> (Male, Year 10)

This might give one kind of sense of inevitability as to what will happen after school, but there are also others:

> My mum says I'd probably be pregnant by that time and having loads of kids, so...
>
> (Female, Year 10)

There are many ways in which parents express concern for their children but, in whatever way they do so, they are far more involved in the long term than schools. Whilst they might say 'It's up to you', as school can, this does not abrogate their responsibility or at least their connection. Breaking off relations entirely is unusual. Schools, on the other hand, only rarely demonstrate any interest in what happens afterwards, and then often by chance. Schools come to an end. Whilst there are some schools that are interested in what happens beyond the place, this, as with university, can be for the purposes of financial connection. Whilst it again might seem obvious that the parental connection is different, its consequences are not often taken into account. The interest in the long-term future and in the immediate happiness makes a different kind of influence on the mind-set of pupils. The family continues to shape their ways of thought. Whatever form this takes, the influence and the distinctions expressed are significant:

> In my family no one goes for a good job. Well, they earn good cars and good money, but they haven't got good jobs. They want me to be educated, well educated, good job, money coming in. That's what they want me to do. That's why. . . to get me higher education. Yes, I feel pressurized. I have to pass because a lot of people are watching me, see what I can do.

> (Male, Year 11)

The connection between good jobs – or earning good cars – and education is made clear. This leads to the awareness of pressure and the self-consciousness of being 'watched'; the expectations are not just to make money but to do something 'better'.

The influences of other people are subtle because they can operate at a variety of levels. They can take the form of personal expectation and hope, or a more complacent acceptance that the children will 'do all right'. The ways in which such influences work are made clear by the different kinds of example or support. There are a number of instances where the most powerful influence or attitudes towards work, or towards the future, came not from parents but from other members of the family. Encouragement and a personal interest in talent can come from various sources:

> My parents, they'd just tell me to do what I can really, as long as it's not just being at home or getting on the dole or anything. My aunty, she always, since I was little, I've always liked writing – she's always asking me to write stories and things,

> so she most influenced me. My mum as well and my dad's
> just as long as you're happy.
>
> (Female, Year 10)

The real influence that is recognized as formative is that which is specific and personal rather than a placid acceptance of being happy or fulfilled. All pupils want to find their own way of pursuing what will stimulate them, so any recognition is welcome.

Pupils do not just react to what is said to them, but observe. The examples they receive are mixed:

> My oldest brother, because he's the one who's been to tech, and got all his money, nice and rich, buy a car. He still lives at home. He's just in bed most of the time.
>
> (Male, Year 10)

At first it could be thought that this scene encapsulates all that is desirable in the alternatives to school: a big car and not having to get up. This is not intended as a good example, but it nevertheless makes an impression, like any insight into a particular, or unusual, way of life:

> My uncle. He's a fitter. He's been all over the place. They fly him out free and he gets paid double time, with his engineering, the trade that he does. He gets £12 an hour in Britain, over here, and then when he goes across it like he can get up to £30 an hour where he works. He comes out with a good wage at the end of it.
>
> (Male, aged 17)

Example is powerful. Clearly the word has spread like an anecdote about the rewards for a particular way of life. This is the kind of information that would also have been passed around the peer group, an insight into the 'real' world beyond school.

Particular examples can make a powerful story, a palpable glimpse into the surprises of life. Examples can also be clear warnings, equally taken to heart, if not so publicly discussed:

> My brother, because he was like on the dole at first and since he's gone to London, he's like grown up more and he cares more about himself but here he was like hanging round town

and on the dole and getting up out of bed at three in the morning, three in the afternoon.

(Female, aged 16)

Individual examples from people observed, leading their own lives, leave a deeper impression than the abstract erudition of the curriculum, or the multiple figures of teachers who rarely emerge from the shadowy impressions to become palpable people. People are like stories, far more influential even in a short glimpse than the facts. Like anecdotes, they draw themselves to pupils' attention and draw on all the connections with their own lives more than passive description can ever do. The real influences, and these could be teachers in certain circumstances, are those people who have a life of their own, who without designs on their observers explain and demonstrate what otherwise is at best blandly described.

There is always a dichotomy in school between the lists of subjects to be taken, the accumulation of fact, and the more personal demonstration of the teacher's style or interest. It is this more human side, of personality, of engagement, of conversation, that seems to be missing in the routine monotony of school. When pupils reflect on who influences them, therefore, they have to consider the difference between what they have been told and what has been demonstrated. It says something about the nature of schooling that there is a distinction made officially between the subjects that are being studied and their application in terms of career. This would be understandable if schools were not so geared to employment, with the implication that the relevance of each subject has just one ultimate measure. Despite the concern with future careers it is interesting to note that advice of a personal nature is left not to the already overstretched teachers but to careers advisers. They can be useful. They listen to an individual. They give the chance for pupils not only to talk but to connect what they are doing to the choices they have to make.

Parents can offer support and, more tellingly, their example, but there are sometimes others who can give advice:

They would like me to do well, but they've said to me, whatever I decide they'll back me up on it. Probably the lady at the careers convention because she made me decide between these options. I've always not let people push me into something and tell me what to do. I've always made my own decision at the end of the day.

(Female, Year 10)

Personal autonomy is important. The decisions will always be made in one way or another by the individual, even in reaction against those who are 'pushing'. There are also times when being made to see the personal opinions can be useful. One person can be the necessary trigger to action.

Careers teachers can have an important, if minor, part to play. They have the luxury not of knowledge, but of time. They can focus on the wishes and needs of the individual rather than the curriculum. The centre of their attention is the individual:

> I don't know. . . People at school when you ask them like careers teachers, and because we've started doing more careers work now in school, and you've got to start thinking more seriously about what you're going to do when you leave school, so it's just careers teachers, that's all.
>
> (Female, Year 10)

The explicit question 'What are you going to do?' gradually makes individuals more self-aware. Their own concerns and their relationship to those who are there to help them are more clear. At last pupils can feel they matter.

Career teachers are useful in their advice because they have time to listen. They rarely emerge from this role into the kinds of personalities who could have deeper influence. This is something that teachers could fulfil, but do not have, or are not allowed to have, time for. Like the occasional aunt already outlined, an adult presence, a belief and interest, can be very important. Not every parent fulfils this role, and not always is such interest enough. It needs to be both deliberate and disinterested. It might be only possible from selected teachers but this personal interest is desired from all:

> Mr W at school, he tells me a lot, because we had him for English for ever and I used to be in his form and we got on right well and he was all right. He was always encouraging us all, and I always wanted to do right well. But, I think my dad has most.
>
> (Female, Year 11)

When a teacher does show personal interest the influence this has can be immense. But it is not part of the systematic operation of school. Teachers are seen as being too busy with their subjects and the tests to have time for the 'present' of the individual. Anyone who asks about futures is striking, if inadvertently, at the heart of the individuals' sense of themselves. What happens next is a contract that defines where individuals are coming from and what they are as well as what they aspire to be.

The idea of the future is therefore a powerful notion. It might be couched in terms of employment but it goes deeper than that. Schools as institutions have very ambivalent attitudes towards outcomes. The real result of schooling for a collection of individuals and their futures is that schools are judged on 'results', and that is a different matter. Results in one sense are the ways in which schools display, as institutions, their prowess, thereby attracting clientele and maintaining their reputation for individual success. The more personal results of the experience of schooling derive from a range of different sources of influence, all interpreted personally:

> My dad says OK, you can't get anywhere without qualifica-
> tions, but these days you can be overqualified. My friend got
> turned down from a job because he was overqualified, he was
> too good. . . it's up to me. It was, before I was always trying to
> please him. That's why I've done well in school now.
>
> (Female, Year 10)

The sense of personal authority against an influence is strong and supported by anecdotal evidence. Such evidence, like that of television, is always potent:

> Me and television. Well, I see different jobs on TV, like you see
> *The Bill*, so it gives you an insight into the police, and you see
> lawyers' things so stuff like that, seeing what kinds of job.
> That's why I wanted to be a mechanic because I saw it on a
> film and it looked really good. I wanted to get all greased up,
> all dirty and stuff like that.
>
> (Female, Year 10)

It is impossible to tell from where influence will come. Some sudden second-hand insights are revealed, of personal predilections. These could coincide against the prevailing pressure of advice, using the particular warning – 'You can be overqualified' – to advantage. Just as in the delicate balance between the over-controlling and the extremely *laissez-faire*, so pupils react against one form of advice or another, finding their own way. They do so with very sparse information.

What pupils are left with is the message that a particular phase in their life is over. They must be moved on. It is the *end*, not the beginning, of a passage. This is odd, considering the focus on *one* kind of future, however impersonal. It is, however, in all kinds of forms, very powerful:

> My dad says he just wants me to get a job so I can move out and stop bugging him all the time.
>
> (Female, Year 11)

> Well, I've told them that I was to be a motor mechanic and they say that's all right then, because people's cars break down every day and you make lots of money out of it.
>
> (Male, Year 10)

There are so many personal interpretations of this particular time, derived from many sources. The future intrudes on school life in a number of ways. Part of the hidden curriculum is the connections made by pupils between what they are learning, its effect on their own lives and what essential additional changes are occurring. They keep hearing the underlying messages: 'It's up to you', 'If you work hard you will be rewarded' together with 'Do whatever you want' and, more particularly, the general need for the school as a whole to do well. One reason that parents and others continue to have such an influence is the fact that they have a personal interest in the individual, whereas the conditions of school make such an interest very difficult for schools (Egan, 1988).

Conclusions

The experience of school that emerges from what the pupils themselves tell us creates a different picture from that of the rhetoric of policy makers and their publicists. There is a world, real enough, of achievements and failures that can be summarized in tables and statistics. Some schools are at the top of the league and others so low as to warrant 'special measures' or closure. So many teachers are named and shamed. Ever-changing targets are set and ostensibly met. There are increasing numbers of truants and excluded pupils and a growing teacher shortage. There are many new initiatives, from Surestart to the National Leadership College. All these are marks of success or failure. The outcomes, heavily inspected and accountable, are measured and either lauded or condemned.

All this is very well and a matter of great and constant attention. The question remains whether such a public account of measurable outcomes gives a true hearing to the personal experience of pupils. Listening to what pupils have to say forces us to the conclusion that their world is a very different version of the one that is officially presented. If we hear what they express and describe, we might have to come to very different conclusions about the actual effects of policies.

The gap between the rhetoric of the educational system and its personal reality is not just a temporary problem or a matter of ephemeral policy decisions. The contradiction between the semi-independence of schools in 'local management' and the heavily centralized control of the curriculum and even of teaching styles might exacerbate the problem – many think it does – but what we are uncovering here goes deeper than that. It raises the question of what education is for. It must make us reconsider the nature of schooling and its purpose in the system we all take for granted. We also need to explore more fundamental issues such as those perennial ones that are so rarely tackled, like whether the human experience hinges around constant education and living curiosity, the desire to understand, and whether we are encouraging human beings to live fulfilled lives or fitting items for the needs of society, or both.

What pupils learn in school has an important effect on their future lives, on their views of society and their place in it, on their views of themselves and their relationships with other people and on their deep-seated hopes and expectations. These are not part of the formal curriculum but personal perceptions gathered individually, unsystem-atically and often inadvertently. These views, these implicit theories that they gather together and share, are very consistent, for all the individual differences.

When asked to summarize the experience of school, even in the most encouraging of circumstances, pupils cannot bring themselves to rate it very highly. School does not emerge as the best years of their lives – but then we cannot judge what will happen to them later. If, with hindsight, schooling actually was a highlight, then that says something about the condition in which people live and supports the notion that we lead lives of quiet desperation. The problem is not so much that we have a tendency to romanticize the past, especially our own, but that we rarely look at the past objectively. For pupils actually in school the experience is generally unpleasant. There are moments of extreme emotions of joy or humiliation, but the general monotonous reality is of time passing by, being filled in, of routines and minor irritations. Whilst this fact is not to belittle the resilience of young people, to which we will return, it does suggest a submission to schooling rather than a celebration of it.

'It's all right' is the most that can be said for school. Looked at objectively, the social and academic demands come across as alienating, as excluding the individual, and without a strong or palpable sense of shared values. From the point of view of the individual, schooling is associated with waiting in a queue, with staring at a blank sheet of paper trying to force inspiration, with being told what to do and what to think. Schooling is a matter of trying to discover the instructions, implicit as well as explicit, and guessing both what is required and what can be got away with. School is itself a clash of two cultures: the personal, private but shared mixture of associations and anecdotes, and the formal, public and usually impersonal demands of the formal curriculum and imposed discipline. Pupils usually accept their power-lessness in the face of these implacable demands. Those who do not either exclude themselves or are excluded. Many more submit to what is required but are psychologically excluded. In one way, the two cultures of school coincide: the ultimate goal of schooling is to leave.

Leaving school summarizes the purpose. This is, at least, what pupils have learnt. From the beginning, the idea of school has been dominated by the notion of the outcomes, for jobs and therefore for qualifications. Each exam is a step towards the next one. At least, all who are employed in school know what this obvious purpose is, so that it is rarely questioned. Perhaps it should be taken for granted. Perhaps to imply that there can be other experiences in education than learning the skills for employability is absurd. Yet we are left with a sense that pupils would have liked to have had some other sense of shared values and ideas, connecting their own lives with those of the formal curriculum. We are not talking of mission statements here, most of which are very impressive, but of the actual experience of school, of engaging all pupils in the practical outcomes of values.

Pupils certainly regret the absence of discussion about what schooling or education is for. If the conclusion is that the only real purpose of education is to survive in a harsh economic world of competition, that would be fine. But such conclusions are never made explicit. They are formed in the minds of pupils for want of anything else. The inadvertent remark, 'You are on your own', becomes the more powerful in that context. The world beyond school beckons. It is both feared and desired. It is a quite different place.

The absence of discussion about the purpose of school is echoed in the absence of discussion about the curriculum. This formal body of knowledge appears to be another 'given' that does not need scrutiny. Instead of any discussion about the curriculum in the statutes, the hierarchy of subjects, with three dominating, is set before pupils as a *fait accompli*. Naturally they have to accept what they are given and what they are told. They hear about the significance of literacy and numeracy (and science). They have had special hours set aside to reinforce the notion of key skills and the core curriculum. They are often reminded about the needs of presenting potential employers with these essential requirements. Pupils have no choice but to submit.

This absence of discussion is a pity, because if the reasons for making certain subjects more important than others were fully explored all kinds of personal connections could be made. The sense of purpose would relate to their own lives and their futures. The implicit understandings that relate one subject to another could be clarified. Personal motivation could be involved in the curriculum. The social aspects of education could be related to the academic requirements. The pity of it is that the pupils would like to share in the thinking behind the presentation of the curriculum. They wish to do more than merely submit to it.

Discussion about the purpose of subjects is related to the sense of what is actually learnt in school and what is useful. 'Relevance' does not refer merely to a utilitarian interpretation of necessary skills, but a personal engagement with learning. It cannot be the fault of pupils that they find much of what they learn seemingly lacking in purpose or irrelevant. They demonstrate clearly the value of certain skills, but these skills are much more to do with personal social matters, of motivation and behaviour. There are useful skills learnt in school, including mechanical ones, but none as powerful as those social relationships that will inform how pupils deal with other people for the rest of their lives.

The most powerful learning that takes place in school is through observation. School is a social experience of being organized into groups and sets, into classes and queues, or being repatterned into gangs and friendships, into teams and rivals. Beneath the mass control are its entanglements of personal connections including the impact on private moods and emotions. Whilst the most emphatic daily relation-ships are with peers, those with teachers are often just as highly charged. When pupils observe teachers, they do not see just a role but a personality with moods and prejudices, peculiarities and weaknesses. On the one hand, pupils accept the teachers' need to fulfil a role and they respect those who carry out their duties without the impediments of personal liking or antipathy. On the other hand, pupils apply that sense almost of patronage as depicted in so many teenage novels, of adults behaving in their own peculiar mood-driven way. The more the teacher has to submit to the demands of delivery, the greater the gap between that and the person. The person, however, remains and it is this gap between system and personality that pupils wish could be overcome; to them a personal sense of purpose could be connected to that of the individual who represents the formal system.

Schools are small societies of a kind. Their differences to the larger communities they are supposed to serve show the kinds of society they are and the kinds of human relationships they foster. In schools, individuals fend for themselves. They are in competition and come first or last, or are isolated or are 'picked on'. At the same time, all the members of the institution are supposed to form a larger homogeneous whole. They adhere to the same rules. In between, there are the constantly shifting patters of group relationships. This symbolic sandwich, with the emotional layer in the middle, is held together by the formalities of individuals' isolation and the formalities of the whole. Individuals are pressed by routines, by set requirements for formal assessment. They are tested as individuals, for whom any kind of collaboration is forbidden. The learning patterns of pupils are supposed to be isolated from those of others. Helping each other is not a central notion when there is so much suspicion of plagiarism. The requirements of being able to work with others, to discuss, to plan, to pool ideas, to share initiatives and to carry out all the working practices for which they are supposed to fit, are all eschewed. Group work cannot be clearly assessed. Pupils, therefore, learn that their most favoured styles of learning, those times when they can combine their emotional intelligence with the requirements of knowledge, are to a great extent disapproved of, for the sake of the formalities of the system. Formality lies with the individual as well as with the collective whole.

Pupils have to accept this. Before they become self-conscious of the fact there are barriers to sharing, they are made to accept that they should learn by themselves, avoid distraction and fulfil the set tasks. This means that the more volatile side to school as a social centre, full of a network of changing interpersonal relations, is associated with distraction, with something that remains to some extent 'hidden'. Other people prevent individuals working. The very skill most prized by pupils – learning to relate to others – is officially diminished. The formality of the tested individual dominates.

The requirements of school are clear and are supposed to pervade all parts of life. There is homework to be done and work to be prepared on the home computer. Pupils are required to come to school physically and mentally ready for the diurnal demands. The support of other people outside school is clearly vital. It is also far more subtle and pervasive than parents' meetings or the occasions when governors are supposed to present the life of the school to outsiders. For pupils the interface between home and school is complex. It sometimes seems as if it were almost schizophrenic since there is an invisible barrier between one and the other. Parents might not be allowed 'beyond this point' but this is more a mental than physical point. When pupils go home, they are notoriously reluctant to say what they have been doing since for them there are two distinct worlds. What they learn and how they behave in school is separate. The way they live their lives and relate to other people is different, and the juxtaposition of one with the other is made symbolically acute by the exaggerated behaviour in the buses on release. Work is rarely discussed outside school, at least with parents. Parents are more welcomed by teachers than by their own children within the confines of school. At one level the two worlds are distinct.

The worlds of school and of home also overlap and influence each other. The influence of what takes place outside school, on attitudes, motivations and behaviour, is the stronger for being less obvious. In the early years the significance of home conditions is taken for granted, but it never leaves and is only partly diminished. The influence helps forms the pupils' mind-set about their futures and about themselves. Parents give a more personal, more idiosyncratic meaning to the outlook of pupils, who are constantly seeking general life opinions from others outside school. By 'life opinions', I mean all those prejudices and deep-seated assumptions that are rarely formally examined in the school curriculum and that are learnt more powerfully through anecdote and personal story than through the systematic deconstruction of facts. The 'two worlds' of school and home, including the community as a whole, particularly peer groups, are not so much physically as mentally and emotionally separate.

This leads pupils to adapt their behaviour naturally to where they are and they can be most embarrassed if they forget themselves and bring one mode of behaviour into the other place. There is more than a hint of learnt instinctive adaptability to circumstances in that pupils can be, at the most extreme, deliberately dissembling. It is part of what is most profoundly learnt in school.

Learning to behave according to formal instructions is obviously different from the self-control (or lack of it) demanded by different conditions. The formalities are also the sooner forgotten. They do not have such a deep influence. The very formality of what is learnt is overrated. The formal curriculum's effect can easily be exaggerated when compared to learnt modes of behaviour. If we think back to what we learnt at school, or if we hear someone else talk about a subject they once knew about, we will find the touches of erudition both surprising and unused. These were matters that were once known about. We can conjure them up, these old subjects, but we know that their place lies in the past. What is consciously learnt is quickly put to one side, even if it can be deliberately recalled. The implicit theories of thinking and behaviour that have been absorbed over the years are applied again and again. What is actually learnt in school is more profound than the set curriculum.

What, then, does school really teach? There are many cultural messages, many of which are uncomfortable or disconcerting. These messages are deeply imbibed: sometimes used, sometimes rejected, as well as interpreted in various ways. The pupils make it clear that the messages are there, whatever they do with them. It might not be easy to summarize them since there are so many contradictions within the patterns learnt. Nevertheless they leave their imprint.

One of the most powerful lessons that schools purvey is that life is full of contradictions, that people say one thing and do another, that people can hold two diametrically opposite opinions at the same time and that to distinguish one person's truth from another's is difficult. The ability to make a distinction between truth and falsehood is one of the earlier signs of young children's social skills. This ability is applied to individuals. Schools give a social gloss to the uncertainties of opinions and points of view. This complication is not a matter of deliberate hypocrisy so much as the inadvertent necessities of social survival in certain circumstances. Some would argue that the emphasis on presentation and defensiveness, which is the shadow of a system of punitive accountability, makes the black market of official falsehood the less easy to resist, but in the ways in which schools operate there are always distinctions between rhetoric and reality.

One of the most important lessons learnt in school is the distinction between intention and outcome. This might be a necessary, even a benign, matter. The individual pupil is aware of the limitations to achievement, however worthy the aspiration. The gap between the well-meaning legislation of government and its actual effects might be a salutary lesson that all pupils should, however sadly, acknowledge. The failure to achieve all that is desired should not be a curb on human aspiration. When the distinctions between the stated intention and the actual situation become commonplace and taken for granted, that is a different matter. Mission statements abound. Schools advertise what they stand for. Inclusive policies are beautifully presented. Against these, pupils measure their tested experience. That they find them wanting might be natural. That they learn a certain cynicism – 'They would say that, wouldn't they?' – is a mark of experience at quite a different level.

The problem for pupils is that they observe in schools the need to respond to outside pressures in a way that makes the society of school no longer complete or enclosed. Schools are not hermetically sealed from the outside, from influences of a far more public kind, whether translated through other people or the media. Neither are schools protected against justifying themselves to the world outside in presenting what they do as small societies to a particular and precise inspection. This leads to the writing up of the intentions. It forces the presentation of precise and measurable outcomes, which inevitably clash with the messy realities of everyday life.

We make no judgement about the efficacy of such learning. It could be that anything is better than to sustain innocent naïvety in a hostile world. The message about society is, however, clear. There are onto-logical contradictions in what goes on. These are heightened by the needs of self-protection, of the individual against others within school and of the school against others outside.

If the main implicit message of school is that there are essential contradictions and that all that seems apparent is not real, the more telling message is that pupils need to accept the fact and adapt to it. This demand for adaptability is also true for the second latent inter-pretation of life presented by school. This is the atavistic culture of competition. Pupils learn that within and outside school they are struggling against others. The inadvertent learning of school lies in the realization that there are significant differences between people, in their attainment as well as temperament, in their well-being as well as their backgrounds. It is the 'differences' that attract teasing and bullying. Individual characteristics stand out and become excuses for attention. This sense of distinction between people is exacerbated by the competitive nature of the academic aspect. Some pupils are better than others and some work harder. Some please the teachers. The crucial fact is the individuality of distinctions between people. The isolation of formal learning is joined by the emphasis on the academic attainment of those picked out in the perception of each other and of the system as a whole. 'You are on your own' is an important latent message.

When the two perceptions of schooling come together, with competi-tion and with a sense that what is said and what is done are two different, if overlapping, frameworks, then there are many possibilities of reverting to cynicism. In the social world of peer groups and of gangs, the art of learning what you can get away with is very important. At one level, this is formalized. The perceptive pupils know just how far to go with teachers. They know at what point a joke becomes dangerous. Their social skills are acute. Again, this might be something to be lauded, but it does suggest that the ability to manipulate, to cajole, to recognize how to adapt to the circumstances, is an essential require-ment for survival. Those who fail to do so cite two clear frustrations. One is the feeling that others are getting away with far worse behaviour than their own because those others are more subtle. The other feeling is the realization that they are particularly vulnerable to teasing. They can be 'picked on' and are easily provoked.

Successful pupils know how to manipulate the system. Teachers are aware of this phenomenon whilst also conscious that it is almost impossible not to pander to it. The quiet children remain in the background, learning how to avoid particular attention. They also learn that notice can be provoked either by them being too slow with their work or too clever. The middle way of almost invisible adaptability is one way of using the social etiquette of the academic system. The smart pupils meanwhile learn how far they can go and test their prowess. They demonstrate their mastery and are observed doing so. Dissembling is successful. The teachers have not got time to pursue every nuance of manipulation. The half-hidden social practices are well understood, as is the cynicism with which they are covered. Submission includes putting up with all the nefarious practices of the difficult, the awkward, the sly and the clever.

The distinction between the formal rules and discipline of school and the undercurrents of pressures and gossip is kept intact because of the essentially hierarchical nature of schools. All the complex social norms would not flourish in the same way, were it not for the rigid systems of authority. What is interesting about the structures of power is that they also exhibit the distinctions between the supposed and the actual. The official framework for a school is simple. The head rules. Teachers carry out his or her wishes. Pupils obey. In fact, pupils realize the greater complexities: the power of outside agencies, like inspectors and governors, so that the hierarchy embraces a greater social reality than the school. At the same time, pupils are acutely aware of which teachers have real weight with each other as well as with pupils. They know when certain pupils carry more real authority than some teachers. Nevertheless, the idea of a hierarchy, of certain people giving orders and the need to accept this, is strong.

The problem for pupils in such manifestations of hierarchy is that they realize that their voice does not count for much. Even in schools where there is an intention to give pupils a sense of democracy, of empowerment by decision making, the realities of power are well understood. Pupils would only be allowed to make comments on certain matters like uniform. On other matters, like the curriculum, they have no say. Even if they make their feelings clear about particular teachers, for instance, there is nothing that can be done about it. It is unlikely that any school would realistically contemplate the *laissez-faire* regime of Summerhill, where the pupils made their own rules including whether they wanted to work or not, or the rigid anarchy of the Thomas Cranmer School, where the political interpretation of the staff went so far as to suggest that the learning of reading was a capitalist act and to be eschewed. For all the occasional difficulties or the protestations of pupils, schools continue in their hierarchical way. This is what all those in them are brought up to expect.

The result of this is not so much an acceptance of authority as a sense of powerlessness that extends to the political system. There is no strong perception that the individual voice is listened to, let alone heard. Such a sense of disenfranchisement does not come solely from the school. There are many other sources of information about the way that political life operates. Schools do, however, reinforce the sense that the power to make changes lies elsewhere and no amount of collective protest will make a real difference to the systematically personal connections of those with power. Schools teach something inadvertently about political parties. They demonstrate the power of knowing the right person, of patronage, of following a particular line. It is the influence of the group that dominates: the organization of numbers of people into pressure groups.

Schools present a series of ontological contradictions. They have conflicting purposes. They take for granted, or ignore, many of the social conflicts and complexities that fill the daily routines. They have a formal curriculum and yet teach the fundamentals of understanding inadvertently. They also expose the implicit vulnerability of children.

All this is not the intention. Usually it is covered from our gaze. This makes the ontological contradictions the more powerful. All kinds of experiences are taking place that are inadvert and unofficial. The formal, proper picture of what takes place in school is one kind of reality. The school has a clear mission statement and a business plan. It is inspected to make sure of this. It achieves results and publishes them. It can measure the input of knowledge and the outcomes. And yet, pupils also give an impression of another, deeper kind of reality that is less well organized, less easy in its rhetoric and far more uncomfortable to live with. For that reason, such reality is customarily denied.

'Denial' is a psychiatric term that can easily be misused, as is the temptation to put someone else's disagreement with your point of view down to their personal problems. It is, however, difficult to avoid involving it in the way in which some of what takes place in schools is deliberately ignored. Those who make policies have their own agendas and their own rhetoric: they want to see results. They do not want to learn about matters that might undermine their policies, just as they would not like to bear criticism. If certain administrative arrangements have the opposite effect to that intended, like Ofsted, it does not mean that the policy is changed in any way.

This unwillingness to accept facts is, however, all too typically human. One of the most difficult ontological facts to take in is the understanding of the complexities and vulnerability of childhood. The 'happiest years of their lives' is a curious reworking or re-creation of the past since a certain amount of self-reflection or a consideration of the numbers of people who have emotional problems will remind us that childhood is not all sweetness and light. Just watching a baby unleash bitter anguish in violent tears is to witness real trauma. At the same time, the anguish is not an unknowing, spontaneous outburst of raw emotions. The child is aware: aware of the world and of other people. An acute emotional intelligence is applied so that failures of understanding of relationships mean the deepest of disappointments. The result of ontological insecurity is twofold. At one level is the vulnerability to being hurt, to humiliations or unfairness. Even the inadvertent has the potential for a deep effect. At another level is the resultant prosperity for self-loathing. When events prove troublesome or things go wrong, it is as natural to fall into self-contempt or despair as to rail against circumstances.

This latent prosperity of self-doubt, as well as the ontological insecurities that go with it, results in moments of vulnerability to being hurt out of all proportion to the cause. It is not difficult to cause pain in others, deliberately or not. The emotional vulnerability, as well as the intellectual confidence that young people bring with them to school, means that their first exposure to the social regime of these years can be, and can remain, very difficult.

The problem for schools is that they give the perfect opportunity for undermining confidence and self-belief. There might be some children who are invulnerable in their self-confidence and the majority have enough resilience to overcome the problems, but the way schools operate, with such emphasis on different kinds of groups, means the pupils will always be exposed to the possibilities of pain. We tend to treat many young people as both innocently cheerful and optimistic, or as tough and insensitive, as if a certain amount of brutality would do them no harm. The propensity for the sense of unfairness and personal failure or humiliation from others goes deep. If we think of schools from this point of view, then we understand better the amount of inadvertent learning that takes place. The implicit vulnerability of children supports their intelligent instincts, which give them other messages than the official ones.

There are three experiences that pupils constantly say they dislike. One is being humiliated, another is being ignored or boycotted and the third is being forced to do something that has no meaning. Schools have the means of influencing all three.

Pupils are aware of their own abilities and those of others. When they explore some of the experiences of school, they mention the way in which they find the constant testing difficult, but they also recall the humiliation they feel when exposed for not understanding something. This can be a trivial incident like the inability to read or it can be laboured in the classroom by the teacher who reveals the humiliation to all. Being thought generally slow is one thing; being exposed for stupidity is another. Whilst the isolated extreme incident might be most emotionally scarring, the school system itself depends on testing, on comparisons, on failure as well as success. No one seems to question the regime of assessment apart from parents, who witness the stress it causes in their children because the way the results are published, as in league tables, seems impersonal and a matter for curiosity. For the individual pupils, however, such exposures are personal. Success or failure matters deeply.

The opportunities for being humiliated also abound in the relationships with peers. Being ostracized by them or rejected by a group or even by a friend is taken very seriously. Pupils talk about this, but what upsets them most is being 'picked on' by a teacher rather than their peers. Worse still, being ostensibly ostracized by a teacher causes real complaints. This is part of the 'unfairness' of school. Being ignored by teachers is nothing deliberate. Teachers do not set out to sideline certain pupils even if they would prefer to ignore them. It is simply that teachers cannot find time to take that kind of interest in every individual or to follow through every social problem. Just as teachers themselves yearn for some praise or even notice, from their head teachers and managers, so pupils long for attention. The circumstances of school make this difficult, if not impossible, but that does not prevent pupils wishing they had it. Many submit to the fact and remain 'invisible', hardly troubling the routines of teachers. Others rail against it, become noticed for the wrong reasons and fall into trouble. None feel that their experience of school is centred on personal relationships or celebrating their individual achievements.

Schools are busy places where the business is directed away from the personalities of those within them. There is a curriculum to be got through, tests to be administered and standards to be achieved. This means that pupils easily feel marginalized. The greatest sense of anonymity and estrangement, however, comes about not just because teachers are so busy doing other things but because the very routines of school take the idiosyncrasies of learning away. If you ask pupils which phrase they associate particularly with teachers, the answer is unexpected. One might have guessed it would be 'Be quiet' or 'Listen!' Instead the telling phrase turns out to be 'Do it again.' Schools are associated with routine drudgery, with writing, with constantly performing tasks that do not have personal meaning. Work has to be done. Pupils must be 'on task', feel they are writing constantly, copying or repeating or being suddenly asked to be creative. The result is a strong feeling that work is associated not with pleasure but with a necessary drudgery.

School could be reasonably described as the embodiment of testing, of time spent on set tasks and of disciplined order. Each of these has potentially hurtful outcomes. Despite this, pupils survive. This says a great deal for the resilience of the human spirit. We should not underrate the personal strength of individuals in not completely submitting to difficult circumstances. Some people will, no doubt, argue that schools themselves force a certain kind of toughness on their pupils, that the whole idea is to give them an insight into the world of self-help, of competition and of difficulties. The system might not be perfect but the people in it still survive. The pupils who have given their analysis of schools have revealed the inadvertent learning that takes place. They have exposed some of the attitudes, some of the anguish and a lot of disappointment. Given their ontological insecurity, it is the more impressive that they survive. They take what they can. They realize in their own unofficial way what they have learnt. They make the best of the circumstances and learn in their own individual, idiosyncratic ways in places where little allowance is made for different learning styles. They do their best despite the system.

The same juxtaposition of well-meaning and resilient individuals working in unsympathetic and difficult circumstances can be seen in teachers. They keep things going despite the system, not because of it. For all the moments of unhappiness expressed by pupils, for all the feelings of frustration at the lack of interest and despite their sense of marginalization in the fact of impersonal role-playing, pupils understand the plight of teachers. They even pity them. Part of the learnt

203

cynicism of the structures of society derives from the observation of teachers being put upon, bullied and harassed by those in control of them. Pupils witness the change of tone as a result of Ofsted inspections. They sense the trepidation at the approach of examination results. They witness the stress and the demoralization. They also appreciate the remains of dedication, the signs of personal interest, the learning of individual names, the encouragement of endeavour. Pupils know that teachers would also prefer different conditions.

This interest in teachers as people is central. It explains the pupils' regrets of never having had enough time to know them properly. It also explains the ways in which real influence works. The most positive learning that ever takes place in school is not of the subject matter as such but in the teachers demonstrating their own love of learning. An enthusiastic lesson where the teacher is caught up in his or her own excitement of learning and where the relish of understanding is palpable makes the deepest impression on pupils. Seeing a teacher driven by the love of a subject and wanting to communicate reminds pupils of all that is possible and is the mainspring of any motivation that they themselves develop.

We only need to think back to our own school experience to acknowledge the memory of the single exciting lesson. We do not remember the daily tasks of undergoing particular subjects. When we think of those subjects that we like or dislike, we can also picture the individuals who helped form such attachments or destroyed all interest in the subject. If enthusiasm was really being learnt, then the accretion of facts could look after itself. The question is whether teachers are allowed to develop their own enthusiasms.

Pupils witness teachers labouring in an unsympathetic system. They see the age-old conundrum of how, as Bourdieu so often asked, well-meaning individuals become caught up in such disappointing systems.

What then are the policy implications of such findings? The answer is that what pupils actually experience should be taken seriously and that there should be a willingness to look closely and realistically at what is going on. This would mean a willingness to let observation reign and to learn from the empirical evidence. Of course, this is a lot to ask, especially of politicians. But the implications are many and obvious.

At one level, this is a practical handbook for teachers and demonstrates what we need to know about the pupils' experience and what the pupils need. It should provide as much hope in doing what is right as despair at the prevailing conditions. It should also give comfort in the integrity of a profession peculiarly beleaguered. There are certain fundamental influences that teachers have, despite the system.

This book does not conclude with the idea of 'de-schooling'. It questions what we are doing and tries to go deeper than a short-term change to the balance of the curriculum or class size. It raises the fundamental question of what schools are for and, particularly, what education is for. It also explores the real ways in which people learn, at levels that the educational system only touches obliquely or by chance. At the moment, deliberately or not, we are trying to turn pupils into the most hidebound of party politicians. They learn all kinds of skills that are not in the formal curriculum. Survival is one of them, submission another.

One day the age of schooling as now understood will naturally come to an end. One day, surely, people will apply all the ingenuity that is directed at technology to the subject of the human experience.

References

Alderson, P and Goodey, C (1996) Research with disabled children: how useful is child-centred ethics?, *Children and Society*, **10** (2), pp 106–16

Alexander, R (2000) *Culture and Pedagogy: International comparisons in primary education*, Blackwell, Oxford

Alexander, R, Rose, J and Woodhead, C (1992) *Curriculum Organisation and Classroom Practice in Primary Schools: A discussion paper*, Department of Education and Science, London

Aries, P (1962) *Centuries of Childhood*, Knopf, New York

Attenbrough, R, Engel, D and Martin, D (1995) *Caring for Kids: A critical study of urban school leavers*, Falmer Press, London

Bandura, A (1973) *Aggression: A social-learning analysis*, Prentice Hall, New Jersey

Barnes, D, Britton, J and Rosen, H (eds) (1969) *Language, the Learner and the School*, Penguin, London

Barry, M (2001) *Challenging Transitions: Young people's news and experiences of growing up*, Save the Children, Plymbridge

Bennett, N and Cass, A (1988) The effects of group composition on group interactive processes and pupil understanding, *British Educational Research Journal*, **15** (1), pp 19–32

Bennett, N and Dunne, C (1992) *Managing Classroom Groups*, Simon & Schuster, London

Bennett, N *et al* (1984) *The Quality of Pupil Learning Experiences*, Lawrence Erlbaum, London

Berkowitz, L (1962) *Aggression: A social psychological analysis*, McGraw-Hill, New York

Berndt, T and Keefe, K (1996) Friends' influence on adolescents' adjustments to school, *Child Development*, Netherlands, **66** (5), pp 1312–29

Bettelheim, B (1987) *A Good Enough Parent*, Thames and Hudson, London

Black, P (1997) Whatever happened to TGAT?, in *Assessment versus Evaluation*, ed C Cullingford, pp 24–50, Cassell, London

Blatchford, P and Martin, C (1998) The effects of class size on classroom practices: 'It's a bit like a treadmill – working hard and getting nowhere fast', *British Journal of Educational Studies*, **46** (2), pp 118–37

Blatchford, P and Mortimore, P (1993) The issue of class size for young children in schools: what can we learn from research?, *Oxford Review of Education*, **20** (1), pp 411–28

Blatchford, P and Sharp, S (eds) (1994) *Break-Time and the School: Understanding and Changing Playground Behaviour*, Routledge, London

Boulton, M (1995) Playground behaviour and peer interaction patterns of primary school boys classified as bullies, victims and not involved, *British Journal of Educational Psychology*, **65** (2), pp 165–77

Bourdieu, P (1990) *In Other Words: Essays towards a reflexive sociology*, Cambridge Publicity Press, Cambridge

Bowles, A and Gintis, H (1976) *Schooling in Capitalist America*, Routledge & Kegan Paul, London

British Psychological Society (1993) *Ethical Principles for Conducting Research with Human Participants*, British Psychological Society, London

Bronfenbrenner, U (1974) The experimental ecology of education, *Teachers College Record*, **78** (2), pp 157–204

Bronfenbrenner, U (1978) *Two Worlds of Childhood*, Allen & Unwin, London

Bruner, J (1967) *Towards a Theory of Instruction*, Harvard University Press, Cambridge MA

Burgess, H (1989) The primary curriculum: the example of mathematics, in *The Primary Teacher*, ed C Cullingford, Cassell, London

Butroyd, B (2001) Secondary subject teaching and the development of pupil values, in *The National Curriculum and it Effects*, eds C Cullingford and P Oliver, pp 79–101, Ashgate, Aldershot

Campbell, J (1998) Primary teaching: roles and relationships, in *How Shall We School Our Children? Primary education and the future*, eds C Richards and P Taylor, pp 75–85, Falmer Press, London

Chandler, M, Fritz, A and Hala, S (1989) Small-scale deceit: deception as a mark of two, three and four year olds: theories of mind, *Child Development*, **60** (6), pp 1263–77

Charlton, T, Jones, K and Ogilvie, M (1989) Primary, secondary and special school teachers' perceptions of the quality of good schools, *Educational Studies*, **15** (3), pp 229–39

Chukovsky, K (1963) *From Two to Five*, University of California Press, Berkeley, CA

Cole, M (ed) (1988) *Bowles and Gintis Revisited: Correspondence and contradiction in educational theory*, Falmer Press, London

Coulby, D and Ward, S (eds) (1996) *The Primary Core National Curriculum: Policy into practice*, Cassell, London

Crank, K (1988) *Teacher–Pupil Conflict in Secondary Schools*, Falmer, London

Crawford, R (2002) Factors associated with high levels of ICT capability among pupils aged 14–16 in English schools, EdD thesis, Leeds University

Cress, K (1992) Why not ask the students? Urban teenagers make the case for working, *Phi Delta Kappa*, **74** (2), pp 172–76

Croll, P and Hastings, N (1996) *Effective Primary Teaching: Research based classroom strategies*, Fulton, London

Cullingford, C (1984) *Children and Television*, Gower, Aldershot

References

Cullingford, C (ed) (1985) *Parents, Teachers and Schools*, Royle, London
Cullingford, C (1986) *Parents, Teachers and Schools*, Robert Royce, London
Cullingford, C (1990) *The Nature of Learning*, Cassell, London
Cullingford, C (1991) *The Inner World of the School*, Cassell, London
Cullingford, C (1992) *Children and Society*, Cassell, London
Cullingford, C 1994) Children's response to television advertising: the magic age of eight, *Research in Education*, 51, pp 79–84
Cullingford, C (1996) *Parents, Education and the State*, Ashgate, Aldershot
Cullingford, C (ed) (1999a) *An Inspector Calls: Ofsted and its effects on school standards*, Kogan Page, London
Cullingford, C (1999b) *The Causes of Exclusion: Home, school and the development of young criminals*, Kogan Page, London
Cullingford, C (1999c) *The Human Experience: The early years*, Ashgate, Aldershot
Cullingford, C and Oliver, P (eds) (2001) *The National Curriculum and its Effects*, Ashgate, Aldershot
Cuthell, J (2002) *Virtual Learning*, Ashgate, Aldershot
Dalin, P *et al* (1994) *How Schools Improve: An international report*, Cassell, London
David, M, Edwards, R and Alldred, P (2001) Children and school-based research: 'informed consent' or 'educated consent', *British Educational Research Journal*, 27 (3), pp 347–65
Davies, B (1982) *Life in the Classroom and Playground: The accounts of primary school children*, Routledge & Kegan Paul, London
Davies, M and Edwards, G (1999) Will the curriculum caterpillar ever learn to fly?, *Cambridge Journal of Education*, 29 (2), pp 265–75
Department for Education and Employment (DfEE) (1998) *Guidance on School Attendance and the Role of the Education Welfare Services*, HMSO, London
Doyle, W (1977) The use of non-verbal behaviours: toward an ecological model of classrooms, *Merrill-Palmer Quarterly*, 23, pp 179–92
Dunn, J (1988) *The Beginnings of Social Understanding*, Basil Blackwell, Oxford
Dunne, E (ed) (1999) *The Learning Society: International perspectives on core skills in higher education*, Kogan Page, London
Egan, K (1988) *Teaching as Storytelling*, Routledge, London
Egan, K (1997) *The Educated Mind: How cognitive tools shape our understanding*, University of Chicago Press, Chicago
Elias, N (1978) *The Civilising Process*, Basil Blackwell, Oxford
Elias, N (1982) *The History of Manners*, Basil Blackwell, Oxford
Elliot, J (1998) *The Curriculum Experiment: Meeting the challenge of social change*, Open University Press, Buckingham
Farrington, D and West, D (1990) *The Cambridge Study in Delinquent Behaviour*, Springer Verlag, London
Galloway, D *et al* (1996) Unadaptive motivational styles: the role of domain specific task demands in English and mathematics, *British Journal of Educational Psychology*, 66 (2), pp 197–207
Galton, M and Simon, B (1980) *Progress and Performance in the Primary Classroom*, Routledge & Kegan Paul, London
Galton, M, Simon, B and Croll, P (1980) *Inside the Primary Classroom*, Routledge & Kegan Paul, London

Galton, M and Williamson, J (1995) *Group Work in the Primary Classroom*, Routledge, London

Galton, M *et al* (1999) Changes in patterns of teacher interaction in primary classrooms 1976–96, *British Educational Research Journal*, **25** (1), pp 23–37

Ghaye, A (1986) Outer experiences with inner experiences: towards a more holistic view of group work, *Educational Review*, **28** (1), pp 45–56

Gill, I and Howard, S (2001) Old school ties: schooling and the construction of allegiance, Paper presented at the Australian Association for Educational Research Conference, Fremantle

Gilroy, P and Wilcox, B (1997) Ofsted, criteria and the nature of social understanding: a Wittgensteinian critique on the practice of educational judgement, *British Journal of Educational Studies*, **45** (1), pp 22–38

Gramsci, A (1977) *Selections from Political Writings*, Lawrence & Wishart, London

Gramsci, A (1978) *Selections from Prison Notebooks*, Lawrence & Wishart, London

Gray, J (1997) A bit of a curate's egg? Three decades of official thinking about the quality of schools, *British Journal of Educational Studies*, **45** (1), pp 4–21

Hacker, R and Rose, M (1998) A longitudinal study of the effects of implementing a National Curriculum project upon classroom processes, *Curriculum Journal*, **9** (1), pp 95–103

Hammersley, M and Atkinson, P (1983) *Ethnography: Principles in practices*, Tavistock, London

Hargreaves, D (1967) *Social Relations in a Secondary School*, Routledge & Kegan Paul, London

Hartap, W (1996) The company they keep: friendships and their developmental significance, *Child Development*, Netherlands, **67** (1), pp 1–13

Haviland, J (ed) (1988) *Take Care, Mr. Baker*, Fourth Estate, London

Hodkinson, P, Sparkes, A and Hodkinson, H (1996) *Triumphs and Tears: Young people, markets and the transition from school to work*, David Fulton, London

Holden, A and Cullingford C (2002), An analysis of parent–teacher relations in primary schools, *Education 3–13*, in press

Hollingshead, D (1975) *Elmtown's Youth and Elmtown Revisited*, John Wiley, New York

Holt, J (1964) *How Children Fail*, Penguin, Harmondsworth

Holt, J (1972) *Freedom and Beyond*, Penguin, London

Illich, I (1971) *Education without School: How it can be done*, Holt Rinehart, New York

Jamieson, J, Johnson, F and Dickson, P (1998) *Every Pupil Counts: The impact of class size on Key Stage One*, NFER, Slough

Jeffrey, B (2001) Valuing primary students' perspectives, European Conference on Educational Research, Lille

Jeffrey, B and Woods, P (1996) Feeling deprofessionalised: the social construction of emotions during an Ofsted inspection, *Cambridge Journal of Education*, **26** (3), pp 325–44

Kelley, P, Mayall, B and Hood, S (1997) Children's accounts of risk, *Childhood*, **4** (3), pp 305–24

Kinder, K (1997) Causes of disaffection: the views of pupils and educational professionals, *EERA Bulletin*, **3** (1), pp 3–11

King, R (1989) *The Best of Primary Education? A sociological study of junior/middle schools*, Falmer Press, London

Latané, B and Darley, J (1970) *The Unresponsive Bystander*, Appleton, New York

Lee, C (2001) Bullying in a primary school: a case study, PhD thesis, University of Plymouth

Lewis, C (1995) Improving attendance – reducing truancy, *Educational Psychology in Practice*, **11** (1), pp 36–40

Lovat, R (1994) The implications of bio-ethics for teachers and teacher researchers, *British Educational Research Journal*, **20** (2)

Manke, M (2001) Defining classroom knowledge: the part that children play, in *Developing Pedagogy: Researching practice*, ed J Collins, K Insley and J Soler, pp 26–38, Paul Chapman, London

McCullum, B, Hargreaves, E and Gipps, C (2000) Learning: the pupils' voice, *Cambridge Review of Education*, **30** (2), pp 275–89

McFadden, M (1995) Resistance to schooling and educational outcomes: questions of structure and agency, *British Journal of Sociology of Education*, **16** (3)

Measor, L and Woods, P (1984) *Changing Schools: Pupils' perspectives on transfer to a comprehensive*, Open University Press, Milton Keynes

Meighan, R (1989) The parents and the schools – alternative role definitions, *Educational Review*, **41** (2), pp 105–12

Meighan, R (1995) *John Holt: Personalised education and the reconstruction of schooling*, Educational Heretic Press, Nottingham

Milgram, S (1974) *Obedience to Authority: An experimental view*, Tavistock, London

Morrow, V and Richards, M (1996) The ethics of social research with children: an overview, *Children and Society*, **10** (2), pp 90–100

Mortimore, P *et al* (1979), *School Matters: The junior years*, Open Books, London

Nutbrown, C (1998) *The Lore and Language of Early Education*, USDE Papers in Education, University of Sheffield Department of Education, Sheffield

Oliveus, D (1993) *Bullying at School: What we know and what we can do*, Blackwell, Oxford

Pearson, M (2000) Children's responses to computers: concept mapping, European Union Representation Project, Brussels

Peters, F (2000) The modernisation of the youth phase: educational, professional and family careers of Dutch youth in the nineties, in *Childhood and Youth in Germany and the Netherlands: Transitions and coping strategies of adolescents*, ed M DuBois-Reymond *et al*, pp 3–39, Walter de Gruyter, Berlin

Petherbridge J (1997) Work experience: making an impression, *Educational Review*, **49** (1), pp 21–27

Plummer, K (1983) *Document of Life*, Allen & Unwin, London

Pointon, P and Kershaw, R (2001) Organising the primary classroom: environment as a context for learning, in *Developing Pedagogy: Researching practice*, ed J Collins, K Insley and J Soler, pp 54–67, Paul Chapman, London

Pollard, A (1985) *The Social World of the Primary School*, Holt, Rinehart & Winston, London

Pollard, A with Filer, A (1995) *The Social World of Children's Learning: Case studies of pupils from four to seven*, Cassell, London

Pollard, A *et al* (1994) *Changing English Primary Schools: The impact on the Educational Reform Act at Key Stage 1*, Cassell, London

Pugh, G (1997) Early childhood education finds its voice: but is anyone listening?, in *The Politics of Primary Education*, ed C Cullingford, pp 15–33, Open University Press, Buckingham

Pye, J (1989) *Invisible Children: Who are the real losers at school?*, Oxford University Press, Oxford

Reubens, B (1977) *Bridges to Work: International comparisons of transitions services*, Marston Robinson, London

Rosenhahn, D (1973) Questions on being sane in insane places, *Science*, 179, pp 250–58

Ruddock, J, Harris, S and Wallace, G (1994) Coherence and students' experience of learning in the secondary school, *Cambridge Journal of Education*, **24** (2)

Rutter, M *et al* (1979) *Fifteen Thousand Hours: Secondary schools and their effects on children*, Open Books, London

Saunders, L, Stoney, S and Weston, P (1997) The impact of the work-related curriculum on 14 to 16 year olds, *Journal of Education and Work*, **10** (2), pp 151–67

Sharp, R and Green, A (1975) *Education and Social Control: A study in progressive primary education*, Routledge & Kegan Paul, London

Siraz-Blatchford, J (1996) *Learning Technology, Science and Social Justice: An integrated approach for 3–13 year olds*, Education Now, Nottingham

Slavin, A (1978) Student teams and achievement divisions, *Journal of Research and Development in Education*, 12, pp 39–49

Slavin, A (1983) *Cooperative Learning*, Longman, New York

Slee, R (ed) (1998) *School Effectiveness for Whom? Challenges to the school effectiveness and school improvement movements*, Falmer Press, London

Sluckin, A (1981) *Growing Up in the Playground*, Routledge & Kegan Paul, London

Smith, D (1994) *The Sleep of Reason*, Century, London

Smith, P and Sharp, S (1994) *School Bullying: Insights and perspectives*, Routledge, London

Spradley, M (1979) *The Ethnographic Interview*, Holt, Rinehart and Winston, New York

Stern, D *et al* (1990) Quality of students' work experience and orientation toward work, *Youth and Society*, **22** (2), pp 263–82

Tight, M (1995) Education, work and adult life: a literature review, *Research Papers in Education*, **10** (3), pp 383–400

Tooley, J with Darley, D (1998) *Educational Research, A Critique*, DfEE Survey of Published Educational Research, Office for Standards in Education, London

Turner-Bisset, R (2001) *Expert Teaching for Knowledge and Pedagogy to Lead the Profession*, David Fulton, London

Underwood, J and Underwood, G (1990) *Computers and Learning*, Basil Blackwell, Oxford

Unwin, L and Wellington, J (2001) *Young People's Perspectives on Education, Training and Employment: Realising their potential*, Kogan Page, London

References

Wharton, D (1997) Learning about responsibility: lessons from homework, *British Journal of Educational Psychology*, **45** (1), pp 8–27

White, C, Bruce, S and Ritchie, J (2000) *Young People's Politics: Political interest and engagement amongst 14 to 24 year olds*, Joseph Rowntree Foundation, York

White, R with Brockington, D (1983) *Tales Out of School: Consumers' views of British education*, Routledge & Kegan Paul, London

Whitney, I and Smith, P (1993) A survey on the nature and extent of bullying in junior/middle and secondary schools, *Educational Research*, **35** (1), pp 3–25

Willan, P (1998) Whatever happened to entitlement in the National Curriculum?, *Curriculum Journal*, **9** (3), pp 269–83

Williamson, I and Cullingford, C (1998) Adolescent alienation: its correlates and consequences, *Educational Studies*, **24** (3), pp 333–43

Willis, P (1977) *Learning to Labour: How working class kids get working class jobs*, Saxon House, Farnborough

Wilson, J and Cowell, B (1990) *Children and Discipline*, Cassell, London

Index